STRATEGIC
THINKING
and the
MANAGEMENT
of
CHANGE

STRATEGIC THINKING
and the
MANAGEMENT
of
CHANGE

International Perspectives on
Organisational Dynamics

Ralph Stacey

KOGAN
PAGE

First published in 1993

Kogan Page Limited
120 Pentonville Road
London N1 9JN

© Ralph Stacey, 1993

British Library Cataloguing in Publication Data

A CIP record for this book is available from the British Library.

ISBN 0 7494 0683 6

Typeset by Saxon Graphics Ltd, Derby
Printed in England by Clays Ltd, St Ives plc

Contents

Contents

List of Contributors

Roger Bennett PhD is a company director, author and lecturer with special interests in European marketing and business. He has written several books on European and general management, including *Selling to Europe* (1991), *Handbook of European Advertising* (1993), *Choosing and Using Management Consultants* (1990) (all published by Kogan Page), and *Small Business Survival*, *Management*, and *Organisational Behaviour* (all published by Pitman in 1991). Currently he teaches at London Guildhall University and is engaged on a major study of the implications for European companies of the formation of the European Economic Area.

Midi Berry, with degrees from Cambridge University, has been in line management and consulting and has taught in business, academia and the community. She has done pioneering work linking Jungian and process-oriented psychology to management and organisation development. She co-founded the Mosaic Management Consultancy Group Limited, and after ten years with that group left to practise psychotherapy, write and consult internationally. She now works in Europe, the US and Africa, specialising in developing facilitative styles of leadership, creating cultural awareness, and conflict resolution.

Andrew Campbell is a founding Director and Fellow of the Ashridge Strategic Management Centre. Previously he was a Fellow in the Centre for Business Strategy at the London Business School, and a consultant at McKinsey & Co. He is co-author of *Strategies and Styles* with Michael Gould, 1987, Blackwell, *A Sense of Mission: Do You Need a Mission Statement?* with Marion Devine and David Young, 1990, Hutchinson, and *Mission and Business Philosophy* with Kiran Tawady, 1990, Heinemann.

Magdolna Csath is Professor of Strategic Management at Shopron University in Hungary and also organiser of courses at the Institute of Management in Salzburg, Austria. She has been Professor of Strategic Management at the University of Stirling in the UK and in the USA. She is the author of a number of articles on strategic management, particularly in relation to Eastern Europe.

Geraldine Healy is a Principal Lecturer in industrial relations and human resource management at the Business School of the University of Hertfordshire. She has researched and published in the area of labour market studies and employment aspects of discrimination. She has also led policy developments in equal opportunities policies.

Bengt Johannisson is Professor of Entrepreneurship and Business Development at Växjo University and also at the Institute of Economic Research at Lund University, both in Sweden. He is the author of numerous articles on entrepreneurship.

William Keyser has been in European management consulting practice for many years including two years' secondment as a senior official of the UK National Economic Development Office. He has written and edited several books on public enterprise. He co-founded the Mosaic Consultancy Group Limited and was variously its managing director and chairman for 11 years. The firm specialised in organisational change and development. His work was concentrated at senior management levels on strategic and policy issues. He is now an independent consultant and writer.

Paul Kirkbride is a Client/Programme Director at Ashridge Management College and a Visiting Professor at the University of Hertfordshire. He currently directs the 'Making Change Work' programme at Ashridge as well as tailored programmes that focus on strategic reassessment and organisational change. Previously he was British Aerospace Professor of Organisation Development at Hatfield Polytechnic Business School, spending most of his time as a specialist consultant to senior management at BAe (Commercial Aircraft) Limited. He has published many articles and has recently written three books.

Eric Miller MA PhD carried out research as a social anthropologist in India and Thailand and spent five years as an internal consultant with textile companies in the USA and India before joining the staff of the Tavistock Institute in 1958. Organisational design and change are his main interests and his consultancy and research have taken him into a wide range of settings in the public, private and voluntary sectors in Britain and overseas. His many publications include the classic *Systems of Organization* co-authored with A K Rice, 1967, Tavistock Publications.

Ralph Stacey is Professor of Management at the Business School of Hertfordshire University and a strategy consultant to the boards of directors of major companies. He was previously the Corporate Planning Manager for John Laing plc. He is the author of *Dynamic Strategic Management for the 1990s, The Chaos Frontier, Managing Chaos* (published in the US by Jossey-Bass as *Managing the Unknowable*) and *Strategic Management and Organisational Dynamics*. His books have been translated into Spanish and Italian.

John Sykes is Professor of International Marketing and Management at the Institut de Management Européen des Affaires, Besançon, France. He is also a management development consultant to major European companies.

Preface

It is now widely recognised that the single most important competence which senior managers must develop, if they are to be effective, is an ability to think strategically. Before such a competence can be deliberately developed, however, it is necessary to try to identify what that competence actually is. From what seems to be today's most popular perpective, strategic thinking is the process of applying some general prescriptive framework, derived from observing best practice, to each new specific stragetic situation encountered: that is, the application of a set of step-by-step analytical rules or other procedures, such as formulating visions and missions, which are learned and installed in advance of taking strategic action. So, before managers actually enter a new market, they should, in this view, develop the skills of analysing market structures in order to identify whether the proposed market is attractive or not, and if it is attractive, which of a limited number of strategic positions is likely to lead to success. The notion is that successful people think and decide what is to be achieved before they act.

The contributions to this book have been assembled from a different perspective. In turbulent times, when we are faced with a rapidly changing world, a succession of ambiguous situations, and actions with unknowable consequences that generate continuing conflict, it becomes impossible to think before we act. Strategic thinking then has to become reflecting *while* we act. When managers face unique situations of great uncertainty, analytical rules and procedures cannot be applied simply because the very regularity they presuppose does not, by definition, exist. The crucial contribution of managers is then the judgement of when and how to break and abandon the analytical rules, how to frame the issues, create meaning and discover what should be achieved. And the necessary skills of judgement are based on the ability to reason by analogy, relating one situation to others previously experienced, that have some similarities to the current situation but are not the same. Such intuitive skills, the ability to reflect-in-action, are acquired through experiencing and developing insight into a wide range of situations, many of which may not at the time appear to be relevant.

This book aims to provide busy senior managers with an alternative perspective on the nature of strategic thinking. It sets out the latest thinking on a number of key concepts that should now be commanding the attention of senior managers – notions such as organisational networks and learning organisations, that have recently become part of management vocabulary but which lack clarity of meaning for many. The various contributions to this book summarise concepts, explain their relevance and identify the state of the debate around them. The contributions identify the paradoxes and contradictions, what it is that the manager needs to reflect upon and think about in order to achieve long-term success.

The contributions to this book reflect three closely related sets of concerns that modern senior managers have. This triangle of concerns covers discontinuity, interconnection and complexity, and is shown in the figure.

Discontinunity is probably today's most talked-about concern. It is the perception (probably also the fact) that the rate of change is accelerating, that the outcomes of change are becoming more uncertain and unpredictable, that change nowadays tends to be an abrupt departure from the past rather then a continuous development from it. Managers and commentators talk about turbulence, chaos, shattering change, unpredictability and uncertainty. Evidence is provided by shortening product life cycles, more rapid application of new technology, greater global competition, more political instability. At the same time, continuity has increased in importance. It is more important than ever to deliver consistent quality, high service levels and low cost.

The growing interconnectedness of the business world, bringing with it the need for integration, is another management concern. This is apparent on a geographic level as industries globalise and geographic market integration (eg the European Community) proceeds. It is apparent at other levels too as business becomes more intertwined with

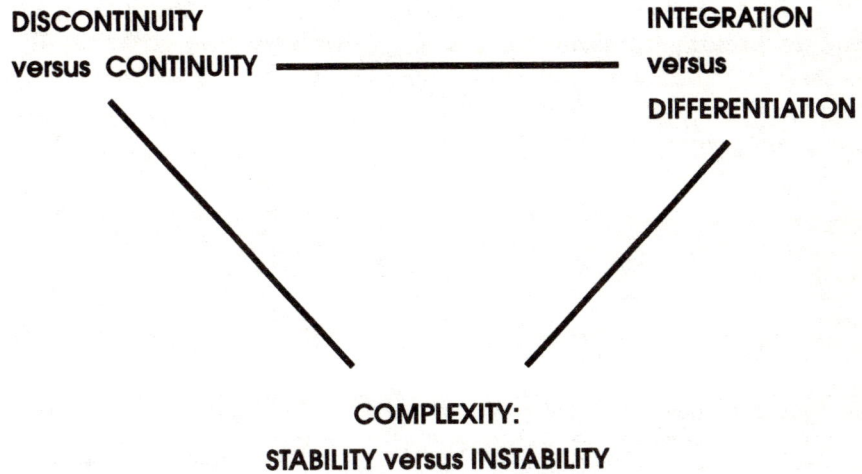

DISCONTINUITY   INTEGRATION

versus CONTINUITY ─────────────── versus

                                                     DIFFERENTIATION

COMPLEXITY:

STABILITY versus INSTABILITY

Figure 1 *Discontinuity, interconnection and complexity*

environmental policies, ethics, positive discrimination in favour of women and minorities. It is apparent at a political level with deregulation and privatisation on the one hand and increased intervention in some areas (for example, environmental issues) on the other hand. It is apparent at an intellectual level as changing paradigms in the natural sciences come to affect thinking about organisations. It is apparent at the pracital level as firms cooperate and build alliances. But, at the same time, fragmentation and differentiation have also increased in importance. On a geographical level there is the fragmentation of Eastern Europe. At a business level there is the emphasis placed on differentiation and segmenting markets.

Closely connected to the interconnectedness of the business world and the increasingly discontinuous changes it faces is the issue of complexity. Larger corporations operating in a great many market segments in many countries, some of which are integrating and others of which are fragmenting, face the problems of complexity. What kinds of structures will secure stability in the complex system that is a modern corporation? Is stability consistent with the requirement for continuing innovation in a successful organisation?

The key point about these three sets of concerns is that each consists of a contradiction or paradox; each creates tensions that have to be managed, resolved or orchestrated in some way. Successful organisations have to deal with and use both continuous and discontinuous (predictable and unpredictable) changes; with integration and fragmentation; with stability and instability. The contributions to this book explore some of the paradoxes and contradictions that should drive the strategic thinking of managers in today's turbulent times.

Part 1

Introduction

1

Introduction

Ralph Stacey

In the 1960s, the fashionable way for managers to deal with the future was to prepare long-range corporate plans. The plans were prepared by expert planning staffs rather than line managers. Those plans consisted of financial objectives and sequences of intended actions that would achieve the objectives. The intended actions were selected after considering the likely consequences, based on quantitative forecasts of the future, of a number of options. However, the manifest inability to forecast accurately enough what would happen and the fact that elaborate long-range plans were hardly ever implemented led to widespread disillusionment with this whole process. In the 1970s, therefore, corporate planning departments were reduced in size and power, and responsibility for strategy formulation was placed firmly on line managers, sometimes assisted by much smaller staffs of strategy experts.

As well as a shift in the focus of responsibility for strategy formulation there was also a shift in the primary concern, from quantitative forecasting to:

- a more qualitative analysis of the purpose of an organisation, leading to the establishment of its mission and a vision of its future;
- a qualitative analysis of the firm's markets and its capability, and how that capability could be fitted to market requirements so as to secure competitive advantage.

To signal the shift in the locus of responsibility and in the primary focus of the analysis, managers talked about strategic management as opposed to corporate planning.

However, many soon realised that even these changes in the conduct of strategic management were not leading to significantly better strategy implementation. During the 1980s, therefore, a concern with the impact of organisational culture and internal political activities on strategy formulation and implementation was added to the emphasis on analysing market structures and organisational capabilities. Many major European companies followed this new fashion and tried to carry out comprehensive culture change programmes to remove behavioural and cultural obstacles to strategy implementation.

But the experience of the 1980s has shown just how difficult it is to change cultures and so the problems with strategy implementation continue. The realisation of just how ineffective the accepted strategic management processes are has led many to emphasise the importance of strategic thinking. It is argued that although the procedures and analytical techniques of modern strategic management may not be of much direct practical use, they do create a framework for strategic thinking and, it is assumed, managers who think strategically are bound to act more effectively in dealing with the future.

What, then, is strategic thinking? In a recent article in *Long Range Planning*, Noel Zabriskie and Alan Huellmantel say:

Specifically, senior executives *think strategically* when they:

- visualize what they want their organization to become
- are able to reposition their resources to compete in tomorrow's markets
- assess the risk, revenues, and costs of the strategy alternatives open to them
- think about and identify the questions they want the strategic plan to answer
- think logically and systematically about the planning steps and model they will use to activate their strategic thinking in the company's operations (1991, p26).

These authors then go on to set out a model consisting of six steps managers must take in order to think strategically and they conclude:

An important challenge for top management in the 1990s is *to develop the strategic thinking ability of senior managers*. By performing the tasks and answering the questions listed in the model, leaders will have developed the contents of a strategic plan... . The questions in the model are designed in such a way that when answered, they will have automatically stated the relationship that the organization hopes to establish with its external environment... .

A similar view of the nature of strategic thinking is presented by Gordon Pearson in his book *Strategic Thinking* (1990). He outlines a number of strategic thinking frameworks: product and technology life cycles; product portfolios; industry and competitor analysis; steps to strategic marketing; models for analysing technology change, innovation, organisational structure, culture, symbolism; and the elements of entrepreneurial strategy. He then identifies which of these frameworks is likely to be applicable in the kind of environment managers are likely to face over the next few years.

What we have, then, is a very widespread view that strategic thinking is the application of general frameworks of analysis to specific strategic situations. There is admittedly not simply one framework but many perspectives. However each perspective consists of step-by-step procedures or rules providing, to some extent at least, automatic ways of identifying what to do strategically speaking. There is also the implicit assumption that strategic thinking precedes action – successful managers think about the long-term future consequences before they act.

This is however a curious view. We all know that everyday organisational life continually throws up exceptions to the frameworks, rules and procedures that have been set up in advance to govern an organisation's tasks. The real job of managers is to judge when to apply the previously established frameworks, when to bend them, when to ignore and break them, when to develop new ones. If we could rely on previously designed frameworks to work most of the time, the job of management could be carried out very effectively by computers.

Furthermore, strategic situations are by definition ambiguous, uncertain, paradoxical and unique – a specific situation is strategic because it has never before been encountered in that form and this makes it difficult to frame objectives, problems and opportunities. It follows that managers have to develop new ways of understanding each new strategic situation. Step-by-step thinking completed before action is taken is in fact impossible in unique situations. Instead, managers must think while they act and they have to think, not in a step-by-step way towards a known goal, but in irregular ways proceeding from one analogy with the situation they face to another, in order to frame and find both goals and ways of achieving them. Moreover, unique situations inevitably generate conflict and, to cope with this, strategic thinking has to encompass political manoeuvres and insight into the dynamics of group behaviour. Effective strategic thinking draws on a very wide area as far as subject matter is concerned – it is impossible to know in advance what may or may not turn out to be relevant.

Analytical ways of thinking can handle only the less interesting and less important problems facing managers. When it comes to the strategic, managers cannot apply a science; instead, they have to exercise skills of intuition and judgement; they have to practise the artistry of strategic thinking while they act, and they can learn this only through experience. Donald Schön (1987) has coined the term 'reflection-in-action' to describe this artistry of the professional practitioner.

If we are persuaded that strategic thinking cannot be practised through analytical frameworks put in place prior to action, then we have to look for insight to a number of alternative views of strategic management that have so far had little impact on the great majority of practising managers. These alternative views are now gaining ground but they still do not occupy the centre stage as far as practitioners are concerned.

For example, some academics claim that strategies are managers' attempts to make sense of what they have done, rather than what they intend to do. This view is based on the notion that managers create, or enact their own future and they can only know what they are doing when they have done it (Weick, 1979). Those pursuing this approach use the findings of cognitive psychology to illuminate how managers act according to mental models, or recipes they share on what their world is like. Those recipes function like filters so that managers frequently see only those changes they expect to see and consequently experience strategic 'drift' until the changes build to crisis proportions to provoke revolutionary alterations in strategic direction, or failure (Johnson, 1987).

Pursuing another tack, other academics see an organisation as a complex system where it is frequently impossible to pursue deliberate or intentional strategies. Instead, strategies emerge from the complex interaction between people within an organisation, and with people across its boundaries with the environment (Mintzberg & Waters, 1985). This change in the whole way that strategic management is viewed is consistent with changes in the natural sciences where scientists are increasingly coming to understand natural systems as operating in chaos and using processes of self-organisation to create new forms of behaviour. Some are now arguing that states of chaos and processes of self-organisation provide more useful ways of understanding how organisations evolve than the old concepts of strategy formulation and implementation aimed at maintaining some kind of stable equilibrium with the environment (Stacey, 1991, 1992).

Views such as these lead to the notion of the learning organisation – an organisation in which managers learn in groups (Brown and Duguid, 1991). Learning here involves processes through which managers surface their tacit knowledge, become aware of their mental models and change them (Nonaka, 1991). It is a notion of managers creating, discovering and exploring their own future. The learning organisation is closely connected to the notion of informal, or shadow organisations, now known as network organisations. Such networking, or political-activities are self organising and it is through informal political and social networks that managers identify and progress strategic issues to produce emergent new strategic directions. The self-organising net-works coexist with the formal organisation, through which managers carry out the day-to-day management of their existing business.

As soon as one starts to see organisations as creating and learning about their own futures through the learning activities of groups of people, one has to become concerned with group dynamics and the psychology of group behaviour. Some are now therefore researching organisational behaviour from a psychodynamic point of view, identi-fying how people in organisations use fantasy defences to protect themselves against anxiety (Kets de Vries and Miller, 1984; Hirschorn, 1990). It can be seriously argued that the formal and analytical techniques that most understand as constituting strategic thinking are just such a fantasy defence.

The purpose of this book is to provide practising managers with brief surveys and discussion on some of the key areas and concepts that modern strategic thinkers need to be aware of.

In the next chapter of this introductory part, Paul Kirkbride surveys the different approaches which may be adopted to the management of change. The key question posed in his chapter is whether change can be managed in an overall, systematic way at all, or whether it is more realistic to think in terms of interventions which may well have unpredictable consequences.

Part 2 is concerned with some key concepts to do with the dynamic nature of managing and organising. Strategic thinking as reflection-in-action takes place within a fluid network structure, and it is conditioned by the human dynamic. More effective strategic thinking is thinking conditioned by insights into shadowy informal, unconscious processes of organising and managing as well by insights into human behaviour in groups.

In the first chapter of Part 2 (Chapter 3), Bengt Johannisson explains what a network organisation means, using his research into the development of small communities in Sweden. He shows how innova-tive and entrepreneurial behaviour is fostered, and indeed made possible in the first place, by the social networks of contact that people build up between themselves. The important point is that innovative behaviour emerges from the self-organising activities of people in a community, not from any prior, shared intention or from any centrally imposed policies and plans. These ideas provide powerful analogies for managers in large corporations to utilise in their strategic thinking. The chapter concludes with the observation that in the end we may have to rely on individual capacities beyond organisational control.

Chapter 4 looks at one of the central functions of the political and social networks that people in all organisations develop, that of learning. The key points here have to do with:

- the self-organising ways in which people in an organisation use tacit knowledge to learn
- the inseparable connections between complex learning and social activity
- the importance of the group dynamic to the progress of learning and thus of the strategic development of any organisation.

Eric Miller explores the nature of the human dynamic in Chapter 5. He explains how the strategic thinking and learning work of a group of people can be overwhelmed by unconscious processes and blocked by shared defences against anxiety. He puts forward the concept of the 'citizen' of the organisation.

Part 3 turns to matters that are not usually seen to be part of strategic thinking – the moral dimension. However, the disappearance of universally accepted moral codes creates the need for judgment about the moral aspects of strategic changes. The increased mixing of communities and the changing role of women cannot be safely ignored if strategies are to be framed successfully.

Chapter 6, by Andrew Campbell, takes up the moral dimension mainly from the management and staff motivation point of view. He points out the modern Western 'action man' embarrassment about reflecting on moral and spiritual matters and contrasts it with the unashamed attitude of Japanese managers to these matters. This chapter is about how leaders must create a sense of mission if their organisations are to succeed. It stresses the importance of emotion and the need to take a wider perspective than the pursuit of profit. Strategic thinking here is depicted as a process of thinking about the nature of leadership and about the role of purpose, value and ethics. Questions this chapter poses are:

- Can we plan the installation of a mission and a sense of mission, or do these things emerge from the interaction between people in an organisation?

- How do we deal with the paradox that a strong sense of mission is necessary for concerted action, but that that strong sense then blocks ability to change?
- Is mission a statement of timeless values rather than a vision or picture of a future state?
- Is a sense of mission best understood as an emotional driving force taking the form of challenges or aspirations?

In Chapter 7, Midi Bery and William Keyser broaden the concern with ethics and point out how managers now need to exercise judgment over a wide range of ethical matters because simple moral codes have gone. Ethical judgment of what they are doing is now an essential part of people's strategic thinking process.

Geraldine Healy, in Chapter 8, focuses the moral dimension on matters to do with discrimination. She identifies why it is good business to pay attention to matters of discrimination, explains how discrimination becomes institutionalised and what triggers action to deal with it.

Then Part 4 turns to the international dimension. Chapter 9, by John Sykes, reviews the main concepts that were prescribed for strategic thinking in the 1980s – industry definition and structure, competitive advantage, generic strategies and value chains. He shows how these concepts take a simplistic 'either/or' view of strategy which is out of keeping with the complexity of the world where 'both/and' choices are required for survival. The chapter emphasises the need for systems thinking and concludes with a discussion of globalising markets.

Chapter 10, by Roger Bennett, explores one of the key issues facing managers today – the integration of Western Europe. He explores the impact of a common currency on the financing of operations and the wide range of strategic issues that common policies and legislation give rise to. He recommends the incorporation of a European dimension in all of the sub-systems of an organisation.

In Chapter 11, Magdolna Csath looks at the mirror image of an integrating Western Europe, the fragmenting countries of Eastern Europe. Her account of the deteriorating social fabric and the economic decline of the region is a sobering one and she makes the powerful point that the activities of Western companies are contributing to this process of decay. The potential consequences of this for Western investments provide food for strategic thought.

References

Brown, J S and Duguid, P (1991) 'Organizational Learning and Communities of Practice: Toward a Unified View of Working, Learning and Innovation', *Organisational Science*, Vol 2, No 1, Feb, 40–57.

Hirschorn, L (1990) *The Workplace Within: Psychodynamics of Organizational Life*, MIT Press, Cambridge, Ma:

Johnson, G (1987) *Strategic Change and the Management Process*, Blackwell, Oxford.

Kets de Vries, M F R and Miller, D (1984) *The Neurotic Organization*, Jossey-Bass, San Francisco:

Mintzberg, H and Waters, J A (1985) 'Of Strategies Deliberate and Emergent', *Strategic Management Journal*, 6, 257–72.

Nonaka, I (1991) 'The Knowledge-Creating Company', *Harvard Business Review*, Nov–Dec, 96–104.

Pearson, G J (1990) *Strategic Thinking*, Prentice Hall, Hemel Hempstead.

Schön, D A (1987) *Educating the Reflective Practitioner*, Jossey-Bass, San Francisco.

Stacey, R D (1991) *The Chaos Frontier: Creative Strategic Control for Business*, Butterworth-Heinemann, Oxford.

Stacey, R D (1992) *Managing Chaos: Dynamic Business Strategies in an unpredictable World*, Kogan Page, London (published in US as *Managing the Unknowable*, Jossey-Bass).

Weick, K (1979) *The Social Psychology of Organizing*, Addison-Wesley, Reading, Ma.

Zabriskie, N B and Huellmantel, A B (1991) *Long Range Planning*, Vol 24, No 6, pp25–32.

2

Managing Change

Paul Kirkbridge

Introduction

A cursory review of both academic and managerial literature reveals that the need for change is now taken for granted and is seen as the hallmark of the late twentieth century. Organisational theorists, from Alvin Toffler (1970, 1981, 1984) and Warren Bennis (1970) to, more recently, Gareth Morgan (1989) and Tom Peters (1987), have pointed to the accelerating pace of change in society. Toffler refers to the 'death of permanence' and the associated 'future shock' while Morgan talks about how managers will have to develop new competencies to cope with the turbulence caused by the 'waves of change'. Tom Peters has typically and alliteratively referred to the current decade as the 'nanosecond nineties' to draw attention to the accelerating pace of environmental change. Change is thus seen as omnipresent and organisations are seen as facing ever-changing economic, technological, social, political and cultural environments. Organisations are thus constantly seeking to adjust to their environmental context if they want to survive in the increasingly competitive world economy.

It is interesting to contrast this recent orthodoxy with earlier views of change. In the immediate post-war period change tended to be viewed as a discontinuous phenomenon. Change was something which 'disturbed' normal situations. Thus, organisations tended to be seen as existing in relatively static environments which were occasionally punctuated by brief periods of revolutionary destabilising change. Indeed, this is reflected in perhaps the most famous process model of change described by Lewin (1951).

Lewin saw change as passing through three phases: unfreezing – change – refreezing. Thus, in order to change, organisations had to be 'unfrozen' from their relative equilibrium and then changed before the required changes were then 'refrozen' and perpetuated. This view is still quite commonly held by managers. As a production manager from a large organisation undergoing major technological and cultural change recently remarked, 'We've been through massive changes on the shop floor in the last 18 months; we now need five to six years to "bed-down" the new systems and methods of working.' Needless to say, his wish was not going to be possible and the organisation has subsequently ceased to exist in its original form.

Increasingly, the traditional 'punctuated equilibrium' model which underpins most traditional theories of change has been turned on its head. Change is now seen as a continuous phenomenon and many organisational environments are seen as being characterised by flux, fluidity and chaos. Organisations, particularly in certain industries, are seen as facing long periods of environmental turbulence and revolutionary change punctuated by rare and brief periods of comparative stability.

The Need for Change

Change within organisations is therefore seen as being driven by external environmental pressures and the role of strategic management is thus one of ensuring a degree of 'fit' between the organisation and its operating environment.

Environmental Pressures

One way of examining the need for change is to consider the possible sets of relationships between organisations and their environments. Allaire and Firsirotu (1985) have developed an elegant model of the potential organisation–environment linkages (see Figure 2.1).

In the first scenario, *'Harmony and Continuity'*, the firm's strategy is well adjusted to its present environment resulting in sound performance. The future is an evolutionary predictable version of the present, for which the firm is able to prepare and change in an incremental manner. In the second scenario the firm has a strategy which is inappropriate for the present situation and results in poor performance. However, it is anticipated that the future will be fundamentally

FIGURE 1
MODELS OF ORGANISATION-ENVIRONMENT LINKAGE

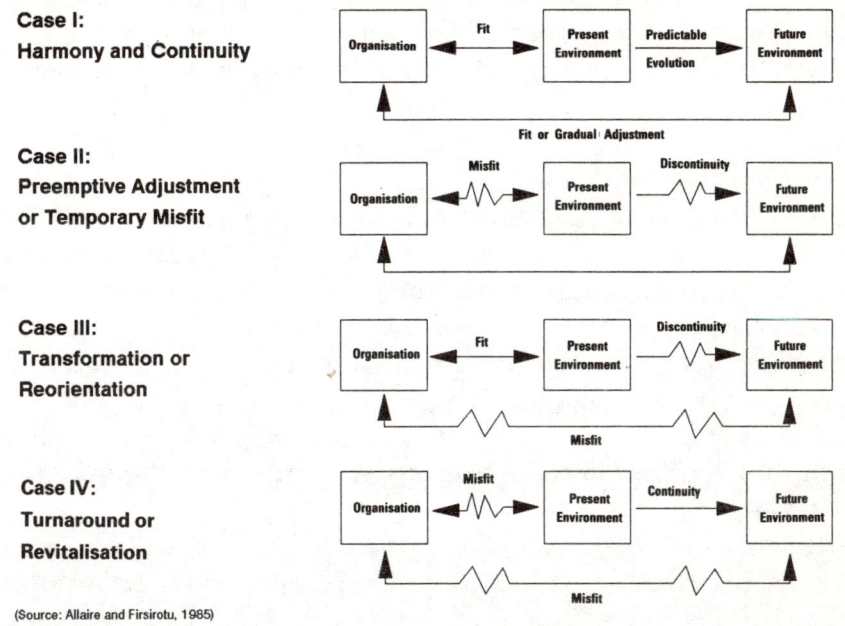

Case I:
Harmony and Continuity

Case II:
Preemptive Adjustment
or Temporary Misfit

Case III:
Transformation or
Reorientation

Case IV:
Turnaround or
Revitalisation

(Source: Allaire and Firsirotu, 1985)

Figure 2.1 *Models of organisation-environment linkage*

different from the present situation and will suit the existing strategy. At this stage the firm will reap the benefits. This is therefore a case of 'Preemptive Adjustment or Temporary Misfit'.

In the third scenario the firm is well adjusted to its current environment and enjoying success but predicts that in the future the environment will radically change. To meet this challenge the firm must change and this is where planned organisational change and development becomes necessary. This scenario is thus one of 'Transformation *or* Reorientation'. Finally, we have the worst scenario where the company is misaligned with its current environment and the future appears to be simply more of the same! If the situation is one of loss of performance and declining market share then we can talk of the need for 'Revitalisation', while if the situation is one of immanent bankruptcy then we can talk of the need for 'Turnaround'.

We can see that change is necessary in each of these situations but it may take rather different forms. In the case of Harmony and Continuity the organisation faces a scenario where evolutionary and incremental changes are all that is required because there is no immediate threat to the organisation's economic well-being and plenty of time is available to think through desired changes and plan ahead. In the second scenario the organisation has, in fact, anticipated the changes required but perhaps acted too soon. The problem with such anticipatory change is that, while there is plenty of time available, this very fact may make it difficult to create and sustain the change process. It may be difficult to persuade staff of the need for what may be seen as minor and unnecessary changes.

Transformational or Reorientation scenarios require more immediate action. There is little time available before the organisation will experience economic damage from the radically changed environmental circumstances. This is thus a case of a requirement for reactive, rather than anticipatory, change. Such reactive changes may be easier to accomplish than anticipatory changes but they may still be relatively difficult. People within the organisation may simply refuse to believe that the environment is about to change and may deny the validity of evidence and data adduced to prove the point.

Finally in the Revitalisation and Turnaround scenarios the organisation is facing a crisis change situation. The organisation is in difficulties and can see no respite. Thus, there is no room for delay or procrastination. Action must be swift and decisive. Paradoxically this may be the easiest form of change to accomplish. If the current external threat is large enough and real enough it may be relatively easy for top management to create a sense of discomfort and urgency. As long as management have a clear and believable plan for survival it may be possible to create a strong focus around the direction for change and to energise and mobilise most staff.

A recent Ashridge Management Research Group survey (Wille, 1989) investigated the 'triggers' that had stimulated organisational changes. As can be seen from Table 2.1, these triggers fall into two main groups. On the one hand triggers occur when 'bad news' from the environment in terms of declining profitability or loss of market share finally percolates the organisational consciousness. On the other hand change sometimes seems to stem from an assessment of potential threats and opportunities and thus results in proactive action. Examples of these potential threats could be the increasing obsolescence of the firm's production technology, increasing tariff barriers, or new entrants into the market, while potential opportunities would include factors such as political changes which open up new markets, declining competition in specific markets, and favourable exchange rate movements.

Table 2.1 *Triggers for change*

	%
Financial losses	24
Drop in profits	
Increased competition	23
Loss of market share	
Industry in recession	6
New chief executive officer	16
Proactive	23
(opportunities or threats foreseen)	
Technological development	8
Staff utilisation	5
N = 178	

Source: Wille, 1989

Internal 'Triggers' for Change

Of course, not all organisational change is directly environmentally driven. Changes are also a function of internal organisational factors such as employee demands, organisational politics, and top management changes. It is interesting to note, for example, that change often accompanies the arrival of a new chief executive. Kotter and Hesketh (1992) have pointed out how major cultural change within large organisations is often created by the appointment of CEOs who are either outsiders or unconventional insiders. Examples would include Lord King and Sir Colin Marshall (British Airways), Sir Michael Edwards and Sir Graham Day (British Leyland/Rover), Jack Welch (General Electric), Sir John Harvey-Jones (ICI), and Jan Carlzon (SAS). The very fact that these executives were relatively untainted by the previous history of their corporation allowed them both to diagnose the organisational deficiencies more clearly and to take decisive action in the form of either breaking accepted recipes and organisational routines or radically downsizing and de-layering the organisation.

Types of Change

While change is increasingly acknowledged as being endemic, it is unfortunately also often seen as a monolithic phenomenon. Yet, as we have already seen, there are many different forms of change. We could simply distinguish between the more macro-level organisational changes such as major strategic changes of direction, mergers and acquisitions, and changes in technology and the micro-level changes that occur constantly at the operational level. We can also distinguish between the 'what' and the 'how' of change or between the content of a

Table 2.2 *Types of Change*

	%
A. Organisational	
Culture	30
Organisational structure	44
B. Market-led issues	
Customer market orientation	30
New products	8
Reduction to core	10
Internationalise	14
Quality emphasis	11
C. People issues	
Communications/participation	23
People matters	10
Reward development	6
Emphasis on training and development	25
New work practices	15
Teams/groups/task forces	8
D. Technology	
Technology	16
E. Entrepreneurial-creative	
Innovation	4
Entrepreneurship	5
F. Economics	
Cost cutting	6
Staff reductions	9
Productivity	7

N = 178

Source: Wille, 1989

change and the process by which it is achieved. The recent Ashridge survey (Wille, 1989) mentioned above has produced some data on the kinds of changes pursued by organisations. As can be seen from Table 2.2, the organisations in the survey had engaged in a variety of different forms of change. Most common were *organisational* changes involving either changes in organisational structures or cultures followed by various market-focused or people issues.

Why is Planned Change Necessary?

Unfortunately, environmental signals and stimuli concerning the need for organisational change do not automatically trigger internal change responses. Similarly, change pressures from within do not always feed smoothly through to the whole organisation. For these reasons, it is usually necessary for someone within the organisation deliberately to plan for the intended changes and direct the various interventions designed to deliver them.

Resistance to Change

It is often asserted that people within organisations generally resist change. This is probably a little extreme, but the common mindset generated by a conception of change as an 'abnormal' disturbance to the equilibrium of organisational stability would perhaps naturally lead to a certain degree of resistance. In reality, of course, resistance is a continuum rather than an either/or. Organisational members do not simply resist or embrace change, but they can also adopt a range of intermediate responses. At one extreme, organisational members can enthusiastically embrace and welcome the proposed changes. Moving away from that extreme, people may merely accept proposed changes in a more neutral fashion or simply acquiesce out of a feeling of fatalism. Resistance may begin with surface and public acceptance but with staff at lower levels working to modify the effects of the change. Resistance may also take the form of ritualistic acceptance without follow-up action. As we escalate up the resistance continuum we come to outright opposition to the proposed changes via mechanisms of delay, the withholding of resources and the creating of defensive coalitions through to more active responses such as direct action, striking, and sabotage. Ultimately, or at an earlier stage, resistors may feel the need to leave the organisation because of the proposed changes.

Why do organisational members resist change? Essentially there are two related explanations. On the one hand, members may be unable to see the need for change and, on the other hand, they may see the need but fear the consequences. Organisational members may be unable to see the need for change for several reasons. First, their organisational roles may not necessarily involve examination of the external environment, so they may well be unaware of changes in the organisation's environment which require an appropriate response. Second, they may feel that current organisational success precludes the need for change even though senior management or organisational planners have identified potential shifts in the external environment which cause concern and require anticipatory change. Third, they may be vaguely aware of the pressures for change, but it is often easier to deny that the pressures are real or will ever happen, or that they potentially affect one's own area, than to internalise the pressure and produce appropriate actions.

Even if employees begin to 'own' the need for change, they may be constrained by an inability to act appropriately. They may be totally confused as to what is required, or clear about the required actions but unwilling to proceed because of fears of the unknown. In the change process, therefore, the 'f' word is . . . fear! Organisational members may fear redundancy, reduced remuneration, different working conditions, new skill requirements, decreased job satisfaction, higher performance standards, or simply the uncertainty of the unknown. Of course, not all the blame for resistance can be placed at the level of individual employees. In addition to human barriers one can identify system, technological, and organisational political barriers to change.

Overcoming Resistance

Restricting our analysis to the human factors, there are clear indications as to how these barriers to change can be overcome. Obviously one implication is the need for clear organisational communication. Employees may be persuaded of the need to change if they can see what is driving the change in the external environment. If they are denying the relevance or validity of the external pressures, then activities such as visits which enable them actually to see such things as new technology in action or competitor performance may 'unlock' their resistance. Thus the first essential step is to communicate clearly the nature of the change problem. Only when this is owned by the majority of the employees can one successfully move to communicating the preferred solution. The second major implication is the need to involve employees in the change process. Consultation and participation can be extremely effective at the stages of problem diagnosis, solution identification, and planned implementation.

Models of the Change Process

The voluminous literature on change contains a plethora of different models of change, most of which are simply variations on a basic theme and amplifications of the seminal Lewinian model. Thus most models consist of a series of discrete stages over a period of time. One simple yet elegant version of this core theme is provided by Phillips (1983), and his model (derived from McKinsey consulting practice) will be used here as an exemplar of this approach.

A Phase Model of Change

The model (see Figure 2.2) assumes that top management of the organisation have diagnosed the need for change(s) and thus the key issue is how to create the required change(s) within the organisation. The first stage consists of creating a sense of concern throughout the organisation. While senior management may be aware of the potential problems or opportunities offered by environmental changes and industry dynamics, it is not necessarily the case that such perceptions are communicated clearly throughout the organisation or accepted by the majority of the workforce. Yet that is the situation which must be brought about if the required changes are to be achieved. Employees must be convinced of the need to change and there must be a potent core group of managers pushing the change forward.

The second stage consists of developing a specific commitment to change. Here the generalised sense of concern developed in the first stage has to be channelled and focused towards specific actions and areas. It is often at this stage that the senior management of the organisation seek to redefine the core values and vision of the organisation and to codify them in some form of corporate mission statement. A common failing of such processes in many organisations is that employees 'learn' the corporate mission but are unable to articulate exactly how this affects them and their sections and to describe how their own behaviour needs to change to deliver the mission. This is the central thrust of this second stage of the change process.

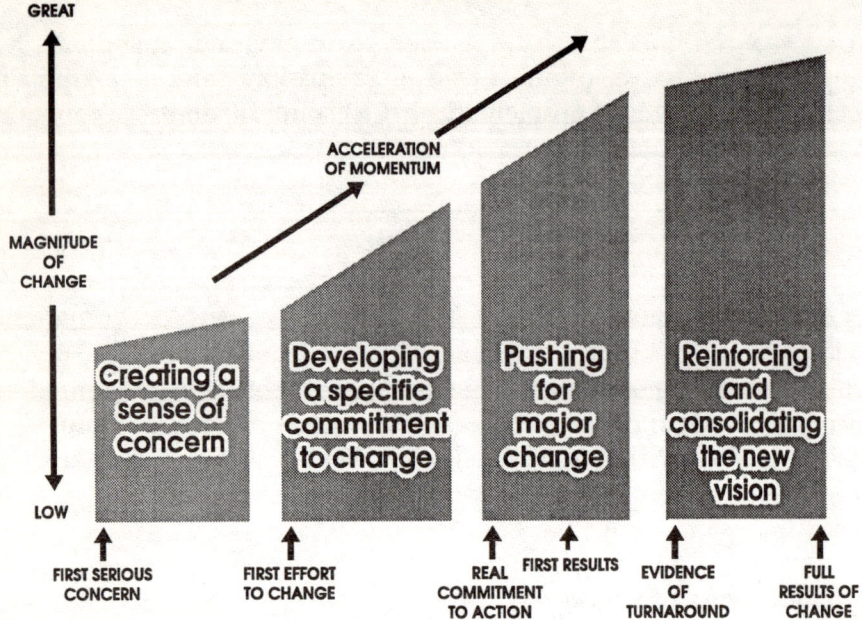

Source: Phillips, 1983

Figure 2.2 *The phases of organisation change*

The third stage consists of pushing for major change on a number of fronts. It is hoped that during this phase the organisation will achieve its intended competitive position by motivating virtually all managers to be active in changing organisational behaviour in key areas. How is this to be accomplished? Essentially, managers have successfully to pull, in unison and in the same direction, the series of 'change levers' which are available to them.

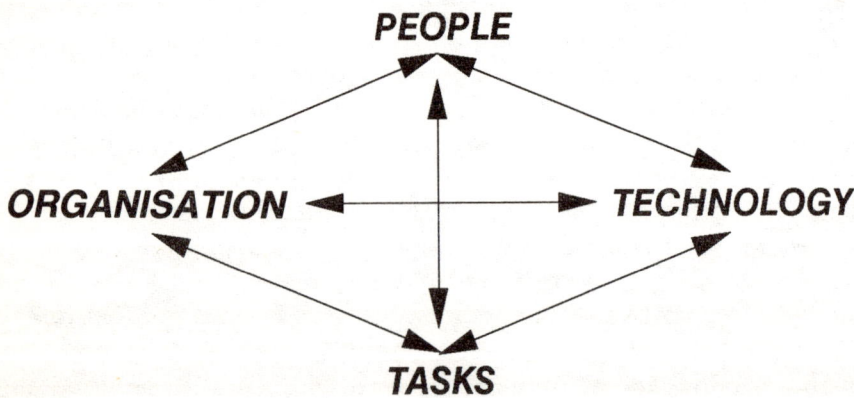

Figure 2.3 *Leavitt's diamond*

What are these levers of change? One traditional model is what has become known as Leavitt's diamond (1964) (see Figure 2.3). This suggests that one can intervene in the organisation to create change in four distinct areas. These are people, technology, tasks and organisation. The manager or consultant implementing change can intervene in terms of people by replacing key staff, reducing or expanding staffing levels, or (re)training staff. Interventions in the technology area may involve new equipment, work methods or information systems. Changes can be made to tasks ranging from goals and strategies at high levels down to individual job design. Finally, in the organisational area, managers can make changes in organisational structures, systems and procedures. It should be noted that each area of potential intervention is linked to the other three. This implies the need to anticipate the fact that first order changes in any area will have consequential secondary and tertiary order changes in the other areas. For example, the introduction of new information technology systems may change job tasks for particular staff with the consequent need for retraining, and structural changes in reporting relationships and accountabilities to take account of the new roles.

Finally there is a need to reinforce the new sets of learned behaviours and to consolidate the new organisational vision. Individuals who exhibit the appropriate behaviours need to be rewarded and sub-units which begin to operate in the 'new culture' need to be held up as exemplars. The outcome of this final phase should be a modified corporate culture with management now routinely acting in accordance with the new vision and values. Obviously, as we have already noted, change will probably be ongoing. Thus, another purpose of this phase of the change process is to create a continuing capacity for further change and to maximise the learning achieved so that subsequent changes may be handled more effectively.

A Completely Integrated Change Programme.

With many organisations facing increasingly turbulent environments and seeking desperately to initiate change there has been a corresponding increase in consultants offering change advice. Unfortunately in some cases this has tended to be of the 'quick fix' variety. One academic/consultant has proposed to go 'beyond the quick fix' and to create a 'completely integrated program' for organisational change (Kilmann, 1989a; 1989b). Like most other theorists Kilmann sees the change process as consisting of a series of discrete temporal stages (see Figure 2.4).

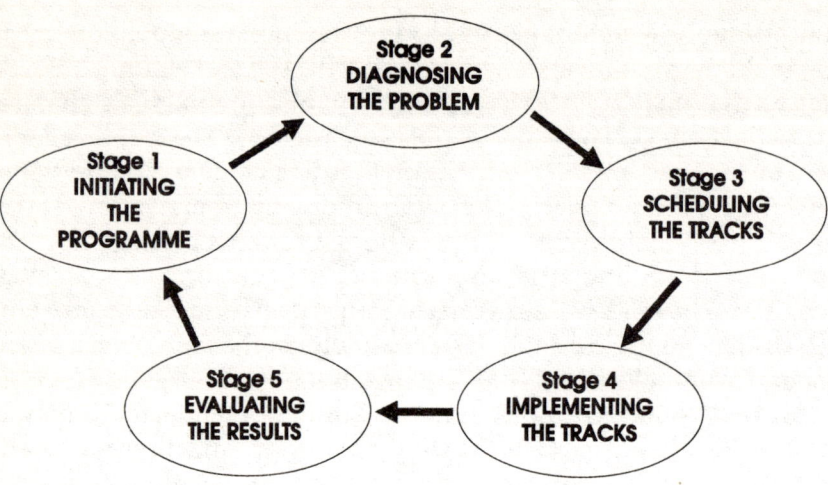

Source: Kilmann, 1989a

Figure 2.4 *Planned organisational change*

The first stage, initiating the programme, essentially consists of ensuring that the key requirement for organisational change, top management commitment, is present and that senior managers will take responsibility for the programme. The second stage then involves an organisational diagnosis focusing on potential barriers to the success of the change programme. Kilmann sees the next stage of planned change as the process of scheduling the five 'tracks' of culture, management skills, team-building, strategy structure, and reward system. Scheduling involves: selecting the first organisational sub-unit to participate; selecting the methods to be used; and then implementing the 'tracks' in a strict sequence. Kilmann suggests that:

> . . . the five tracks, in all cases, are scheduled in the prescribed order. The first three tracks (culture, management skills, and team-building) adjust the behavioural infrastructure of the organisation – the blood and guts of how people behave toward one another on the job. The last two tracks (strategy structure and reward system) adjust the organisation's tangible features – the documents, technologies, systems and resources that guide people's behaviour toward an agreed-upon mission. Without first developing an adaptive *inner* organisation, any adjustments to the outer organisation would be cosmetic and, therefore, short-lived. (1989b, p13)

The fourth stage of this systematic planned change approach is to implement the tracks. Kilmann sees each of the tracks making specific contributions in an additive manner. Thus:

> The culture track enhances trust, communication, information sharing, and willingness to change among members – the conditions that must

exist before any other improvement effort can succeed. The management-skills track provides all management personnel with new ways of coping with complex problems and hidden assumptions. The team-building track infuses the new culture and updated management skills into each work unit – thereby instilling cooperation organization-wide so that complex problems can be addressed with all the expertise and information available. The strategy-structure track develops either a completely new or a revised strategic plan for the firm and then aligns divisions, departments, work groups, jobs, and all resources with the new strategic direction. The reward-system track establishes a performance-based reward system that sustains all the improvements by officially sanctioning the new culture, the use of updated management skills, and cooperative team efforts within and among all work groups. (Kilmann, 1989b, pp 13–14)

The final stage involves attempting to evaluate the planned programme in order to monitor progress, identify remaining barriers, and determine relative success and failure.

Revitalising Mature Corporations

Kilmann offers his model as a generic process applicable to all organisations undergoing major change. His model is essentially top down, cyclical, participative, moving from 'soft' issues to 'harder' ones, and processual. A useful contrast is provided by a model which specifically focuses on change in a particular type of organisation. Richard Beatty and Dave Ulrich (1991) propose a five-stage model (see Figure 2.5) for 're-energising' the large mature corporation facing the decline stage of the organisational life cycle.

Obviously the first stage of an organisational renewal process for the 'bloated' mature corporation starts with some form of restructuring usually in the form of cuts in both headcount and organisational levels ('downsizing' and 'delayering' in modern consulting parlance). This is followed by the second stage of 'bureaucracy bashing' which involves attempts to:

. . . get rid of unnecessary reports, approvals, meetings, measures, policies, procedures, or other work activities which create backlogs. By focusing on bureaucracy reduction, employees throughout the organisation experience changes in how they do their work. Often, sources of employee work frustration come from being constrained by bureaucratic procedures and not being able to see or feel the impact of their work on others. (Beatty and Ulrich, 1991, p 25)

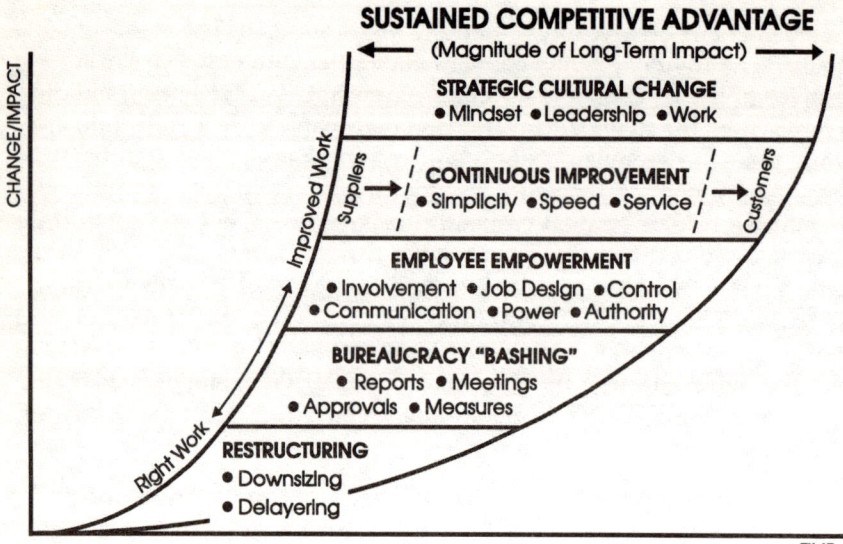

Source: Beatty and Ulrich, 1991

Figure 2.5 *A process for re-energising mature organisations*

During this stage the organisation needs to ask itself two critical questions:

1. To what extent does each work activity add value to customers?
2. To what extent are the work activities performed as effectively as possible?

One rationale for beginning the re-energising process with such harsh steps is that as such cuts have to be made at some stage then they should be done as soon as possible. This reduces uncertainty, reduces operating costs, refocuses the business on customer needs, and clears the ground for later more participative stages. It also sends a clear cultural message throughout the organisation that change is for real this time and that all employees will from now on be required to operate in different and more productive ways. The central focus of the first two stages is thus that of identifying 'right work'. With this done the organisation can proceed to the last three stages which focus instead on 'improving work'.

The third stage is one of removing barriers between managers and employees and involving employees directly in the processes of work improvement. Out of this stage the next flows naturally and consists of implementing a series of continuous improvement processes and efforts. As Beatty and Ulrich note:

The final stage of renewal is really an outgrowth of the other four. Fundamental cultural change means employees' mindset – the way they think about their work – is shifted. Employees do not feel part of a 'mature' company, but they see themselves as having faced and overcome the renewal change challenge. They feel the enthusiasm and commitment of trying new approaches to work and, as a result, they bring more desired changes into the organization. (1991, p 28)

While this model is also top down in orientation in a manner similar to that of Kilmann there are a number of crucial differences. The Beatty and Ulrich model is more linear, is only participative in the later stages, moves from 'hard' issues to 'softer' ones, and is much more task focused.

A Critique of Top-down Attitude Change

Despite the consistent advocacy of such programmatic top-down change initiatives both in the business and managerial press and by change consultants, there appears to be little objective evidence that such programmes are ever successful. To what extent do they ever finally produce the behavioural changes and business results that are desired? While the managerial journals are replete with 'how we did it at XYZ Corporation' articles and many such programmes begin in the glare of publicity, there tends to be a paucity of articles reporting systematic evaluation studies and most such change attempts appear to fizzle out quietly in private.

Michael Beer and his colleagues at Harvard (Beer, Eisenstat and Spector, 1990a, 1990b) believe that this is because such top-down programmatic attempts at change are fatally flawed. They suggest that:

> [most] change programs don't work because they are guided by a theory of change that is fundamentally flawed. The common belief is that the place to begin is with the knowledge and attitudes of individuals. Changes in attitudes, the theory goes, lead to changes in individual behavior. Any changes in individual behavior, repeated by many people, will result in organizational change . . . This theory gets the change process exactly backward. In fact, individual behavior is powerfully shaped by the organization roles that people play. The most effective way to change behavior, therefore, is to put people in a new organizational context which imposes new roles, responsibilities, and relationships on them. This creates a situation that, in a sense, 'forces' new attitudes and behaviors on people. (1990a, p159)

Table 2.3 *Contrasting assumptions about change*

Programmatic change	Task alignment
Problems in behaviour are a function of individual knowledge, attitudes and beliefs	Individual knowledge, attitudes and beliefs are shaped by recurring patterns of behavioural interactions
The primary target of renewal should be the content of attitudes and ideas; actual behaviour should be secondary	The primary target of renewal should be behaviour; attitudes and ideas should be secondary
Behaviour can be isolated and changed individually	Problems in behaviour come from a circular pattern, but the effects of the organisational system on the individual are greater than those of the individual on the system
The target for renewal should be at the individual level	The target for renewal should be at the level of roles, responsibilities and relationships

Source: Beer, Eisentat and Spector, 1990a

Thus Beer *et al* offer the process of what they term 'task alignment' as a corrective and alternative to programmatic change. This approach completely alters the point of focus in change attempts. Whereas programmatic change believes the target for change should be the individual in an attempt to change attitudes and thus behaviours, task alignment focuses on the level of structural and task arrangements in the belief that these can determine and constrain behaviour and that ultimately such behaviour changes will result in consequent shifts in attitudes and values (see Table 2.3).

Beer and colleagues see the role of top management in task alignment approaches as one of creating a market for change rather than specifying the change methods and approaches. The most effective way of creating such a market is to set demanding standards for all operations and then hold managers accountable to them. As particular sub-units then begin to tackle change as a means of delivering the required performance standards, then these should be held up in the organisation as exemplars. Finally, they suggest that top management needs to develop career paths which foster leadership development:

At our best-practice companies, managers were moved from job to job and from organization to organization based on their learning needs, not on their position in the hierarchy. Successful leaders were assigned to units that had been targeted for change. People who needed to sharpen their leadership skills were moved into the company's model units where skills would be demanded and therefore learned. In effect, top management used leading edge units as hothouses to develop revitalization leaders. (Beer, Eisenstat and Spector, 1990a, p166)

6 Monitor and adjust strategies in response to problems in the revitalisation process

5 Institutionalise revitalisation through formal policies, systems and structures

4 Spread revitalisation to all departments without pushing from the top

3 Foster consensus for the new vision, competence to enact it and cohesion to move it along

2 Develop a shared vision of how to organise and manage for competitiveness

1 Mobilise commitment to change through joint diagnosis of business problems

Source: Beer, Eisenstat and Spector, 1990a

Figure 2.6 *Six steps to effective change*

While the Beer model, with its concentration on changing task behaviour and starting change at sub-unit levels, can be seen as a useful corrective to the more common top-down and attitude-focused models, it appears odd that the authors should seek to position their model as a critique of 'programmatic' change. Indeed their 'six steps to effective change' (see Figure 2.6) appears suspiciously 'programmed' and not, in fact, totally dissimilar from the Kilmann model in certain respects.

A Multiple-Method Approach to Organisational Change

We saw earlier that it was important to make clear distinctions between the 'types' of change that an organisation is facing. We have also seen that there is a good deal of debate about the potential differences in the 'methods' used to deliver change. One useful distinction, as we have seen, is the level in the organisation at which change attempts should begin. Some theorists and consultants advocate starting at the top of the organisation with a 'trickle down' effect and suggest that the essential prerequisite for change is top management involvement and commitment. Others suggest that the initial change attempts should focus on small groups or sub-units with the purpose of gaining 'early wins' which can then be used to spread change both laterally and vertically through the rest of the organisation. Another clear dichotomy exists between those who advocate a 'hard' approach to change, focusing on the use of force, edict, pressure, threat and actions such as imposed downsizing and de-layering, and those who prefer a 'softer' approach which involves persuasion, consultation, employee participation and 'buy-in'. Putting these two dimensions together we can identify four core styles of change (cf Bate, 1990) (see Figure 2.7).

The Conciliative Approach

The conciliative approach consists of the application of consultative, collaborative and participative interventions targeted at groups, teams and organisational sub-units. It is therefore typical of traditional organisational development (OD) approaches in the process-consulting mode derived from the theory of small group dynamics. The key features of this 'Bing Crosby' theory of change (Bate, 1990; p9) are that proponents believe that change can be achieved via non-dramatic, gradual and routine means. There is a clear attempt made to avoid potential confrontation and to smooth over and manage any conflicts which occur during the change process. The conciliative approach believes that often change processes involve the classic mistake of

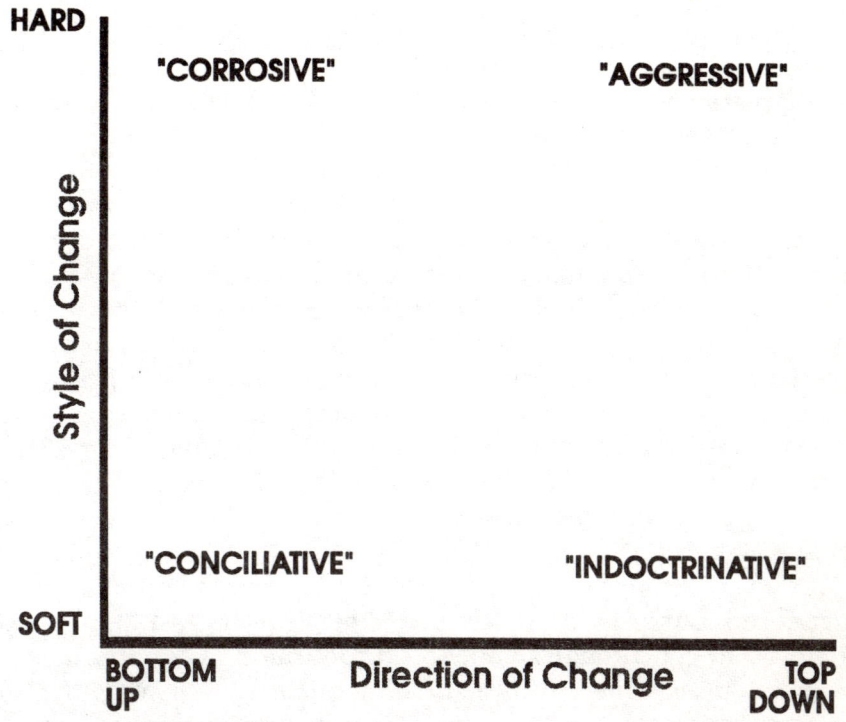

Source: Derived from Bate, 1990

Figure 2.7 *Types of cultural change*

'throwing the baby out with the bathwater'; thus good elements of the existing organisational culture are sacrificed deliberately or accidentally erased in the process of establishing a new and improved culture. Instead the conciliative approach suggests that 'the old can be put to good use in the construction of the new: only when you get the brickwork up can you take the scaffolding down' (Bate, 1990; p13).

The advantages of the conciliative approach are clear. Such an approach tends to unite employees and can create increased trust. As the approach retains the best features of the old culture and a continuity with past tradition it may lead to increased 'buy-in' and high levels of organisational commitment. The approach also treats people as adults and is non-dogmatic and flexible, being capable of adjustment to particular sub-unit circumstances. However, there is a danger that the change 'message' will become diluted and eventually 'wishy-washy' as a result of extended processes of consultation and participation. The message may thus result in a lot of detail but an absence of 'core truths'. In addition, the process is extremely time consuming and thus organisationally expensive.

The Aggressive Approach

In complete contrast, the aggressive approach to change consists of more directive, authoritarian and radical interventions targeted at the whole organisation. As Bate notes, this 'might be described as cultural vandalism, a wilful attack on the traditional values of the organization that aims to break a few windows. Its purpose is to create disruption among the local population, and to give notice of the intention of establishing an entirely new cultural order' (1990, p2). This approach has been aptly tagged 'leadership with a machine gun' (Brissy, 1989). It is often justified on the basis that the organisation is in crisis and about to go 'over the brink' and thus a final radical solution is needed to solve the organisation's problems and to bring it back from the edge. Thus it may be asserted that 'radical times demand radical remedies'. Such an approach is often implemented by leaders with heroic and messianic pretensions.

The main strengths of the aggressive approach to organisational change are that it deals in plain and simple messages and may be the only way to get through to affect behaviour and thus performance in crisis situations. The focus is on tackling existing problems with radical and innovative solutions. Often such approaches are adopted by new CEOs brought in to turn around ailing corporations and are seen as a new broom sweeping clean. The problems of this approach are that it can (does?) lead to strong resistance and creates rancour and discord. The process is fairly inflexible with the need for the strong messages to be spread and applied consistently throughout the organisation. There tends to be little initial 'buy-in' by employees and little ownership of any changes achieved in this manner. Often the changes evaporate when the initiator leaves the organisation or retires.

The Indoctrinative Approach

Also top down and directed centrally, but with a softer focus, is the indoctrinative approach to change. This '1984' theory of change is based on the central premise that ideas can influence behaviours. Thus an attempt is made in this method to teach employees core values via systematic socialisation and training initiatives. As Bate notes, this approach has:

> . . . one great claim to respectability in that it follows the teachings of mainstream organization development (OD). It shows a perfect fit, for example, with Beckhard's (1969) classic definition of OD as a) a planned

and deliberate attempt to introduce change, b) managed and led from the top, c) introduced system-wide, and d) based on an educational strategy. (1990, pp 22–3)

The key advantage of this approach is that it communicates clearly certain core messages to employees in a systematic and structured format. It is thus a total immersion strategy. The problem with such an approach is that few people appear actually to go through the 'conversion' process envisaged by the designers of the programme. People appear remarkably resistant to such manipulation. Even where employees do either internalise or superficially parrot the messages, there is little evidence that this level of rhetoric actually feeds through into different job and task behaviours. Another problem is the fact that if the messages are not constantly reinforced then any effects which are apparent soon dissipate. This makes this change strategy potentially very expensive. A final problem is that many individuals appear to react very badly to these kinds of approaches, feeling that they are being excessively programmed and that the system is inflexible and cannot tolerate deviant behaviour.

The Corrosive Approach

Finally, we come to the approach which focuses in a fairly 'hard' political manner on promoting change either from the bottom up or at lower levels of the organisation. This is known as the 'corrosive' approach to change. In contrast to the indoctrinative approach, it takes the view that behaviour influences attitudes and values and not the reverse. Thus the key issue is to intervene in the organisation in order to make changes which force changes in behaviour which will eventually feed through into attitudinal and belief changes and consequently a new culture. Obviously Beer's task alignment model (see Table 2.3) is an exemplar of this approach.

We may argue that there are perhaps two distinct variants of this approach. In the first, disaffected middle managers adopting the dictums that 'you can succeed from the inside' and 'you can't wait for direction from the top' turn inwards on their own departments and sections and seek to make changes to ensure improved productivity, performance and satisfaction. This we can call the 'organisational subversion' approach. The advantage of this approach is that changes can occur quickly where they are needed without waiting for a corporate response which may never materialise. It is also very empowering for those involved. From the point of view of the organisation it may lead to a haphazard change scenario as various parts of the organisation do their own thing.

In the second variant, top management wish to create change but wish it to be seen to be coming from lower levels in the organisation. They thus quietly encourage and enable a particular sub-unit to effect change in the hope that this will 'corrosively' spread to other parts of the organisation. While such an approach has the advantage of distancing management from unpopularity and failure, it does have the potential to get out of control as sub-units make changes which were not intended.

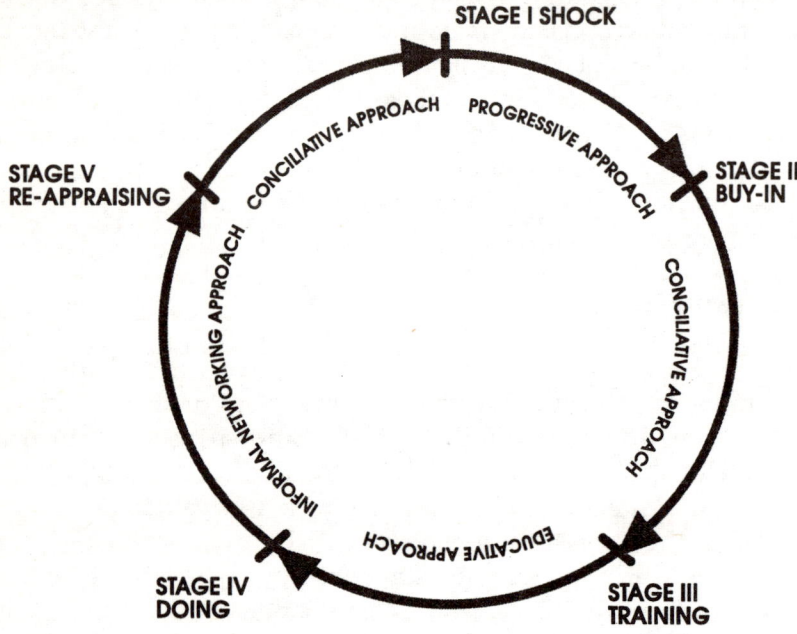

Source: Adapted from Bate, 1990

Figure 2.8 *A multiple-method model of change*

Combining the Approaches

As we have seen, each of the four preceding approaches has particular strengths but also specific weaknesses. Unfortunately there is a tendency for managers and consultants to adopt one, and only one, of these approaches, to persist with it throughout a change programme, and to apply it invariably in all situations regardless of the circumstances. Yet as Bate perceptively argues:

We must recognize that cultural change is episodic, characterized by abrupt transformations rather than gradual evolution. It thus requires qualitatively different methods for handling each episode, and a definite switch of approach as one episode supersedes another; at the appropriate moment, one approach should be ready to 'hand over the baton' to another. (1990, p 31)

What would such a fluid, change-oriented and environmentally sensitive model look like? A tentative outline is suggested in Figure 2.8. Stage I consists of 'shocking' the organisation out of its current routines, recipes and rituals by the application of the aggressive, or perhaps a slightly milder and more acceptable progressive, approach. This is followed by an attempt to create 'buy-in' and to smooth over the schisms and ruptures caused by the first stage. If the first stage corresponds to Beatty and Ulrich's phases of restructuring and bureaucracy bashing, then Stage II can be seen as an attempt to obtain the commitment of those staff who remain in the organisation. This conciliative stage is then followed by the educative Stage III where training and development interventions are used to spread the new culture. This, again, can be seen as a milder and organisationally more acceptable version of the 'pure' indoctrinative approach. Stage IV consists of using an informal networking or corrosive approach to spread the new attitudes, values and behaviours through the organisation. This is followed by Stage V where the organisation reviews, in a conciliative and participative manner, the extent of cultural change and the emergence of appropriate behaviours.

As Bate argues:

> [The] justification for the sequence runs briefly as follows: the Progressive Approach is arguably the best method for getting the whole process underway, but it tends to lack follow-up and finish. The Conciliative Approach is weak in the above area but provides excellent follow-up by allowing everyone to have a say, exert some influence and thereby gain ownership of the ideas. The Educative Approach draws these ideas together and enables them to be systematically incorporated within participants' personal frames of reference. In following the Conciliative Approach it can no longer be indoctrinative; the emphasis shifts from teaching to learning. The Corrosive Approach that follows cannot enjoy unfettered freedom to roam at will because there should now be some parameters within which it is constrained and directed. It is still, however, one of the best ways of translating the new culture into action and adapting it as necessary. The Conciliative Approach . . . is now put to good use again, this time to give shape and form to the emergent culture. It thus guarantees a degree of durability until such time as the system is shaken up all over again! (1990, pp 32–3)

A Post-modern Critique of Change Theory

So far in this chapter I have attempted to provide a review of the central features of the management of change literature culminating with the exposition of a sophisticated model which appears to integrate the key themes and issues in a coherent and powerful manner. Yet it may be argued that this whole canon is built upon a series of, often unacknowledged, presuppositions which may be open to challenge. To put it simply, the vast majority of the literature and theorising on change can be located centrally within a 'modernist' perspective (Clegg, 1990). Such a perspective is predicated upon the power of reason, the search for fundamentals or essentials, the machine metaphor of organisation, and a faith in progress and universal design (Gergen, 1992).

Modernist Assumptions about Change

Despite the surface heterogeneity of much of the organisational change and development literature, a set of common core assumptions is revealed upon closer examination. First there is a conception of time as linear and sequential, as summed up in Heraclitus's contention that 'no man steps in the same river twice'. Thus many theories of organisational change portray the process as a series of logically interrelated steps in sequence over time with distinctive points of conception and completion. Associated with this is the notion that change involves the inevitability of progress and development. Thus OD is seen as a process of moving organisations from present 'unhealthy' states to future 'healthy' ones (Beckhard, 1969). This view of linear progression lies at the heart of modernist philosophy which advocates the inexorable rise of reason and the subsequent improvement of society. As Burrell notes:

> . . . it is clear that the unilinear progression of organisational forms has been assumed by many Western writers. 'Unilinear' because forms are seen as following in sequence, with the origins of the new fashionable mode being visible in the previously fashionable way of organising. The antecedents of the present are seen in what is the immediate past. 'Progression' because what is contemporary and fashionable is often seen to represent a 'higher' level of development as well as a newer level. (1992, p 169)

A second major tenet of the modernist view of change is that change is an incremental and gradual process of adjustment. Such periods of revolutionary change that do exist are seen as 'abnormal' shocks to the 'normality' of relative stability. This assumption naturally leads to a belief that various social actors (eg managers and consultants) can intervene purposively into organisational processes in order to produce desired change. Given a state of comparative stability, engineered incremental change becomes possible.

The final core assumption of modernist theories of change is the importance of maintaining a degree of 'fit' between the organisation (strategy and structure) and the external environment in which it operates. Thus the role of OD is one of reacting to environmental change to ensure continuity of 'fit' between the organisation and environment. We can perhaps sum up the modernist approach to change as one of 'managing change'.

Challenges to Modernist Assumptions

In recent years there have been a number of authors who have drawn attention to the problematic nature of these core assumptions of modernism. For example, Tom Peters (1987) has challenged the view of change as gradual and incremental, arguing instead for revolutionary change to keep pace with an increasingly chaotic environment. Similarly, a variety of writers (Burns, 1978; Bennis and Nanus, 1985) have sought to distinguish the transactional leadership style suitable for gradual and incremental change from the transformational style required to deliver revolutionary changes which transform the organisation. Others (Clark, 1990), have pointed to the existence of cyclical conceptions of time and the associated implications for organisational change processes. Finally, yet others, such as Pascale (1990), have suggested that there are dangers in the pursuit of excessive 'fit' and that what is required is the creative management of 'critical vectors of contention' in a dynamic and constructive tension. Excessive 'fit' leaves organisations extremely vulnerable to revolutionary environmental shocks in that they can move from positions of perfect fit to total lack of fit extremely quickly.

While these theorists all offer useful corrections to modernist assumptions, it may be suggested that they fail to transcend the modernist paradigm. We may therefore refer to this group as 'sophisticated modernists'. They are more likely to believe in the existence of chaotic environments and cyclical time and to accept the need for transformational and revolutionary change to break organisational recipes. Thus their central orientation to change can be seen as one of 'creating change'.

Change in a Post-modern World

Increasingly, however, both modernist and sophisticated modernist approaches are coming under attack from a growing 'post-modernist' perspective which rejects the primacy of reason and the concepts of unity and progress (Gergen, 1992). What, then, would constitute a post-modernist view of change? Dictates of space in this chapter prevent a full answer but an attempt will be made to sketch some of the contours of such a perspective. In essence, the post-modernist approach would reject the notions of progress, linearity, and regular patterning. Change could occur in any direction at any time, which itself could be conceived of in new ways such as 'spiral time' (Burrell, 1992). But, perhaps centrally, change would be seen as chaotic in the pure scientific sense (Stacey, 1991). Thus the key issue is not just the increasing pace and scope of change as noted by the sophisticated modernists, but that, in fact, the organisational world is better described in terms of disorder and unpredictability. In a post-modern world change simply *is*. It cannot be 'managed' or even 'created'. At best it can be observed and diverted. As Massarik has suggested;

> . . . we now face frequently, more so than even in the immediate past, that *point of discontinuity* where old rules – or even fairly-well learned approaches for dealing with conventional change – fail us. The 'force field' once so neatly conceptualized by discrete and identifiable arrows, falls apart. Erratic turbulences embrace us.. . . The task of high-intensity diagnosis, therefore, becomes one of finding the way – for OD and for other purposes – through the paradox of 'regularity within chaos'.

What does all this mean for post-modern change agents? On one level of analysis we might suggest that the role of the change agent becomes one of commentator, interpreter and high-speed interventionist. Perhaps the role of the change agent will be to help managers reflect upon their own mental maps and frameworks and to help them adapt and reframe them as they face change and seek to influence its direction and outcome. It may be asserted that the real issue revolves around the certainty of the outcomes in change attempts. The modernist tends to believe in simple cause and effect relationships and thus in the possibility of 'pulling levers' to deliver desired outcomes. In a post-modern world, intervention remains possible but there can be no certainty about outcomes. Thus the motivation changes: one no longer intervenes in order to produce desired results; instead one intervenes in a belief that something, generally better than worse, might result. As Massarik suggests, but perhaps in more of a 'sophisticated modernist' vein than a post-modernist one:

. . . the top-notch OD practitioner of the next decade will need to become rapidly and responsively adaptable to a world that will not hold still, not even long enough for traditional diagnostic process and normal intervention design. High speed heuristics, sometimes virtually on the spot, but rooted in a thorough understanding of underlying concepts, will become the order of the day. Versatility will count, in drawing from a suitable repertoire of intervention types; and team effort and networking among practitioners of varied fundamental styles will count to assure responsiveness to the demands of irregularity and chaotic transformation. (1990, pp 7–8)

On another level of analysis we might suggest that change agents will not exist in a post-modern world as the term becomes an oxymoron. Agency disappears in pure post-modernism. Change agents simply become 'voices' without authority and change plans become 'texts' to be 'read' in many different ways. This world-view would not preclude intervention in organisational affairs, but the motivation for such intervention would now simply be the intervention itself.

How seriously should we take the post-modernist critique? Some theorists (Clegg, 1990) appear to view post-modernism as an epoch of time and to take the view that we are currently in transition from a modernist world to a post-modernist one. Others would argue that post-modernism is a method of viewing our current realities and more accurately describes the organisational world in which we live. If you are a modernist you may wish to wait for the unfolding of linear time and the accumulation of evidence to prove or disprove post-modernist assertions. On the other hand if you are of a post-modernist inclination you may read this 'text' in any way you desire.

References

Allaire, Y and Firsirotu, M (1985) 'How to implement radical strategies in large organisations', *Sloan Management Review*, 26, spring, p 3.

Bate, S P (1990) 'A description and evaluation of four different approaches to the management of cultural change in organizations', *Proceedings of the Fourth Annual Conference of the British Academy of Management*, Glasgow.

Beatty, R W and Ulrich, D (1991) 'Re-energizing the mature organization', *Organizational Dynamics*, 20, p 1.

Beckard, R (1969) *Organization Development: Strategies and Models*, Addison-Wesley, Reading, Mass.

Beer, M, Eisenstat, R A and Spector, B (1990a) 'Why change programs don't produce change', *Harvard Business Review*, 68, 6, Nov–Dec, pp 158–66.

— (1990b) *The Critical Path to Corporate Renewal*, Harvard Business School Press, Boston.

Bennis, W G (1970) 'A funny thing happened on the way to the future', *American Psychologist*, 25, 7, pp 595–608.

Bennis, W and Nanus, B (1985) *Leaders: The Strategies for Taking Charge*, Harper and Row, New York.

Brissy, J F (1989) 'Leadership in the courtroom: A Belgian experiment in "responsive law"', *Paper presented at the 4th International SCOS Conference on Organizational Symbolism and Corporate Culture*, June, INSEAD, France.

Burns, J M (1978) *Leadership*, Harper and Row, New York.

Burrell, G (1992) 'Back to the future: time and organization', in M Reed and M Hughes (eds), *Rethinking Organization: New Directions in Organization Theory and Analysis*, Sage, London.

Clark, P (1990) 'Chronological codes and organizational analysis', in J Hassard and E D Pym (eds), *The Theory and Philosophy of Organizations*, Routledge, London.

Clegg, S R (1990) *Modern Organizations: Organization Studies in the Postmodern World*, Sage, London.

Gergen, K J (1992) 'Organization theory in the postmodern era', in M Reed and M Hughes (eds), *Rethinking Organization: New Directions in Organization Theory and Analysis*, Sage, London.

Kilmann, R (1989a) 'A completely integrated program for creating and maintaining organizational success', *Organizational Dynamics*, 18, 1, pp 5–19.

— (1989b) *Managing Beyond the Quick Fix*, Jossey Bass, San Francisco.

Kotter, J P and Hesketh, J L (1992) *Corporate Culture and Performance*, Free Press, New York.

Leavitt, H J (1964) 'Applied organizational change in industry', in W W Cooper, H J Leavitt and M W Shelly (eds), *New Perspectives in Organizational Research*, Wiley, New York.

Lewin, K (1951) *Field Theory in Social Science*, Harper and Row, New York.

Massarik, F (1990) 'Chaos and change: Examining the aesthetics of organization development', in F Massarik (ed), *Advances in Organization Development – Volume 1*, Ablex, New Jersey.

Morgan, G (1989) *Riding the Waves of Change*, Sage, London.

Pascale, R T (1990) *Managing on the Edge: How Successful Companies use Conflict to Stay Ahead*, Viking, London.

Peters, T (1987) *Thriving on Chaos: Handbook for a Managerial Revolution*, Pan, London.

Phillips, J R (1983) 'Enhancing the effectiveness of organizational change management', *Human Resource Management*, 22, 1/2, pp 183–99.

Stacey, R D (1991) *The Chaos Frontier: Creative Strategic Control for Business*, Butterworth/Heinemann, London.

Toffler, A (1970) *Future Shock*, Bodley Head, London.

— (1981) *The Third Wave*, Pan, London.

— (1984) *Previews and Promises*, Pan, London.

Wille, E (1989) *Triggers for Change: Report on Patterns in the Management of Corporate Change*, Ashridge Management Research Group, Berkhamsted.

Part 2

Strategic Thinking and the Dynamics of Managing and Organising

3

Organisational Networks and Innovation

Bengt Johannisson

Introduction

An entrepreneur is an individual who personifies and orchestrates the creative process through which a new venture is realised in the marketplace. That creative process is one of trial and error out of which innovations may emerge and through which the entrepreneur successively and interactively ensures that the new concept and the targeted market match. It is a process in which entrepreneurs act while reflecting on their actions and so learn, making sense in ambiguous settings. It is also a process through which entrepreneurs essentially upset that which is taken for granted by generating path-breaking initiatives – for example, introducing a genuinely new product, process technology, logistical system or organising procedure.

The new venture organiser, the entrepreneur, must possess special personal attributes such as perseverance and a positive attitude toward risk. However, despite the clear need for personal independence and personal achievement, creativity is not a sufficient condition for the entrepreneurial process to occur. The realisation of an innovation is in practice a complex process in which independent, motivated individuals require external support in terms of information, resources and influence. And this is true no matter whether the entrepreneur operates in a newly established small firm or in a mature large corporation.

Since entrepreneurs are necessarily egocentric and since the processes they must employ are those of trial and error, only a very flexible organisation can provide that external support which is vital if the entrepreneurial process is to occur. The only feasible form for this purpose is a network structure; that is, an interpersonal set of contacts that tap into business, social and power resources – in short, a political and social system. The entrepreneur's distinctive competence, whether in a major corporation or in an individual new venture, is a capability for envisaging new realities and making them come true; that is, enacting them through active real world experimentation. This is a form of experiential learning that can be performed only in a flexible network context through which resources and commitment are mobilised. Planning, that is, freezing an optimal action repertoire derived from forecasts of outcomes, is dysfunctional for everything but routine issues.

Developments at Målerås

To ground what I mean, take the example of Målerås (Johannisson, 1991). At the end of the 1970s the small community of Målerås in southern Sweden had a population of 300 that had declined by two-thirds over a 30-year period. The dominant glassworks had come under external control and had shrunk to a fraction of its former size. However, a strong local identity had survived, due to geographic isolation and to kinship ties among the inhabitants reaching back several generations.

One of the 300 inhabitants, Mats Jonasson, was active in various local arenas such as the sports association, the local orchestra and the village committee. He recognised the potential of the social resources of Målerås and perceived that they could be mobilised to create businesses and jobs. So, Mats founded a local organisation, Project Målerås. People taking part in this project collectively approached banks, local author-ities and various other organisations for venture capital, inexpensive premises and professional advice. Mats supplied ideas and designs for new products to the local leather industry, to a small iron foundry and to a trading company. The iron foundry and a local metal manufactur-ing company became subcontractors to the glassworks. Mats also formulated the idea of taking over the local glassworks.

Over a period of five years the number of companies and the number of locally employed workers more than doubled in Målerås and the number of inhabitants increased slightly. The glassworks became a local company owned by employees and the local people. But it was not all plain sailing: there were close-downs and bankruptcies; the second largest company in the community came under external control and its workforce was reduced. The commercial success of the glassworks provoked a hostile takeover bid from one of the major corporations in the glass industry and this led Mats Jonasson to acquire the majority of the stock. Local ownership was thus retained but Målerås is again approaching the status of a one-company town.

This example, with its intertwined activities of a talented individual and a social network, with its spontaneous and self-organising characteristics and its irregular patterns of development, is typical of the many entrepreneurial incidents studied in an extended programme of research into the entrepreneurial process in Sweden. This programme is being conducted jointly by the Centre for Small Business Development at Växjö University and the Institute of Economic Research at Lund University. Combined with this there is also a major experiment concerning management training for owner managers in small firms. The purpose behind that experiment is to tap academic knowledge by building strategic alliances with owner managers that include academic institutions and the confidants of those owner managers such as bank managers and company accountants. The emphasis of the research and the training programme is on the process, the 'how', of entrepreneurship and this has led to a focus on the personal networks that provide the context for the entrepreneur's experiential learning.

The purpose of this chapter is to highlight the key conclusions that are emerging from the research and training programme. The next section will elaborate on the characteristics and manageability of entrepreneurial activity. The key point to be made is that entrepreneurs are essentially dealers in paradox. In the section following that, independent and corporate entrepreneurship will be contrasted and the nature of the required 'organising context' will also be discussed. The key point there is the essentially spontaneous and self-organising nature of the social networks that create the context for entrepreneurial activity. After that there is a section on educating entrepreneurs and in the concluding section some lessons are provided for the practice of entrepreneurial management.

Entrepreneurs: Dealers in Paradox

Entrepreneurs as organisers of innovations and markets can be studied from a number of perspectives: we can focus on the personal characteristics of the entrepreneur as a person, or on the entrepreneurial deed, or on the process of realising the entrepreneurial innovation (Stevenson and Jarillo, 1990). Research has not succeeded in unambiguously isolating the personal attributes of entrepreneurs from those of other people (Gartner, 1989). In other words, it seems to be impossible to separate the entrepreneur as a person from the process of realising an innovation. I therefore intend to focus on how entrepreneurs operate in their context, not on who they are or why they are motivated to be in business.

The 'how' of entrepreneurship can be clarified by contrasting the entrepreneur with the traditional artisan owner manager and with the professional manager in a corporation. Traditional artisan owner managers are similar to the conventional picture of entrepreneurs in that they operate on a small scale in their own businesses, where they are able to apply a holistic view, but they differ from entrepreneurs in that they repeat the same skill without change. Professional managers bear some similarity to entrepreneurs in that they too use trial and error and reflection-in-action (Schön, 1983) when they are faced with unique, ambiguous and conflicting situations, but they can be contrasted with entrepreneurs because they primarily administer the ongoing business of a firm rather than change it. It is differences of this kind, summarised in Table 3.1. that are important in identifying the nature of the entrepreneurial process.

Table 3.1 makes the following points:

Table 3.1 *The entrepreneur, the artisan owner manager, and the professional manager*

	Entrepreneur	**Artisan**	**Professional**
Mission	Urge to create	Independence	Company career
Guide	Vision and action	Action	Planning
Environmental Orientation	Interaction	Reaction	Proaction
Risk Orientation	Ambiguity management	Risk avoidance	Risk reduction
Time Orientation	Synchronisation	Time as a buffer	Time management
Focal Resources	Social	Physical	Financial
Generic Competence	Intuition	Imitation	Professional experience
Education/Training	Organic, qualified practice	Formal and practical	Institutionalised

- Entrepreneurs have an innate need to launch ventures, while artisan owner managers refrain from growth in order to stay independent, and professional managers accept the role of administrators, pursuing professional careers within or between corporations.
- Entrepreneurs combine visionary thinking and concrete action in their enactment of revolutionary concepts (Mintzberg, 1973a), while owner managers work long hours at repetitive activities, and professional managers draft, implement and evaluate plans.
- Entrepreneurs cope with their environments by interactively redefining them wherever possible, while owner managers react to changes in the commercial and institutional environment, and professional managers attempt to be proactive through plans.
- Entrepreneurs regard risky, ambiguous situations as providing a potential for imposing their own ideas on others (Johannisson, 1992a), while owner managers avoid risk taking by staying with familiar technology, products and markets, and professional managers in large corporations cope with uncertainty by attempting to reduce it.
- Entrepreneurs look upon time as a continuum where the challenge is to synchronise their own initiatives with changes in the environment in a favourable way, while owner managers think in terms of hours invested in the business as a buffer, to be increased when times are bad and reduced when times are good, and professional managers consider time itself to be a precious resource, the use of which is to be planned.
- Entrepreneurs combine internal and external resources flexibly through networking and consider financial surpluses to be an indicator of capability in the marketplace, while owner occupiers have a personal and proprietorial attitude to resources, and professional managers focus on the financial dimension of the enterprise.
- The key to entrepreneurial competence is intuition based on experience, unconsciously refined by self-awareness and sensitive 'readings' of the environment, while the key competences of both artisan owner managers and professional managers have to do with skills, concepts and practices that are acquired through formal training. Since the role of the entrepreneur is to identify new niches and disobey established industry recipes, formal training with respect both to form and substance may well counteract entrepreneurial activity.

The Paradox of Change and Stability

These distinctions between entrepreneurs on the one hand and owner and professional managers on the other, all have to do, in one way or another, with the fact that the primary task of entrepreneurs is to bring about change while the primary tasks of the others are to secure stability of operations. All organisations, however, must be able to deal with both stability and change. Change may dominate in the emerging organisation, but without some stability that organisation will be unable to sustain high quality, timely delivery and low cost. Stability may be assured in large, mature organisations with substantial resources and influence, but without continual change and innovation, such organisations will stagnate and die. This need for simultaneous stability and change raises a challenge: entrepreneurs are indispensable as initiators of new ventures and organisers of resources into new patterns; professional managers too are indispensable because they ensure that these new ventures and resources are employed in an efficient manner; but the entire process of entrepreneurship stands in stark contradiction to the process of management. An organisational paradox therefore clearly emerges when we consider the contrasting logics of the entrepreneurial and managerial processes as shown in Table 3.1.

A paradox consists of dual statements that are equally true, taken one by one, but contradictory when combined. The fundamental paradox of organising is the simultaneous need for entrepreneurial flexibility on the one hand and the need for professional management, with its inevitable inflexibility, on the other. This intrinsic contradiction creates organisational tensions, but it is such tensions that generate the variety needed to cope with the complexity of modern management. It is therefore necessary to recognise the inherently contradictory character of entrepreneurship: the management of paradox in the marketplace is the entrepreneur's main task. This fundamental paradox of change and stability is reflected in many other paradoxes of entrepreneurship, as follows (Johannisson, 1990).

Entrepreneurs Are Both Independent and Dependent

Typically, an entrepreneur claims an independent niche in a market. However, entrepreneurs usually have limited owner-controlled resources and can therefore only defend their niche through the creation of strategic alliances with others, for example supplementary market suppliers. The enlarged resource base and legitimacy thereby achieved are prerequisites for the realisation of strategic ambitions but they do mean increased dependencies. Would-be entrepreneurs are also dependent upon different kinds of support, including role models; for example a father who is also in business (Shapero and Sokol, 1982). This contradictory need for both independence and dependence can be seen in the way that successful Swedish entrepreneurs have introduced their companies on the OTC stock exchange only to withdraw them after a few years. A major reason for such decisions seems to be that entrepreneurs cannot accept the anonymity of external control: entrepreneurs only accept dependencies on a recognisable flesh and blood counterpart. The conflict between dependence and independence is also reflected in ambivalent attitudes toward partnership: the majority want to keep ownership and control within the extended family (Johannisson, 1992b).

Entrepreneurship Reflects Both Personal Attributes and Organising Processes
We have already noted that research on the personal attributes of entrepreneurs has failed to discriminate unambiguously between entrepreneurs and others. However, that research does seem to indicate that certain attributes are significant factors in the entrepreneurial personality, even though they are not unique to entrepreneurs. The notion of entrepreneurs as egocentric is supported by findings suggesting that self-confidence is the most important of their attributes. For entrepreneurs, then, the locus of control is internal, but in addition they also have to develop and sustain a large set of live contacts with others.

Entrepreneurs Are Both Anarchists and Organisers
Entrepreneurs defy existing norms and business recipes – they are robber barons who bring confusion to the market (Schumpeter, 1934). In challenging the existing order they are anarchists who take collective action within voluntary networks rather than formal organisational structures. But they are also organisers of resources who alertly exploit available opportunities (Kirzner, 1973) and as leaders and organisers of new markets, they give meaning and thereby reduce uncertainty for others just as professional managers do (Smircich and Morgan, 1982; Bennis, 1984).

Entrepreneurship Implies Both Revolution and Evolution
The entrepreneurial mode of strategy making is characterised by discontinuous radical changes guided by a tunnel vision (Mintzberg, 1973a). An entrepreneurial culture is also characterised by revolutionary exploitation of opportunities, in contrast to the administrative

culture of the professional manager where changes in the environment are recognised incrementally (Stevenson and Gumpert, 1985). However, entrepreneurs are also experiential learners (Lessem, 1986) who recognise emerging market niches and successively build up an organisation to exploit them, often recycling resources to form new patterns (Binks and Vale, 1990). All of this implies that entrepreneurs realise step by step, balancing small winnings and mistakes just as professional managers do (Weick, 1984).

Entrepreneurial Venturing Means Both Growth and Non-growth
Entrepreneurship is usually associated with growth, and growth in the size of a venture is regarded as synonymous with its success. But it is important for the entrepreneur to stay in control, to maintain feelings of being the creator of the business. By keeping the operation relatively small, 'economies of overview' can be tapped, for example, to make fast internal decisions and quick moves in the market. This is probably the reason why most (Swedish) family businesses never grow beyond ten employees. Expansion by acquisition is especially critical since it means bringing an alien party into the nest. An alternative is different cooperative arrangements where the same amount of resource can be made available, but where network control substitutes for ownership.

Entrepreneurs Are Both Globally and Locally Oriented
The entrepreneurial project is centred around the individual and in practical terms this means that all entrepreneurs are locally oriented due to a restricted time budget. But, in the immediate socioeconomic setting, the entrepreneur also mobilises social resources in addition to those available in the market. In this sense the entrepreneur has a sense of community.

Entrepreneurs Are Both Prophets and People of Action
Entrepreneurs are designers of new realities, whether in terms of creating a genuinely new image (such as the effect that the introduction of fast food had on restaurant habits) or introducing a new product or process (Drucker, 1985). In contrast to the rational, linear logic of the manager, entrepreneurs apply intuitive, holistic approaches to challenges. The act of entrepreneurial creation has neither prototypes nor any methodology to copy. The entrepreneur's mission is highly internalised, implicit even to the person concerned. In all these regards an entrepreneur is somewhat like a prophet. But entrepreneurs also have a strong bias for action and this makes them outwardly oriented

and visible. Due to the successive nature of the creation of the new venture, most actions mean exchanges with other external actors. The objective, the launching of innovation, and the restricted means to achieve the objective (eg restricted owner resources) require persistent and frequent actions: initiatives to convince others about the unique qualities of the product and the successive procurement of means for production. Note that professional managers also have a bias for action. Swedish research suggests, however, that when managers are surprised by radical environmental change, they too apply intuition rather than rational, linear logic in order to meet the need for flexibility in identifying and implementing responses (Kylén, 1989).

Entrepreneurial Action is Driven Both Commercially and Socially
Successful Swedish entrepreneurs consider themselves to be primarily creators and organisers in the marketplace. Since they are existentially motivated, they express little spontaneous concern for economic success. Rather, financial achievement confirms the viability of their personal vision.

Perhaps the most striking feature of the entrepreneurial process, then, is its paradoxical nature. And there are four ways of dealing with paradox: accept that the paradoxical states can never be removed, only rearranged; change the level of analysis so that one state applies at one level and its contradiction at another; change the focus over time so that one state applies at one time and its contradiction at another; or introduce a new logic through which it becomes clear that the contradiction was apparent only and can be removed by rethinking the problem. All of these approaches may be applied to the paradoxes around entrepreneurial activity that have been identified above (Johannisson and Senneseth, 1990). The next section provides a framework for reconciling the paradoxes indicated by the contrasting logics of management and entrepreneurship. It argues that social networks provide an organising context that copes with these paradoxes. It defines social networks and how they function and then goes on to show how they cope with the paradoxes.

Entrepreneurs in Context: the Social Network

Entrepreneurs, like all other individuals, operate in a social setting that imposes restrictions upon their behaviour but also provides support essential for individual action. In addition to their own individual characteristics, therefore, entrepreneurs must be part of a supportive task environment which in essence creates an organising 'context' (Johannisson, 1988; Shapero and Sokol, 1982; Kao, 1989).

The Nature of Networks

The organising context referred to above is in fact a socio-economic network, a web of personal ties between individual entrepreneurs and people in other organisations – customers, suppliers, competitors, regulators, financiers and so on. We can define these social networks in terms of their:

- *Focus.* The focal point may be a local community or industrial district such as Målerås in the introductory example above; or it may a science park, or a corporation, or some other social form.
- *Orientation.* The primary orientation may be social (eg family and friendship ties), commercial, or professional.
- *Mode of creation.* Some networks emerge spontaneously through self-organising processes: local communities and industrial districts such as Målerås are good examples of this. Other networks may be induced by intentional policies, that are functionally defined, and the innovative corporation may be an example of this. The science park on the university campus appears to be a hybrid combining aspects of intentional policies and emergence.

Most agree that the context for entrepreneurship, whether in the corporation, the industrial district or the science park, calls for an organisational structure that is flexible and permissive with respect to individual initiative. This need for ambiguous and dynamic *organising* rather than unequivocal and static *organisation* is achieved by personal networking. There must be a structure that flexibly provides resources for business venturing and this is provided by personal networking. Ultimately, networks consist of interrelated connections between people which can be specified in terms of nodes and linkages (Barnard, 1938). A linkage – a tie or a relationship – can be thought of as a set of episodes or transactions which sediment over time into an 'institution' of relationships between pairs of people that are built on instrumental reward and trust. Mutual dependence in legal, technical, social and psychological terms is the generic basis for the interaction.

The Social Characteristics of Networks

The entrepreneurial process is one of continual learning and it is also essentially a social process. Research (Johannisson, 1990) suggests that:

- Socially dominated ties are almost as frequent as professional/business linkages in the personal networks of entrepreneurs.
- Entrepreneurs who are about to launch a venture include more social ties in their networks and spend less time maintaining networks than colleagues already in business.
- Entrepreneurs typically build local networks: eight out of ten personal contacts live within a distance of one hour's drive by car.
- Women entrepreneurs build more social networks and invest less time in developing new ties than their male counterparts.
- Cosmopolitan entrepreneurs invest relatively little time in network maintenance and relatively more time in developing new linkages.
- Academic entrepreneurs invest average time in network management and their networks are relatively more social.
- Among new entrepreneurs, network resources and business success are not correlated.

These findings on the one hand reinforce the fact that personal networks are generally crucial to emerging firms, and on the other underline that the structure and function of networks may vary due to entrepreneurial, venture and context characteristics. Network resources seem to provide a necessary but not sufficient condition for entrepreneurial success.

Research has also compared the nature of the networks developed in industrial districts – contexts that emerge spontaneously, with networks developed in science parks – contexts that are intentionally established and planned to some extent. When the Anderstorp industrial district was compared with the Ideon science park at Lund University it was found that the industrial district had a much more densely structured network system – linkages were more numerous, more complex and served more functions. This would tend to indicate that it is difficult if not impossible to create contextual networks by planning. Effective networks emerge spontaneously through some form of self-organisation. That research revealed that while 50 per cent of firms in the science park had commercial exchange with other firms in the park, the figure in the industrial district was 97 per cent Entrepreneurs in the industrial district knew each other better and they talked more with each other on a social basis.

Thus, entrepreneurs use their contexts differently in spontaneously generated settings compared with induced settings. The contextual settings which emerge are to a greater extent social in nature than those which are induced.

The context for entrepreneurial activity, then, is a loosely coupled system of personal networks that enable the paradoxical requirements of both change and stability, both individual local innovation and collective strategic action, to be met (Weick, 1976 and 1979; Burgelman, 1983).

The Functions of Networks

The function of the context, from the point of view of the entrepreneur, is both that of a shock absorber when radical environmental changes occur and that of a springboard once opportunities are there to be exploited. The context also provides regulatory boundaries that frame individual actions, providing security but demanding observance. In the functionally defined, intentionally established network context, the regulatory framework is usually explicit. For example, a company policy may state that innovations relating to that company's distinctive competences are to be given priority. However, even in such intentional networks, the corporate culture provides important implicit regulatory functions. In the spontaneously created context, however, regulation is almost completely implicit. For example, in the local community, the rules of the game are hidden in the values and taken-for-granted behavioural norms of that community. Again, the science park combines formal and informal regulation: on the one hand there are often rules stating that production of goods should not take place within the park; but, on the other hand, the permissive culture of the university is adopted.

Perhaps the key function of the network context, however, is that of resolving the paradoxes of entrepreneurship and providing rewards for entrepreneurial activities. Table 3.2 indicates how the paradoxes of entrepreneurship can be reconciled through the context of personal networks.

Table 3.2 also demonstrates how managing innovation and entrepreneurship is a process of contextual management as well as one of business venturing. The main task is on the one hand that of administering a framework that provides stability and on the other promoting a change process made up by individual anarchic initiatives. Stated more precisely:

- The entrepreneurial initiative as a creative act cannot itself be managed
- The context of the entrepreneurial process can be deliberately influenced
- Any entrepreneurial initiative will benefit from a supportive context.

Table 3.2 *Resolving paradoxes – entrepreneurs in context*

Entrepreneurial Paradox	Solution by contextual logic
Entrepreneurs are both independent and dependent	Entrepreneurs are free to establish any network tie, but strong contextual ties create mutual dependence
Entrepreneurship reflects both a process and personal attributes	Persistence is channelled through networks into creating, recycling and organising resources
Entrepreneurs are both anarchists and organisers	Entrepreneurs use networks to exploit market opportunities alertly and organise resources accordingly
Entrepreneurship implies both revolution and evolution	The contextual network is an instrument for radical change, but is also the means of smooth adaptation
Entrepreneurial venturing means both growth and non-growth	Subcontracting allows network control to replace internal growth and resource control
Entrepreneurs are both locally and globally oriented	Strong social relationships and weak global ties tap resource and product markets
Entrepreneurs are both prophets and people of action	Networks provide ideas for business and a base for learning by doing
Entrepreneurial action is driven both commercially and socially	Networks integrate everyday life and business endeavours into one socio-economic context

From the perspective of the context, the management of entrepreneurship means both stimulating variety and selecting and supporting ventures according to predefined criteria (Weick, 1979; Burgelman 1983). The most critical issue in this management process is to decide when and how to encourage initiatives which enforce the current major strategy, and when to use the innovative capacity to diversify available options in order to create a portfolio of emerging strategy candidates.

Due to differing origins and rationales, the principles of contextual management vary between the three kinds of contexts mentioned above: namely, the corporation, the industrial district and the science park. However, the two generic functions of the entrepreneurial context remain those of legitimising, and of concretely supporting, individual initiatives in the interests of the collective.

Managing Network Contexts

Corporate Entrepreneurship

In the 1980s it was generally argued that individual initiatives could be stimulated and tamed to the benefit of both the individual and the organisation (Lessem, 1986). Most present-day researchers into corporate entrepreneurship attempt to reconcile contextual norms and the entrepreneur's deviant behaviour through consensus-oriented approaches. Some promote the creation of a change-oriented, entrepreneurial culture (Peters and Waterman, 1982; Pinchot, 1985). Others argue that managers must deliberately direct innovative activity according to whatever is needed to maintain the company's competitiveness in the markets being penetrated (Kanter, 1983; Haskins and Williams, 1987). However, some researchers recognise the dilemma of simultaneously promoting spontaneous individual venturing and the corporate need for deliberate focused strategy (Quinn, 1979; Burgelman, 1983).

Pulling this research together, three factors have been identified as essential to the successful development of corporate entrepreneurship:

- top management support
- organisational structure
- resource availability.

This in fact boils down to the need for a network organisation. Networks make and enforce behavioural norms, networking is organising, and resources are made available by networking.

Industrial Districts

In some local communities, where there are prospering, indigenous small businesses, the professional and social dimensions of business life do intermingle organically. This suggests that the context, the industrial district, is furnished with a distinctive competence in the world of business, a genuine entrepreneurial spirit (Pyke *et al*, 1990).

Science Parks

With few exceptions, most science parks established in Europe in the 1980s seem to have been based on role models provided by both corporate entrepreneurship and industrial parks. A minimum of formal structure serves the inhabitants of the park, with most science parks providing premises and supportive administration services. This milieu seems to appeal both to university staff trying to commercialise their findings in a systematic way and to relocated research and development (R&D) departments with members looking for a 'waterhole' far away from everyday routine. Although these two basic categories of science park inhabitants both demonstrate a need to detach themselves – albeit for quite contrasting reasons – neither of them seems to want to abandon their original domicile completely. They evidently aim to combine partial separation with mutual integration, embracing both their original domicile and the science park.

Entrepreneurship and innovation obviously operate differently in the corporation, the industrial district and the science park. The differences between strategic/induced and spontaneous contextual management are, though, to a great extent illusory. Corporate strategies often emerge and are then made to sound intentional after the event and the norms of industrial districts, the role model for entrepreneurial communities, are as efficient as any management control system. In the science park, professional/academic norms and the administrative rules of the park management also give a regulatory framework.

Educating Entrepreneurs

Innovation is essentially the creation and communication of new meaning, and such creation and communication is a fundamentally individual act, holistically integrated with the personal history and contemporary existential conditions of the individual. It follows that entrepreneurial competences cannot be acquired through the administration of general knowledge based on calculative rationality. The art of entrepreneurship is indeed personal (Polanyi, 1983). While others see education and training as a potential for career change, entrepreneurs regard education is a vehicle for concrete problem solving, intimately associated with the operational activities of the venturing process. This suggests that training for entrepreneurs should be as close as possible to the natural context of business operations, ideally applied as one dimension of economic exchange. Entrepreneurs learn through reflection-in-action (Schön, 1983). Entrepreneurship is action learning (Revans, 1982) and is itself the training ground for entrepreneurship. It follows that:

- Entrepreneurs should be provided with contexts for self-organised learning, not with training programmes which are planned in detail.

71

- Entrepreneurial training should be integrated with everyday business operations.
- The personal network of the entrepreneur should be mobilised during the learning process.
- Formal education must be focused on action in order to become an integrated feature of the entrepreneurial rationale.

Promoting the Entrepreneurial Process

The research that has produced the findings set out in this chapter has focused on the entrepreneurial process in a number of industrial districts and science parks in Sweden. Since the entrepreneurial process is presumably the same wherever it is found, these findings have implications for the promotion of entrepreneurship in corporations. Here too there is the fundamental paradox – the need to sustain stability by obeying the rules and the need for change which can come only through breaking the rules and thus causing anarchy and instability. Entrepreneurship must therefore be characterised by the same paradoxes as those we have identified in industrial districts and science parks. Those paradoxes must therefore be coped with by the same mechanism, namely the organising context provided by the personal networks that people form in and across corporations.

The main conclusions of this kind of analysis are as follows. First, the entrepreneurial process cannot be planned, controlled or managed. It is spontaneous and experimental at the individual level and self organising and spontaneous at the group or network interaction level. Second, the network is one of the main keys to the entrepreneurial process in that it provides the organising context, and that context has social and political, as well as professional and commercial, characteristics. Third, high levels of entrepreneurial activity seem to be associated with high levels of network activity including social intercourse and talk that many might regard as inefficient uses of time. Fourth, it does seem possible to manage the context to some extent, by providing suitable conditions for network activity and the science park is an example of this kind of management of context: providing an area of stability in which people can develop social networks and feel secure enough to take risks. Fifth, networking takes time and, even if management is highly efficient, if its resources are stretched there will be no time for networking. Finally, traditional forms of education are quite inadequate for training people in entrepreneurship but some form of mentoring and coaching while people carry out entrepreneurial tasks seems to be the way to foster such activity.

From the perspective of the individual entrepreneur there are also lessons. First the entrepreneur should combine strong (multiplex) contextual ties at the local level, with weak global ties to avoid going 'native'. Second, entrepreneurs must realise that networks take time to build but can dissipate overnight. Third, as much concern must be devoted to maintaining networks as to building new ones. Time is obviously the major restriction on personal networking.

Conclusion

Entrepreneurship will always be dependent upon human creativity and commitment to action in ambiguous settings. Since the visions which guide such action are personal theories known to the entrepreneurs by intuition alone, it is obviously difficult to manage them through external impact or in any other way. The argument of this chapter has therefore been that instead of encouraging and supporting individual entrepreneurship, contexts which are appropriate for entrepreneurship should be created.

The chapter has also argued that viable contexts must themselves be organically structured. This means that the promotion of an entrepreneurial culture remains the basic management tool. In addition to this, it is necessary to construct a distinctive framework, both to provide entrepreneurs with a set of rules and to offer them the needed stability. In other words, contextual management includes a paradox as well. Hypocrisy must be accepted because top management must on the one hand state official corporate policy and on the other encourage 'deviant behaviour' in would-be entrepreneurs.

I have suggested that this paradox and hypocrisy can be dealt with by way of personal networking. The need for personal networking in addition to other tools in management is generally recognised. Such networks are particularly relevant, even indispensable, when it comes to handling innovative processes and this is so because of the ambiguous character of the entrepreneurial phenomenon. Personal networks may bypass formal structures and give access to political centres and they provide a management tool which is sensitive enough to register egocentric needs and the requirements for collective resources in new ventures.

Entrepreneurial management encompasses both manageable issues and those indispensable tasks which rely on individual capacities beyond organisational control.

References

Barnard, C (1938) *The Functions of the Executive*, Harvard University Press, Cambridge, Mass.

Bennis, W (1984) 'The 4 Competencies of Leadership', *Training and Development Journal*, August, pp15–19.

Binks, M and Vale, P (1990) *Entrepreneurship and Economic Change*, McGraw-Hill, London.

Burgelman, R A (1983) 'Corporate Entrepreneurship and Strategic Management: Insights from a Process Study', *Management Science*, Vol 29, pp1349–64.

Drucker, P (1985) *Innovation and Entrepreneurship*, Harper & Row, New York.

Haskins, G and Williams, R (1987) *Intrapreneurship in Action*, Special Report No 1099, EIU, *The Economist*, London.

Johannisson, B (1988) 'Business Formation – A Network Approach', *Scandinavian Journal of Management*, Vol 4, No 3/4, pp83–99.

— (1990) 'Building an Entrepreneurial Career, in a Mixed Economy: Need for Social and Business Ties in Personal Networks', *Paper presented at the Academy of Management Annual Meeting*, San Francisco, 12–15 August 1990.

— (1991) 'Locally Initiated Economic Development – Swedish Experiences'. *Paper presented to the conference Jornados Internationales Desarollo Locale*, Seville, Spain.

— (1992) 'Entrepreneurship – The Management of Ambiguity', in Polesie, T and Johansson, I-L (eds), *Responsibility and Accounting – The Organizational Regulation of Boundary Conditions*, Studentlitteratur, Lund, Sweden, pp155–79.

— (ed.) (1992ab) *Entreprenörskap påa svenska* (Entrepreneurship in Swedish), Liber/Almqvist & Wiksell, Malmö, Sweden.

— and Senneseth, K (1990) 'Paradoxes of Entrepreneurship', *Paper presented at the 4th Workshop on Recent Research in Entrepreneurship*, Cologne, Germany, 29–30 November 1990.

Johansson, J and Mattsson, L-G (1987) 'Interorganizational Relations in Industrial Systems: A Network Approach Compared with the Transaction-Cost Approach', *International Studies of Managment & Organization*, Vol XVII, No 1, pp34–48.

Kanter, R Moss (1983) *The Change Masters*, Simon and Schuster, New York.

Kao, J J (1989) *Entrepreneurship, Creativity & Organization*, Prentice Hall, Englewood Cliffs, NJ.

Kirzner, I M (1973) *Competition and Entrepreneurship*, The University of Chicago Press, Chicago, Ill.

Kylén, B (1989) *Hur företagschefer beslutar innan de blir överraskade (How CEOs Decide Before Being Surprised)*, Dissertation (English summary), Stockholm School of Economics, Stockholm.

Lessem, R (1986) *Intrapreneurship*, Wildwood House, Aldershot.

Mintzberg, H (1973a) 'Strategy-Making in Three Modes', *California Management Review*, Vol XVI, No 2, pp41–53.

Mintzberg, H (1973ab) *The Nature of Managerial Work*, Harper & Row, New York.

Mintzberg, H (1988) 'The Adhocracy', in Quinn, J B *et al The Strategy Process*, Prentice Hall, Englewood Cliffs, NJ pp607–27.

Peters, T and Waterman, R H (1982) *In Search of Excellence*, Warner, New York.

Peterson, R A (1981) 'Entrepreneurship and Organization', in Nystrom, P C and Starbuck, W H (eds) *Handbook of Organizational Design*, Vol 1, Oxford University Press, Oxford, pp65–83.

Pinchot III, G (1985) *Intrapreneuring*, Harper & Row, New York.

Polanyi, M (1983) (1966) *The Tacit Dimension*, Peter, Gloucester, Mass.

Pyke, F, and Becattini, G and Sengenberger, W (eds) (1990) *Industrial Districts and Inter-Firm Co-operation in Italy*, ILO, Geneva.

Quinn, J B (1979) 'Technological Innovation, Entrepreneurship, and Strategy', *Sloan Management Review*, Vol 20, Spring 1979, pp19–30.

Quinn, R E and Cameron, K S (1988) 'Organizational Paradox and Transformation', in Quinn, R E and Cameron, K S (eds), *Paradox and Transformation: Toward a Theory of Change in Organization and Management*, Ballinger, Cambridge, Mass, pp1–18.

Revans, R W (1992) *The Origins & Growth of Action Learning*, Studentlitteratur, Lund, Sweden.

Schön, D (1983) *The Reflective Practitioner: How Professionals Think in Action*, Basic Books, New York.

Schumpeter, J A (1934) *The Theory of Economic Development*, Oxford University Press, Oxford.

Shapero, A and Sokol, L (1982) 'The Social Dimension of Entrepreneurship', in Kent, CA, Sexton, DL and Vesper, KH (eds), *Encyclopedia of Entrepreneurship*, Prentice-Hall, Englewood Cliffs, NJ, pp72–90.

Smircich, L and Morgan, G (1982) 'Leadership: The Management of Meaning', *Journal of Applied Behavioural Science*, Vol 18, No 3, pp257–73.

Stevenson, H H and Gumpert, D E (1985) 'The Heart of Entrepreneurship', *Harvard Business Review*, March–April, pp85–94.

Stevenson, H H and Jarillo, C (1990) 'A Paradigm of Entrepreneurship: Entrepreneurial Management', *Strategic Management Journal*, Vol 11, Special Issue on Corporate Entrepreneurship.

Weick, K E (1976) 'Educational Organizations as Loosely Coupled Systems,' *Administrative Science Quarterly*, Vol 21, pp1–19.

— (1979) *The Social Psychology of Organizing*, Addison-Wesley, Reading, Mass.

— (1984) 'Small Wins: Redefining the Scale of Social Problems', *American Psychologists*, January, pp40–9.

4

Learning Organisations and Emergent Strategy

Ralph Stacey

Introduction

One of the more recent concepts to grab the attention of those concerned with management is that of the 'learning organisation'. The purpose of this chapter is to explain what a learning organisation might be, how such learning leads to emergent strategies and why it is so difficult for organisations to learn. First, however, consider some statements made by practitioners and academics regarding the Western manager's approach to management. These statements make it clear why there is nowadays so much talk about the need for organisations to learn.

In an interview with the writer Richard Pascale, in 1982, Konosuke Matsushita – the founder and leader of Matsushita Electrical Limited, one of Japan's largest companies – gave this combination of explanation and prediction:

> We are going to win and the industrial West is going to lose out; there's not much you can do about it because the reasons for your failure are within yourselves. Your firms are built on the Taylor model [that is, the principles of rational scientific management]. Even worse, so are your heads. With your bosses doing the thinking while the workers wield the screwdrivers, you're convinced deep down that this is the right way to run a business. For you, the essence of management is getting the ideas out of the heads of the bosses and into the hands of labor.
>
> We are beyond your mindset. Business, we know, is now so complex and difficult, the survival of firms so hazardous in an environment

increasingly unpredictable, competitive and fraught with danger, that their continued existence depends upon the day-to-day mobilization of every ounce of intelligence. (Pascale 1990, p27)

But it is not only triumphant Japanese entrepreneurs who reach this conclusion – some senior managers in large Western corporations are saying much the same thing. In an article published in 1986, David Hurd, Executive Vice President of the Canadian company, Federal Metals (with sales of $1 billion), argued that the Western approach to strategic management was bankrupt because it:

> . . . assumes that businesses are like complex, mechanical clockworks operating in an environment that can be objectively determined by senior managers of the business. It is supposed that this knowledge, together with the managers' assessment of their organisation's strengths and weaknesses, can be used to devise a strategy of objectives, plans and so forth. These strategies are meant to allow managers to structure their organizations and adapt and/or take control of the environment. (Hurd, 1986, p13).
>
> But these strategic structures are built on retrospective foundations. They work for the future only so long as the pattern of the future mimics that of the past. Such stability is unusual and does not last for long. (Hurd, 1986, p14).
>
> [The strategic planning] . . . mode cannot tell managers where they are going, only where they have been. It is useful for managing today's business, the business that already exists.. . . [But it] interferes with the strategic managers' ability to discover new business opportunities. (Hurd, 1986, p15)

Western academics have also been busy revising the way we might understand the process of strategic management. Henry Mintzberg, one of the most eminent of management experts, and James Waters identify a number of different modes of making strategies. One option is to plan the strategy in what most managers still think of as the normal way, but these writers argue that this is possible only in reasonably stable environments. In highly turbulent environments where innovation is required, the appropriate approach is what these writers call consensus strategy:

> . . . the consensus strategy grows out of the mutual adjustment among different actors, as they learn from each other and from their various responses to the environment and thereby find a common, probably unexpected, pattern that works for them.
>
> In other words, the convergence is not driven by any intentions of central management, nor even by the prior intentions widely shared by

other actors. It just evolves through the results of a host of individual actions.. . . [The strategy] derives more from collective action than collective intention. (Mintzberg and Waters, p13)

Emergent strategy itself implies learning what works . . . emergent strategy means, not chaos, but in essence, unintended order . . . emergent strategy does not have to mean that management is out of control, only – in some cases at least – that it is open, flexible and responsive, in other words, willing to learn. Such behavior is especially important when an environment is too unstable or too complex to comprehend, or too imposing to defy. Openness to such emergent strategy enables management to act before everything is fully understood – to respond to an evolving reality rather than having to focus on a stable fantasy. (Mintzberg and Waters, p14)

So, what we see from these quotes is disquiet with the notion dominant amongst Western managers that success comes to those who plan their long-term futures – that is, to those organisations whose top managers intentionally set the future point all are to work towards and then ensure, by one means or another, that the intention is implemented. Such a notion, it is argued, is quite inappropriate in times of great uncertainty and the price paid for trying to practice it is the death of creativity and innovation. Instead, the call is to conceptualise the development of successful organisations in different terms; namely, as a process in which communities of people learn together to create and discover the evolving path their organisations follow into the future.

The call is to replace the metaphor of the captain guiding the organisational ship to a known destination with the metaphor of a group of intrepid jungle explorers who set out to discover something new, without knowing what that something might be. If managers are guided by the first metaphor, they design many sets of procedures and complex information, planning and control systems. If, however, they are persuaded by the second metaphor they create conditions that favour organisational learning from which new strategic directions may emerge. The former simply get better at what they have always done, until some imaginative competitor destroys them, while the latter create innovative new strategic directions.

What then does a learning organisation look like?

What a Learning Organisation Looks Like

Perhaps the best way to paint a picture of the learning organisation is through a few specific examples from which some general principles may be extracted.

Matsushita's Dough Machine

In 1985, a group of product developers at Matsushita could not perfect the kneading action of the home bread-baking machine they were developing (Nonaka, 1991). After much unhelpful analysis, such as a comparison of X-rays of dough kneaded by the machine and dough kneaded by professionals, one member of the team, Ikuko Tanaka, suggested a more unusual approach – namely, using a top professional baker as a model. The other team members agreed and so Ikuko trained with a top baker to acquire his kneading skills. After a year of trial and error she was able to help her colleagues reproduce a mechanical kneading action that mimicked that of the professional.

What we have here is a group of people faced with the practical task of developing a new product; this group constituted what we might call a 'community of practice' (Brown and Duguid, 1991). That community of practice found it impossible to accomplish its task through rational planning and careful analysis, but it did succeed through a continuing process of acting and then discovering, as a joint effort, what the actions of its members meant. In other words, the product development team succeeded by learning together as a group.

We can represent what they were doing in a very simple way as a feedback process of choosing some action (accepting the proposal to use a professional as a model), acting (Ikuko training with the professional), discovering what the consequences of that action were (colleagues learning from Ikuko) and making further choices in the light of those discoveries (trying out some variants of mechanical kneading). This feedback loop is depicted in Figure 4.1.

Consider now how this community of practice actually made their discoveries, reached their choices and took their actions.

Discovering and Tacit Knowledge

The most important form of discovering in the process of developing the dough machine involved the movement of tacit knowledge, as opposed to explicit knowledge, from the professional baker to Ikuko and from her to her colleagues.

It is easy to understand the nature of explicit knowledge – it is the formal and systematic knowledge that we consciously express and communicate clearly in written or verbal form. Examples of explicit knowledge are product specifications, repair procedures and computer programs. Tacit knowledge, however, is hard to formalise and very difficult to communicate because it is personal and lies below the level of awareness. It exists in the form of mindsets, mental models, beliefs and

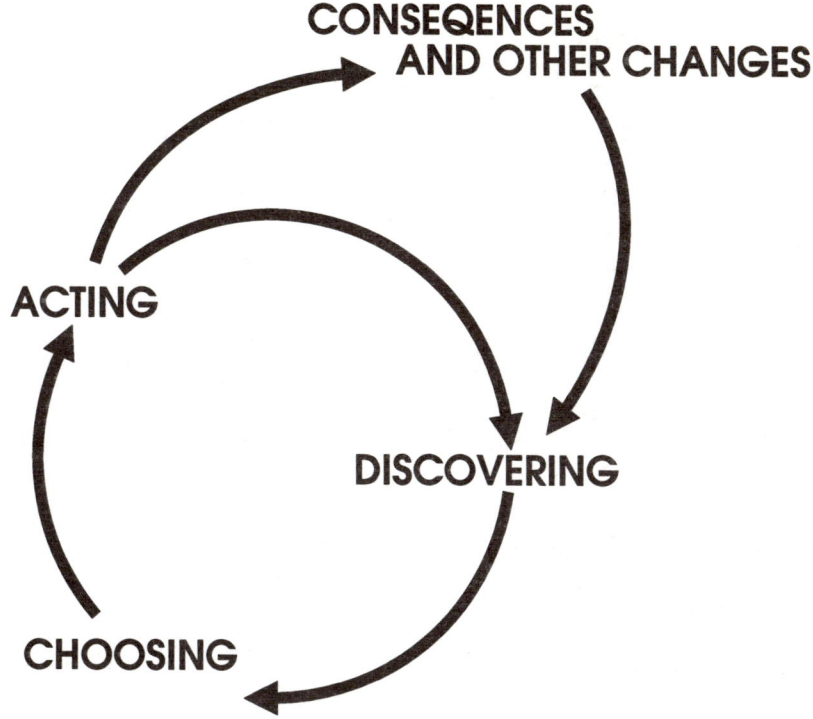

Figure 4.1 *Simple single-loop learning*

perspectives, ingrained in the way people understand their world and therefore act. Tacit knowledge shows itself as skill, or 'know-how'. In short, tacit knowledge is the unarticulated recipe of how to do things that a community of practice shares and the most complex form of learning occurs when that tacit knowledge passes from one community of practice to another, or when a community of practice changes, enhances or creates its own tacit knowledge.

In the case of the dough machine the community of product developers acquired tacit knowledge from the community of professional bakers when Ikuko observed and imitated the professional, so practising, internalising and learning the skill. As she articulated the foundations of her newly acquired tacit knowledge to her colleagues, she transformed it from the tacit to the explicit and by internalising that explicit knowledge, they altered their own tacit knowledge or mental models – in other words, they learned. Then, as the newly formulated product specifications were communicated to the production department and embodied in working models and final production processes, the explicit knowledge of the product development team became the explicit knowledge of the production department. Note how, throughout this creative process, discovery took the form of collaborative transfers of knowledge, choice required social and political interaction in the sense that each team member had to persuade colleagues to follow a particular sequence of actions, and the actions themselves took the form of trials leading to both error and success with both successes and errors generating further discoveries as the basis for yet more action.

We can see from the dough-making example that innovation is the creation of new knowledge, as a result of moving knowledge from one community to another and between one type and another, utilising a continuous circular loop of choosing an action, acting, and discovering the consequences of that action. Furthermore, we can also see from this example how a second loop is involved, namely one in which discoveries of tacit knowledge are made and used to alter the mindsets or mental models that we use to assess the consequences of our actions. The second loop is a process of reflecting upon and changing the mental model that drives the first loop (Argyris, 1990). This double-loop learning process is depicted in Figure 4.2. As individuals work and learn together, moving around the learning feedback loops, they come to share a common mental model. That shared mental model is largely below the level of awareness. It constitutes the culture of a work group and that culture is expressed in symbols and rituals and in the stories that people tell about the history of their group, its past accomplishments, failures, heroes and villains.

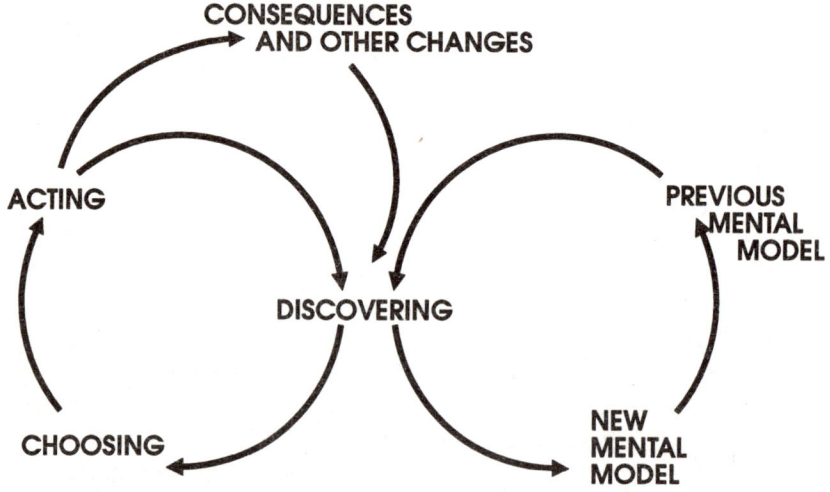

Figure 4.2 *Complex double-loop learning*

What this shows is a complex learning process in which people learn from their past experience by amending both their actions and the way they understand the world. To emphasise the distinction, a group of people may engage in simple single-loop learning, in which case they learn from the consequences of their actions without altering the mindset through which they see their world. Or they may engage in complex double-loop learning in which case they use their experience to understand their world in a different way. Simple single-loop learning is adequate for coping with clearcut predictable situations, but it is double-loop learning that is required for ambiguous unpredictable situations from which innovations emerge. To summarise; innovation flows from the complex, double-loop learning activities of communities of practice, in which tacit knowledge is surfaced and altered and the learning process is essentially social and political interaction.

But how is tacit knowledge, the crucial aspect of complex organisational learning, raised above the level of awareness and how is it transferred between people? Another example will help to answer this question.

The Data Discman

In 1988, a Sony employee, Yoshitaka Ukita, had to accept the failure of the 8 cm single compact disc player that he was responsible for developing; the machine was too late to secure a market against the competition. However, he did not just give up: he tried to think of an alternative use for the machine. As he pondered, he noticed a computerised personal organiser lying on his desk. In his mind he related it to Sony's great success, the Walkman miniature personal entertainment centre. The juxtaposition of the Walkman and the personal organiser led him to the idea of turning the failed compact disc player into the heart of a personal information system that would enable people to carry a reference library around in purse or pocket and call up passages from many books within seconds. Ukita then persuaded his colleagues to support the further development of this idea, which was to become the Discman, a miniature compact disc player that combines pictures in a liquid crystal display with speech and music and plays discs containing books, dictionaries, language lessons, travel guides, quiz games, and other kinds of information.

Ukita was supported by his colleagues who asked publishers to put reference material on compact discs and software writers to prepare the programs for organising and retrieving data. They began to prepare a distribution system that encouraged both book-shops and electronics shops to sell the product. All this time, however, the product was kept a secret even within Sony, partly to preserve the element of market surprise and keep the competition away, but also because the culture encouraged people to take an idea as far as possible on their own initiative. As the product launch date of 1 January 1990 approached, however, it became necessary to inform Norio Ohga, Sony's CEO. He backed the idea, making a design modification that improved the product even though it delayed its launch by six months.

At first Sony expected to sell 5,000 units per month. Instead, they sold 8,000, and at time of writing are producing 20,000 per month. The product was launched in Germany and the United States in November 1991 and in the United Kingdom, France and Spain in the spring of 1992. Ukita expressed his surprise at this outcome. He and his colleagues agree that no one knows how the product will develop from here.

This example illustrates several important points about the process of organisational learning. First, note how the Discman itself emerged from failure through trial and error, rather than being the realisation of a vision or grand design. It is the experience of failure, of contradictions and paradoxes, that provokes people into reflecting upon and changing the way they see things, that is, the tacit models governing how they see things. And note how this trial and error learning process relies on individual insights that come from analogies rather than step-by-step logical reasoning. The beginning of the Discman lay in relating the current problem to the Walkman and to personal organisers. This process of reasoning by analogy is so central to creative learning that it is worth spending some time considering it.

Reasoning by Analogy
It is when we juxtapose seemingly illogical and contradictory things that we are stimulated to look for multiple meanings, to call upon our tacit knowledge, and so develop new insights. And we use metaphors rather than logic to link contradictions to each other and express paradoxes. The ambiguity of metaphors provokes and challenges us to define them more clearly. Metaphors are formulated through intuition, a form of tacit reasoning that links images which may seem remote from each other.

For example, Nonaka (1991) describes how in 1978, top management at Honda inaugurated the development of a new car concept with the slogan 'Let's gamble' indicating the need for a completely new approach. The development team expressed what they should do to deal with this metaphor in the form of another slogan: 'Theory of Automobile Evolution' (a contradictory idea of a car as both a machine and an organism). This posed the question – if a car is like an organism how will it evolve? The designers discussed what this might mean and produced another slogan: 'man-maximum, machine-minimum'. This conveyed the idea that the car should focus on comfort in an urban environment. The idea of evolution prompted the designers to think of the car as a sphere – a car that was 'short' and 'tall'. This gave birth to the idea of a 'Tall Boy' car, eventually called the Honda City.

Once metaphors have provoked new ideas, analogies between one thing and another can then be used to find some resolution (perhaps only temporary) of the contradictions that have provoked us into thinking new things. Analogy is a more structured process of reconciling opposites and making distinctions, clarifying how the opposing ideas are actually alike or not alike.

To illustrate this, Nonaka (1991) recounts the story of Cannon's development of the mini-copier. To ensure reliability the developers proposed to make the copier drum disposable since the drum accounted for 90 per cent of maintenance problems. Team members were discussing, over a drink, the problem of how to make the drum easily and cheaply, when the team leader held up his beer can and asked how much it cost to make one. This led the team to examine the process of making tin cans to see if it could be applied to the manufacture of photocopier drums. The result was lightweight aluminium copier drums.

Control and Self-organisation

The second important point to note about the learning process in the development of the Discman is the role of top executives at Sony: they were not in control of developing the Discman, nor did they expect to be. Indeed they heard about it only when it was ready for launching. The immediate reaction of most Western managers is one of surprise at this failure to seek top management's prior approval for what turned out to be such an important project. Western managers recognise that individuals, given greater freedom, may be much more motivated to develop new ideas, but those managers cannot believe that an organisation can be properly controlled if this kind of behaviour is permitted. Nonetheless, the behaviour of Ukita and his colleagues was controlled; it had a self-organising quality.

Self-organising control is a group phenomenon. It occurs when political interactions and dialogues between members of a group produce coherent behaviour, despite the absence of formal hierarchy within that group, or authority imposed from outside it. Informal groups and networks of managers within an organisation clearly form and conduct themselves through self-organising processes: no central authority organises the network of informal contacts and coalitions that develop in an organisation and yet that network can behave in a controlled way and become a vital part of the organisation's control system. Most managers are not used to the idea that a system, that is, a set of interactions, can control itself. For them, control requires some superior manager to take charge – but when we consider the nature of innovation we see that it is impossible for superior managers to be 'in control'.

New knowledge starts with an individual and its production cannot be centrally designed because no one can know what will be produced until it is produced. Tacit knowledge has to travel from one person to another, in a way that cannot be centrally intended because no one knows what is to travel, or to whom, until it has travelled. New knowledge can therefore only be created when individuals self organise into the unstructured small groups that make up informal networks.

Unpredictability
Thirdly, note how everyone involved in the Discman's development got their forecasts wrong. They simply had no idea whether the product would succeed or how well it might sell. They openly admit that they do not know what the future holds for the product now.

Finally, note how much of the process of developing the Discman took place in the informal organisation through the political network of contacts that existed between Ukita and his colleagues. Complex double-loop learning takes place informally in organisations, often in conflict with the formal organisational procedures. This point can be neatly illustrated by the next example.

The Repair Job

A detailed study (Brown and Duguid, 1991) of the work of service technicians (reps) in a large company in the United States shows quite clearly how actual practice can differ from espoused practice, and in so doing indicates some important points about organisational learning. The primary task of the reps was to answer customer calls for the service and repair of sophisticated machinery supplied by their company. The procedure for servicing and repairing the machinery was set out in great detail in manuals that provided a decision tree for diagnosis and repair. Rep training programmes were provided so that the reps could learn to follow the directive procedures set out in the manual and it was emphasised during such training that any departure from the recognised procedures would be regarded as deviant, unacceptable behaviour.

The researcher observing how the reps actually worked, however, noticed that the mechanistic procedures and training programmes actually obstructed the real work. The prescriptive documentation did not cover all the faults that could arise in the operation of the sophisticated but unpredictable machines the reps had to deal with. The reps coped by using improvised strategies and then concealing what they were doing – they made it look as though they were employing the legitimate procedures.

For example, on one service call, the researcher observed a rep dealing with a defective machine that produced the error codes upon which standard repair procedures were based. But, the error codes did not match the nature of the machine fault and the repair manuals therefore provided no assistance. The correct procedure according to the manual would have been to replace the machine. The rep was reluctant to do this because he realised that he and his company would lose face and the disruption to the customer's work would damage relationships and make the rep's life more difficult in the future. So he ignored the procedures and, since he had not encountered this particular problem before, he sent for a technical specialist who acted as a supervisor. The supervisor too had not encountered this problem before and was also reluctant to assign the machine to the scrap heap.

The rep and his supervisor then began to question the users and to swop stories about similar malfunctions each had encountered before or heard about from colleagues. They approached the task of diagnosis through a story-telling procedure that had nothing to do with formal manuals. Eventually the stories and anecdotes of similar experiences, conducted while the rep and his supervisor tried one experiment after another on the faulty machine, led to correct diagnosis and repair. Subsequently when they met with other colleagues they recounted the story of the repair and that story then became a part of the folklore of the rep community, folklore that would later be used to provide analogies that would assist in diagnosing unpredictable machine failures on future occasions. The reps were dealing with unpredictable problems using a process of narration through which they explored analogies and so jointly discovered an explanation of what had gone wrong. They constituted a community of practice and what they were doing was learning. What they learned was then embodied not in a rigid manual but in a loose story that would be remembered by others.

This example makes it clear how complex double-loop learning takes place through political and social interaction within a community of practice. Organisations are simply communities of such communities of practice (Brown and Duguid, 1991) and organisations develop in innovative new directions when the communities of practice that constitute them are actively learning. Informal collaboration and social construction are essential aspects of this learning process. Furthermore, the example makes it clear that in effective organisations, complex learning takes place at all hierarchical levels – it is not the hierarchical level that determines whether or not complex learning is required, but the level of uncertainty and ambiguity in the situations people are confronted with. Anything that obstructs complex learning at any level cuts down on the amount of uncertainty and ambiguity an organisation as a whole can cope with.

Taken together, the examples of new product development and day-to-day servicing of existing machines indicate how different kinds of learning are deployed by people in organisations to carry out their tasks effectively in different situations. Consider now those different kinds of learning and the situations in which they are appropriate.

Different Kinds of Learning

Learning occurs when people change the way they think and the way they behave and these changes in thinking and behaving can be brought about in a number of different ways.

The simplest kind of learning is based on some form of conditioning. For example, reflex conditioning is learning by frequent association; unless one's addiction to smoking is completely overpowering, one soon learns not to smoke if an electric shock is administered each time one lights up a cigarette and ten pence is paid each time one declines a proffered cigarette. This simple, mindless, learning about the consequences of acting produces obedient behaviour patterns that, once acquired, are hard to change. More complex conditioning occurs when people identify linkages between certain actions and the subsequent satisfaction of basic drives such as hunger and thirst or some other material reward. Reward systems that tie pay to performance make use of this kind of conditioning.

Rather more complex is what we might call incremental learning. This is the conscious rational form of learning in which people collect facts, conduct experiments and add progressively to a bank of knowledge. It is what most people usually mean when they talk about learning.

The key point about these forms of conditioning and incremental learning is that they are basically single-loop learning. They proceed without questioning the mental models through which the world is understood, but are rather concerned solely with adapting current behaviour to the discovered consequences of previous behaviour. Such single- loop learning can only be carried out in situations in which there are clear connections between cause and effect and hence the possibility of prediction. Conditioning and incremental forms of learning are therefore appropriate only when people in an organisation are going about their repetitive day-to-day tasks in the existing business. What people have learned in this way can be embodied in procedures, manuals, plans, policy documents, and cultural symbols and stories.

As soon as people are confronted by the ambiguous, the unpredictable and the uncertain however, they have to switch to more complex, double-loop forms of learning if they are to cope. And that means essentially reflection upon, and change to, the mental models through which they understand their world. The learning process here is essentially one of conflict with the received wisdom, the destruction of current procedures and existing cultures, and the creation of new ones. This kind of learning is partly based on emotion: the motive to learn is provided by emotions of one kind or another and the result is a more complex and less mechanistic form of learning. Emotions are important in a complex learning process because they may act like circuit breakers and allow quick adaptive shifts in understanding. Emotion–based learning is prompted by unconscious needs.

Complex learning is transformational, involving a conscious aspect when information is collected and reflected upon, but also an unconscious aspect in which the material is somehow integrated. We can see the conscious and the unconscious aspects of complex learning when we struggle unsuccessfully to deal with a problem late at night and then wake up in the morning to become immediately aware that we have the answer.

Communities of practice consist of individuals who utilise all these forms of learning. The difference between individual and group learning is of course the social, political and unconscious interactions between the people involved. Ultimately, organisational learning is the unconscious establishment of shared assumptions through people imitating and modelling themselves on each other. And as the tasks they face become more and more uncertain and ambiguous, the people involved have to switch from simple, mechanistic, conditioning types of learning to the more creative transformational kinds of learning that involve complex social interactions and complex unconscious processes.

Key Points about the Learning Organisation

The examples above make a number of key points about organisational learning. The concept of an organisation that learns helps us to understand what is going on when people in an organisation have to deal with tasks that are innovative or unpredictable in some way. They do not have to be weighty strategic tasks; they can be the ordinary everyday tasks of the existing business. It is not the hierarchical level or the strategic nature that calls for the activity of learning – it is the degree of uncertainty and ambiguity, the requirement for creativity and innovation around the task.

The second key point is this. The accepted way of doing things, the manual, the procedures, the plans, are all of no use when people have to operate far from certainty. Step-by-step logic cannot be applied and the recipe, the culture or the stories cannot be applied directly. What happens instead is a kind of drama, an activity of playing and telling stories, using metaphors, analogies and dreams to explore the new unique uncertain situation and test the boundaries and the constraints provided by the rules and procedures. Because the situation is so different, a completely different kind of thinking is required.

Third, the activity of complex learning is spontaneous and self organising: it cannot be centrally controlled and attempts to do so simply destroy it. Instead of trying to exert direct control, superior managers have to create the right kind of psychological and emotional atmosphere in which people are encouraged to embark spontaneously on complex learning processes.

Finally, organisational learning is a political process that takes place in the informal organisation. As purported new knowledge is dispersed through a group and an organisation, it must be tested: that means that there must be discussion, dialogue and disagreement. The dispersion of purported new knowledge threatens people's existing perceptions and positions, raising anxiety levels and perhaps provoking strange group dynamics. Insecurity, anxiety, conflict and confusion must be accepted as inevitable factors in the process of new knowledge creation. They can only be removed by stamping out the creation of new knowledge. It is the function of the informal organisation to use this chaos to generate new perspectives, to learn, and to destroy existing paradigms and create the new. But it is also the role of the informal organisation to contain the instability, to keep it bounded, for without this we get utter confusion (Stacey, 1991 and 1992).

Why Organisational Learning is so Difficult to Achieve

Effective organisational learning is very difficult to sustain and the main reasons for this lie in the minds of the people who make up an organisation. Most of us employ mental models that make it almost impossible to act in a manner that promotes effective organisational learning.

The Control Model of Management

The model that drives most people's behaviour as they act in organisations can be called the control model (Argyris, 1990). The control model is one in which it is believed that:

- a manager's power is derived from position in the hierarchy;
- people are motivated by the task; and
- people respond most to short-term rewards in relation to task achievement.

These beliefs about the source of power and the way to motivate people are closely associated with the suppression of negative feelings and judgements about people's performance. Such judgements are usually not publicly exposed and tested in case they upset and demotivate others, so reducing levels of task performance. Instead evaluations are made privately and covered up in public. All understand that this is what is happening but they accept it as a necessary defence against hurting people's feelings and against the consequent organisational inefficiency.

So, when a manager is fired, this is frequently presented as a resignation due to health reasons or some other factor. Memoranda are distributed thanking the fired person for years of valued contributions. All know that this is a tissue of lies, but none publicly says so. This is an example of a defence routine, a game people play to protect each other from having to face unpleasant organisational truths in public. As a result, the real reason for firing the person, a judgment that he or she is incompetent, is never properly examined: it could well have been unjustified and turn out to be harmful to the performance of the organisation.

These kinds of beliefs about control lead to win/lose dynamics in which people adopt tactics of persuasion and selling, only superficially listening to others. People driven by win/lose behaviour also tend to use face-saving devices for themselves and each other. They save face by avoiding the public testing of the assumptions they are making about each others' motives or statements. This behaviour produces what has been called skilled incompetence: skilled in that the behaviour is automatic; incompetent in that it produces obstacles to work, real learning, effective decision making. These obstacles take the form of organisational defence routines that become embedded in behaviour and are extremely difficult to change. In short, most people in organisations think in a way that ensures the simple, conditioning, incremental forms of learning and they construct defences that prevent the more threatening, complex transformational learning from occur-ring. The main reason why organisations do not learn lies in these defence routines, making it essential to explore further what is meant by them.

Defence Routines

Organisational defence routines are patterns of behaviour that people in an organisation deploy to protect themselves and others from embarrassment and anxiety (Argyris, 1990).

The prime defence routine is to make matters undiscussable and to make the fact that they are undiscussable itself undiscussable. So, subordinates refrain from telling their superiors the truth if those superiors are thought likely to dislike it. Subordinates do not publicly admit that they are doing this and neither do their superiors who, of course, know what is going on because they do it themselves. The result is an undiscussed game of pretence in which all indulge and all know they are doing it. The pretence enables all involved to avoid confronting embarrassing or potentially explosive behaviour.

Defence routines take the form of bypasses, cover-ups and games. For example, a manager may ask a colleague with whom he or she disagrees for comprehensive proof of a proposal outcome when it is quite clear to all that such proof is impossible to provide.

A well-known game is to prevent a decision one dislikes by repeatedly calling for more reports and research, on the grounds that a rational decision can be made only on the basis of the facts. For example, one company familiar to the author played the following game for over a year. One faction in the top management team thought that the company should diversify the range of its activities. Another faction led by the chairman thought that it should not. However, the chairman did not openly quash the idea. He called for a paper setting out general diversification principles. After discussion at the formal executive meeting, the principles paper was held to be too general and specific proposals were called for. When the specific proposals were discussed, the chairman called for a discussion of the general principles. So it went on and, needless to say, no diversification occurred. All involved knew it was a game and, while they admitted this to each other in groups of two's or three's, no one ever raised it at the full meetings.

Long-term plans, mission statements and visions could well be games of a similar kind. They are usually abstract statements without operational content, simply to convey an impression of rational decision making and to keep people quiet or feeling more secure.

Perhaps the most popular cover-up, mostly unconscious, is to espouse a different style of management while actually continuing to use the control model. So, a manager says that he or she is looking for team decision making, that he or she is open to different views, and then becomes visibly annoyed when such views are put forward. That manager makes it clear by behaving in a particular manner that team decision making is not actually to occur despite any statements made to the contrary.

Defence routines become so entrenched in organisations that they come to be viewed as an inevitable part of human nature. Managers make self-fulfilling prophecies about what will happen at meetings. Because, they claim, it is human nature, they indulge in the game playing, so confirming their belief in human nature. The defence routines, game playing and cover-ups can become so disruptive that managers actually avoid discussing contentious open-ended issues altogether. Even if this extreme is not reached, the dysfunctional learning behaviour blocks the detection of gradually accumulating small changes, the surfacing of different perspective, the thorough testing of proposals through dialogue. When they use the control management model with the organisational defence routines it provokes, managers struggle to deal with strategic issues. They end up preparing long lists of strengths and weaknesses, opportunities and threats that simply get them nowhere. They produce mission statements that are so bland as to be meaningless, visions not connected with reality and long-term plans that are simply filed. Or they may decide on an action and then not implement it.

Managers collude in this behaviour and refrain from discussing it. They then distance themselves from what is going on and blame others, the chief executive, or the organisational structure, when things go wrong. They look for solutions in general models, techniques, visions and plans. All the while the real causes of poor strategic management – the learning process itself, the political interaction and the group dynamic – remain stubbornly undiscussable.

People within an organisation collude in keeping matters undiscussable because they fear the consequences if they do not. Consultants too find themselves sucked into defence routines because they are nervous of the consequences of exposing them. They may be fired. The result of the defence routines we have been talking about is passive employees and managers, highly dependent upon authority, who are not well equipped to handle rapid change. In these conditions managers in difficult situations produce vague, impractical prescriptions such as 'we need more training' or 'we need a vision', as a defence against having to do anything. The organisation loses out on the creativity of people because of the management model it uses and that model can quite literally lead to disaster.

The Challenger Disaster

In 1986 a Presidential Commission enquired into the disaster which had occurred when the Challenger shuttle had crashed soon after launching. It concluded that NASA had sound structures, policies and rules to secure safety. What had gone wrong was that those most intimately involved with the launch had focused so heavily on the launch itself that they neglected safety matters. The conclusion was that there was nothing wrong with the organisation: the disaster was due to human failures. These were to be addressed in the future by making it compulsory for all launch constraints, and waivers of launch constraints, to be considered by all levels of management. In other words there was to be more referral up the management hierarchy.

Argyris (1990) analyses this episode to show how the disaster was actually due to organisational defence routines, which both NASA and the Presidential Commission were unwittingly covering up. The recommendation of more referral to higher management levels would do nothing to remove those organisational defence routines. It would therefore most probably be ineffective in preventing another accident.

Using the testimony presented to the Commission, Argyris shows the following. Before the launch, engineers had indicated that the launch should be delayed because of problems with O rings – problems that ultimately caused the disaster. At a meeting with the engineers, one manager understood them to be advising a delay, but his superior concluded that they were simply raising some questions. The two managers did not explore their different understandings with each other: they did not test them publicly. The superior manager decided, without discussing it with anyone, not to report on the meeting with the engineers to higher levels of management. The engineers sounded a number of warnings and then stopped when they realised that no one would listen. Engineers never questioned management as to why they would not listen: that would have been regarded as an affront to management capability.

At each level, the engineers and managers are covering themselves. The engineers raised the problem, but the next level did not heed them. They were defending themselves by drawing attention to a problem and then giving up when it become clear that the next level would not listen. They would not themselves take the matter further up the hierarchy because they knew that this would antagonise their immediate superiors. So, they adopted the routine of raising the matter, knowing it would be ignored, and then dropping it, all in order to defend themselves. If anything went wrong, they would not be to blame. The first manager heard the message but bowed to his superior. He was covered because he was doing what the superior wanted. The superior was covered because he interpreted the points made by the engineers as simply raising questions and no one contradicted him. He probably made this interpretation because he knew those above him did not want bad news that they would have to convey to the President. In the end the disaster was due to all these organisational defence routines and cover-ups. All knew that what was being covered up was important. They do not now need rules to tell them this. Introducing rules is therefore unlikely to prevent this kind of thing from happening again. No rule can stop some manager from interpreting a warning as a question. The only way around this is to require everything to be conveyed up the hierarchy and that is impossible. The real solution is to uncover the defences and discuss them, despite the anxiety and difficulty this involves. Argyris concludes:

> Organizational defence routines make it highly likely that individuals, groups, intergroups, and organizations will not detect and correct the errors that are embarrassing and threatening because the fundamental rules are to (1) bypass the errors and act as if that were not being done, (2) make the bypass undiscussable, and (3) makes its undiscussability undiscussable.

These conditions, in turn, make it difficult to engage the organizational defense routines in order to interrupt them and reduce them. Indeed, the very attempt to engage them will lead to the defensive routines' being activated and strengthened. This, in turn, reinforces and proliferates the defensive routines. (1990, p43)

The Commitment Model of Managing

The way out of this impasse is to switch to a commitment model of managing. The commitment model seeks to take advantage of the inherent creativity of people by emphasising that:

- power flows from expertise and contribution, not simply position in the hierarchy;
- people are assumed to be motivated primarily by their own internal commitment; and
- people are assumed to respond to long-term rewards.

These beliefs about power and motivation tend to encourage the public exposure and testing of relevant feelings and judgements, even if they are negative, in order to ensure that decisions are being taken on valid data. Behaviour according to the commitment model should lead to cooperative dynamics and mutual control, allowing people to put their own creativity to use for the organisation.

The problem is that the attempt to move to the commitment model is just as likely as the control model to provoke defensive behaviour arising from:

- the management fear of losing control
- the clash of vested interests
- the effects of power vacuums
- the effects of unconscious processes.

These loops could quite easily completely immobilise learning, decision making and action. It is possible to specify what needs to be done to create a learning organisation, but actually doing it is a never-ending task.

References

Argyris, C (1990) *Overcoming Organizational Defenses: Facilitating Organizational Learning*, Allyn & Bacon, Prentice-Hall, Boston

Brown, J S and Duguid, P (1991) 'Organizational Learning and Communities of Practice: Toward a Unified View of Working, Learning and Innovation,' *Organisational Science*, Vol 2, No 1, Feb, pp 40–57.

Mintzberg, H and Waters, J A (1985) 'Of Strategies Deliberate and Emergent', *Strategic Management Journal*, No 6, pp 257–72.

Nonaka, I (1991) 'The Knowledge-Creating Company', *Harvard Business Review*, Nov–Dec, 96–104.

Pascale, R T (1990) *Managing on the Edge: How Successful Companies use Conflict to Stay Ahead*, Viking Penguin, London.

Stacey, R (1991) *The Chaos Frontier: Creative Strategic Control for Business*, Butterworth-Heinemann, Oxford.

—(1992) *Managing Chaos*, Kogan Page, London. Also published in the USA as *Managing the Unknowable: The Strategic Boundaries Between Order and Chaos*, Jossey-Bass, San Francisco.

5

The Human Dynamic

Eric Miller

Introduction

We can think of a business or other enterprise as straddling two regions of chaos. Externally, multiple forces interact with each other to produce what in the 1960s was called a 'turbulent environment' (Emery and Trist, 1965). At that time it was still possible to describe the external environment of some enterprises as relatively 'placid'. Since then, such has been the pace of change and the complexities that go with it, that it is hard to think of any examples of placidity: unpredictability has become the norm. The internal environment is a collection of individual human beings whose relatedness to the enterprise is ambivalent; and their interactions too are an intertwining of rational and irrational processes which also defies predictability.

We used to be told that the key to business success lay in being proactive instead of reactive. In today's chaotic world each of these postures is dangerous. Over-responsiveness imports turbulence at an indigestible rate; while the enterprise that tries to impose a proactive strategy is increasingly likely to find itself blown off course by unforeseen forces. Survival and success seem to call for a mixture of both – creating new patterns interactively through continuous engagement with the external environment (Stacey, 1991).

In facing the internal, human environment, enterprises are having to struggle with a similar problem. On the one side there is the picture of human beings as inherently unreliable: they have to be cajoled and controlled to fit the needs of the enterprise. On the other side, they are

98

regarded as a valuable resource whose potentialities need to be tapped. The subject of this chapter is the problem of reconciling these two perspectives – of neither being swamped by, nor trying to eliminate, the chaos of this internal environment, but engaging with it.

First we need to have some understanding of the chaos that we each have to engage with in ourselves in the process of becoming and being individuals. I shall suggest that we are perpetually involved in trying to export chaos from our internal environments (self and group) and to import order from outside. Recognition of this enables us to look at what organisations import from their members. Mathematicians tell us that chaos is not total confusion: the structure of feedback mechanisms is such that certain broad patterns tend to recur (Stacey, 1991). Every hurricane is unique, but we can identify it as a hurricane. It is to patterns of this kind that we need to alert ourselves in our organisations: some can contribute to the task; some can be destructive. Yet, perversely, behaviours that are on the edge of destructiveness may have the greatest potential for creativity.

Human Beings as Group Animals

Our simian ancestry is still part of us. Watch the dependent attachment of a baby – monkey or human – clinging to mother and the maternal breast: there it finds safety and pleasure. Observe the other response, to pain or to a perceived threat: attacking it or fending it off (and 'it' may be the mother's breast again), or arching back to get as far as possible from it. These are the very basic instincts with which we are all born. Here I shall follow through this theme in two directions.

First, we need to consider 'groupishness'. To quote the psycho-analyst, Wilfred Bion:

> The individual is a group animal at war, not simply with the group, but with himself for being a group animal and with those aspects of his personality that constitute his 'groupishness'. (1961, p 131)

The Work Group

Bion's proposition was that every group is always operating at two levels. At the conscious level it is what he variously described as a 'sophisticated group' or a 'work group', whose members are met together for some common purpose. The work group:

- has an explicit and agreed definition of its task

- has an appropriate system of organisation for the task and of communications, internal and external
- uses rationality to deal with reality and also recognises and faces complexity
- values individuals for their contribution: anyone having a contribution is enabled to make it and this is assessed on the merits of the content, not on the status of the contributor, in other words, leadership is not exclusive, mutual dependency is acknowledged, and cooperation – in the literal sense of working together – is fostered
- has mechanisms for identifying and coping with disagreement or discontent
- can tolerate turnover of members without fear of losing its identity
- can identify and face the need for change.

Whether as managers or members, that is surely a model of what we would like to see in the workplace!

Unconsciously Shared Group Assumptions

Bion goes on to explain why we are so often disappointed. Although the work group attracts a strong psychological investment, it expresses only one dimension of mental functioning. Every group, he says, besides being met for the work task, whatever that may be, is also, *at the same time*, unconsciously held together by and operating on an underlying shared assumption – an assumption about the group and about the members' contribution to it. He identified three of these basic assumptions: fight/flight, dependency and pairing.

In fight/flight, the group behaves as if its purpose is to identify an external enemy or threat, which it has either to fight or to flee from. The lynch mob is an extreme example; but we have all at times been in groups united in rage against a common enemy. Sometimes the threat is real; often it is imaginary, and we look back later wondering how we got caught up in that paranoia. A common version of the lynch mob, though usually less fatal, is hunt-the-scapegoat: if only we can get rid of X, our problems will be solved. X goes, amid much rejoicing – and then we discover that the problems are still with us: they belong to the group and X was just a symptom.

The group sharing the basic assumption of dependency is expecting to be fed and nurtured by an omnipotent and omniscient leader. Some chief executives get caught in this role: they are credited with having *the* vision. It has happened to me too, when, as a consultant I was treated as the expert who will solve all problems. It is a seductive experience: at that moment I could almost believe that I *did* have the answers. It is as if the clients had surrendered their capacity to think and given it to me. Some chief executives do get seduced. So long as the vision works, they prosper. But because they have surrounded themselves with acolytes whose capacity for independent thought and criticism has been suppressed, there is no one to warn them when they are making a terrible mistake.

Dependency and flight/fight are fairly obvious group-level manifestations of the infant's drives of pleasure seeking and pain avoidance. In pairing, the third basic assumption, the emotional state of the group is one of expectancy and hope. All attention is focussed on two members, as if they together will generate the solution to the group's problems. Although the pair may not be heterosexual they represent the primitive reproductive drive of the group: their pairing will produce the future leader, the messiah, who will save the group.

It is a characteristic of basic assumption behaviour that group members contribute to it without being aware of doing so. Rationality is out; statements that are plainly false go uncorrected; there is no sense of time. The behaviour is 'instantaneous, inevitable and instinctive'. Physicists use the term 'valency' for the capacity of an atom to combine with others (notably hydrogen). Bion applied it to the human 'capacity for instantaneous, involuntary combination of one individual with another for sharing and acting on a basic assumption' (1961, p 153).

That this is part of our inalienable inheritance as herd animals, I am in no doubt. Many years ago in India (still blissfully unaware of Bion's writings) I was fascinated by a band of langur monkeys whose territory adjoined a nearby mosque. The leader was a powerful male, who, after an initial confrontation in which neither of us gave way, decided that we could coexist, and thereafter I paid regular visits on Sunday afternoons. There were about eight adult females with their young and a similar number of males, but the leader was largely successful in maintaining a sexual monopoly. The recurrent phenomena were striking. One was a tableau of dependency, with the leader sitting on top of a hillock with his band arrayed around him. The other was their management of territory. When an intruder appeared, action was collective and instantaneous. If it was a dog, the whole band as one would rush at it and drive it off. With the arrival of three men with sticks, on the other hand, the band with the same unanimity would flee as a body. If the leader gave any signal, I never saw it.

The Group as a Meeting of Two Types of Mental Functioning

The human group is a meeting of the two types of mental functioning that its members bring to it: the primitive horde response, and the reasoning and reality testing of mature human beings. Or to put it another way, it is a place where each of us is struggling with the conflicting drives of wanting to be an autonomous individual and of needing to belong, to be part of something larger than ourselves. Hence there is always a tension between the work group and the basic primitive group. Commitment to the work group can, as I have said, be quite strong, but the basic assumptions are never far below the surface, waiting to break through and take over.

It often happens that a particular basic assumption is consistent with the task. In some activities, for example, a certain amount of dependence is quite appropriate. If I am giving a lecture I prefer my audience to be orderly and to have some investment in listening to what I have to say, and also to be 'working', in the sense of listening in a critical way. That is calculated mature dependence, within which people are not surrendering their individual autonomy. But it requires an effort not to fall into the assumption state of dependence:

'That was a wonderful speech.'
'What did she say?'
'Oh, I don't remember what she said, but it was a wonderful speech.'

Dependence in a sales team, on the other hand, is usually undesirable: we want them to mobilise 'fight'. Again, however, the effective sales campaign requires sophisticated reasoning and judgment, not the mindless emotion of the basic assumption.

This particular view of group behaviour alerts us to one set of patterns in the chaotic internal world of the enterprise. For example, we can spot a situation where followers have become over-dependent on the leader and lost their capacity for independent judgment; or where a difference of view about strategy has turned into a destructive interpersonal and interdepartmental battle. These phenomena are far more difficult to see and act on when we ourselves are part of them. The leader in the dependency culture is caught in the collusion and actually has an inflated opinion of his/her own wisdom and insight. The fellow-manager whom I disagree with does not simply have a different view: he/she is a traitor to the organisation and it is my duty to try to get rid of him/her. Many years ago, when The Tavistock Institute was in a financial crisis, an emergency meeting was called. We began to look at alternative actions, all of them painful. Then one respected older member described eloquently and at length his vision of where we needed to get. We left feeling much happier. Only later did it occur to us that the crisis remained unresolved. The basic assumption of 'flight' had swallowed us all.

The picture painted so far is of the tension within ourselves and within the group between the mature, autonomous, human adult and the primitive group animal. That is complicated enough. What complicates it still further is that maturity and autonomy are ideals that we never fully realise and that part of what each of us brings to our groups is also our own built-in personal history of a chequered process, from birth on, through which we have struggled towards becoming individuals. That is subject of the next section.

Becoming an Individual

We are not born with a sense of self. The infant's early experience is of a bundle of pleasurable and painful feelings, with no awareness of whether they come from inside or outside. It takes many weeks, even months, to make that distinction. The sense of me is acquired in conjunction with the recognition of not-me, of a boundary between self and other. It probably begins from awareness of the boundary of one's own body as separate from mother's.

What we do seem to be born with, in a more developed form than in our simian cousins, is a need to make sense of our experience, a 'will-to-meaning' (Frankl, 1959). To the infant the initial experience must seem chaotic: food and no food, comfort and pain, alternate in a bewilderingly random way. Students of child development tell us that the first, and unconscious, 'explanation' is in terms of splitting. Pleasure is attributed to a 'good breast' or good mother to whom there is a deep attachment (Klein, 1952 and 1959). Pain is ascribed to a 'bad breast', which is a threat to be attacked – and we have all seen the frustrated baby punching the breast in a rage. Those are raw, powerful feelings. With the discovery of the boundary between self and other comes the disturbing realisation that the good and bad breasts are the same breasts, part of the same mother. So the initial explanation was inadequate; a new paradigm is needed.

Defences Against Anxiety

This is the transition from what one psychoanalyst called the paranoid-schizoid position to the depressive position (Klein 1952, 1959). In that earlier phase, when the young infant could not distinguish between its impulses and their effects, its fantasy was that the objects it wished to attack and destroy – notably the 'bad breast' – were actually damaged and would take their revenge with equal destructiveness. Separation from mother could be terrifying: perhaps she was destroyed and would never come back.

The resultant paranoid anxiety was coped with by the 'schizoid defence', of splitting the good from the bad. What gives the depressive position its name is the pain of coming to terms with ambivalence. The perfect idealised mother – the good breast – seems to have abandoned me; and now I have to relate to a person who is a mixture of good and bad parts – those bad parts that I wanted to attack and destroy . . . Though good mothering can mitigate it, it is a painful learning experience. It marks the beginnings of feelings of guilt and also of reparation.

The wish to repair the damage that the infant feels it has inflicted on the mother leads to a capacity to be caring and loving. So we acquire a caring, loving self alongside that other aggressive, destructive self – an internalised version of the ambivalence towards mother. Those two selves do not sit comfortably together; they generate depressive anxiety. Even the well-mothered baby can stand only so much of it and erects defences against the pain. Others get stuck in the defensive position.

One strategy is to cling on to the paranoid defence: that is, to split one's world – both outside and inside – into good and bad. Thus if I make father bad I am justified in wanting to kill him (the Oedipus complex in males) and I can keep my images of my mother and of myself good; though then I am also frightened that father will punish me for my destructive feelings towards him. That is the problem with projection: it deals with the depressive anxiety at the cost of creating a belief in a vengeful enemy.

The other main strategy is the 'manic defence' – an omnipotent notion that I am totally self-sufficient; the loss of the perfect mother doesn't matter to me. The cost to the baby, and to the adult that it becomes, is the unavailability of those parts of the self that enable one to make a loving relationship with others. A further coping mechanism is the acquisition of obsessional behaviours, which have a kind of magical quality: if I perform this or that ritual, I shall get back what I lost, or be saved from the punishment I deserve.

By the time the baby is a year old, it has had to learn to relate to an array of other people – not only parents, but also siblings, other family members, neighbours and so on. It has also learned an array of ways of categorising and responding to these experiences, such as splitting, projection, introjection and identification, along with a widening repertoire of emotions, such as love, hate, guilt, reparative drives, envy and jealousy (in males the Oedipus complex again).

The Filters of Perception

In fact neither the infant nor the adult ever relates directly to other people. First there is the constraint of perception itself: I can never actually see, hear, touch, smell, taste the other; my senses are processed by a brain that tells me what it is seeing, hearing and so on. That is, perhaps, a pedantic point, though not to be entirely dismissed: colour-blindness is a reminder that we do not all see the same thing. (And I have met a young man who was thought to be psychotic until he was diagnosed as having uniquely acute hearing: his problem was information overload – including the things people were saying about him behind closed doors.) The more serious point is that our perceptions are not simply processed by our brains but they are filtered through our minds, including our unconscious minds.

Our search for meaning has erected the kinds of defences I have described to cope with the contradictions we have experienced from infancy onwards. Maturity might be defined in terms of accepting and integrating all the disparate and conflicting feelings and impressions that experience has evoked inside us: those overwhelming primitive feelings of total attachment, murderous rage and unspeakable anxiety, followed by depression and guilt, along with identification, love, idealisation and hatred. When will humankind reach maturity? Maybe in another 5,000 years? There have certainly been few signs of progress in the last 5,000.

Some of us get closer to genuine integration than others, but all of us to some extent deal with the chaos within ourselves by maintaining the defences through which, on the one hand, we keep some experiences locked away in our inner, unconscious worlds and, on the other, we disown those feelings that do not fit with our picture of self and locate them elsewhere. All that baggage therefore is carried into our adult relationships.

When I meet a new male boss, for example, I am seeing him through a distorted lens: I am carrying with me preconceptions based on my past experience of a series of authority figures in my life, probably starting with father. It is those, more than the evidence in front of me in the here and now, that will shape my responses of trust or suspicion, compliance or rebelliousness. The female boss will resonate with unconscious memories of a 'good' or a 'bad' mother. These behaviours tend to become self-fulfilling prophecies, because I will always be alert to evidence that confirms my preconceptions; and the preconceptions may produce the evidence: if I distrust my boss, she or he will probably be distrustful of me.

As with bosses, so with others in our environment. To maintain a consistent sense of myself as an individual, I populate my world with a whole set of persons and groups in relation to which I locate my self as 'the same as' or 'different from' along all sorts of dimensions. Various parts of me are distributed among the range of my roles and relationships: perhaps caring as a parent, submissive as a spouse and authoritarian as a boss. Each of these is sustained by attributing appropriate characteristics to the other: the child is needy, the partner is aggressive, the subordinates are irresponsible. In that way I can disown and project on to others my own neediness, aggression and irresponsibility.

Beyond that, there are groups and figures 'out there', in society, that I identify with or piously condemn. Of course there are exceptions – 'some of my best friends are Jews but' – . . . And I have the reassurance of knowing that many others share my feelings. The British miners' strike of 1984 threw up two figures for the roles of hero and villain. Half the population was on Scargill's side, half on Thatcher's. When Mrs Thatcher claimed that there was no such thing as society she was not altogether wrong: one can argue that 'society' is no more than a collection of widely used labels which attract our projections, positive or negative: 'the Government', 'the City', miners, blacks, civil servants, and so on. They are characters in a national soap opera that we all not merely watch but create as we go along.

Work Groups and Defences Against Anxiety

Work organisations perform similar functions. It was long ago pointed out that organisational structures and cultures are not only created for the performance of a task but also used and modified to provide their members with defences against anxiety (Jaques, 1953; Menzies, 1959). One fundamental anxiety is loss of boundaries. We need an outside to relate to, in order to define ourselves, our identity. Conferences run by The Tavistock Institute for the study of group processes have shown very clearly that the unstructured large group of people is a dangerous place for the individual, who may experience being made into something other, a caricature of self, or being lost, isolated, excluded, bewildered (Turquet, 1974; Miller, 1989).

First of all, the organisation defines a work role in terms of a set of activities and relationships. If, as some employers recognise, tasks are designed in a way that enables people to feel that they are using their skills and to see the product of their labours, the role is psychologically rewarding; it makes positive use of those early reparative urges. Even without this reward, it at least provides a boundary and a location in a social system. That social system also defines status, represented by differences of rank and pay and positions of superior and subordinate. So 'me' is located in relation to a set of 'not-mes'; and the individual identifies with a number of 'us-es'. These are overlaid on the formal structure and sometimes cut across it: for example, identification with territory. Hence there is much scope for splitting and projection between various configurations of 'them and us', villains and heroes, with all the accompanying myths, rituals and taboos. As we all know, much energy and feeling is invested in resentment at a remote head office or in interdepartmental rivalries. In such ways organisations provide a rich mix of outlets for expressing positive parts of oneself, such as opportunities for comradeship and role models to identify with, as well as channels for discharging the potentially destructive parts, such as aggression, envy and contempt.

Beyond this, it is worth recognising that the employing organisation is an equivalent to mother. If it does not actually provide food it provides the money to buy it. As with mother, one is dependent on the organisation and it evokes correspondingly ambivalent feelings towards the 'management' that personifies it. (The definition of what constitutes 'management' for this purpose depends on one's rank in the system.) The ideal mother's love is unconditional. The organisation's love is conditional: in return for 'food' it demands compliance. Enforced dependence generates rage. Here unions may serve a two-fold function for employees. They can – perhaps as a father-equivalent – put pressure on mother to be more generous with the food and more caring. Secondly, my other role as a union member can siphon off some of my rage at the enforced compliance and make it less likely that I will launch a single-handed attack, which would both be ineffective and probably cost me my livelihood. Unions often help management too, by serving as a common enemy: differences and rivalries get suppressed and management acquires at least a superficial solidarity.

These then are examples of the complex drives and feelings, some of them quite primitive, that we import into organisations and some of the defensive arrangements that emerge. Enterprises such as, say, airlines or hospitals, which process people rather than inanimate materials, tend to produce further defensive configurations to deal with anxieties inherent in the task, including the anxieties imported by the passengers or patients themselves (Menzies, 1959, Miller and Rice, 1967).

Recapitulation of the Argument So Far

Deeply embedded in us as a species is our biological inheritance as herd animals. This leads us to coagulate instinctively around the primitive 'basic assumptions': dependency, fight-flight and pairing. These are a perpetual, built-in handicap to our more specifically human drive to become mature, rational, individual beings, integrating intellect and feeling. To be human is to be caught in that constant pull between individuation and incorporation. By becoming aware of it, we can recognise the repetitive patterns of basic assumption behaviour in groups around us and, with difficulty, even in our own.

Because of our genetic inheritance each one of us is biologically a unique individual. Our actual experience, from birth onwards (and possibly even within the womb), of the process of becoming human individuals starts from the same basic drives of pleasure seeking and pain avoidance. What distinguishes us from monkeys is the emerging *consciousness* of being individual, with all its attendant satisfactions and anxieties. The details of our experience of this process and the ways in which we cope with the contradictions and complexities that go with it are also unique for each individual. But for all of us these are too much to contain within our own skins, as it were. By getting rid of, and depositing somewhere else, the bits that we can't contain – the most disturbing bits – we reduce our internal conflicts to a tolerable level.

Although our individual sets of anxieties and defences are unique, certain constellations recur. Moreover, perhaps because of our inherited 'groupishness', we need to find others who, at least on some dimensions, we can feel are the same as we are. The work organisation, which occupies a large block of our lives, is an ideal institution for this purpose. It usually offers – or at least should offer – the satisfaction of achieving something and being valued for it. And it also offers an array of groupings and categories of people to identify with and to project into. So we use, elaborate and subvert the official structure and culture, designed to perform the official task, so as to construct a system for the unstated task of catering for our need for defences.

The fact that each individual's early internal conflicts and the defences adopted are unique means that when they come together in a large group the outcomes of their interactions are inherently unpredictable. The official structure provides a framework, but there can be innumerable variations around that theme. Some recurrent underlying patterns can nevertheless be spotted. They are more complex than those produced by the basic assumptions – though they tend to build around those – but the range of types of defences that individuals draw on is finite and some, such as splitting and projection, seem universal; so that it is to be expected that institutional defence systems will show some regularities.

Our difficulty in recognising these patterns is because the behaviours are so much taken for granted. We are unsurprised by an interdepartmental feud. We may try to stop it but we often fail to ask basic questions, such as: Why is it happening now? What else has changed? What function does it serve for the people involved, for other departments, for the organisation as a whole? And the defensive behaviours that we ourselves are engaged in are rendered invisible by our rationalisations: 'this is the moment to teach the union a lesson' (because we want to avoid a power struggle in top management); the ritual formality of a board meeting to ratify a decision that everyone knows is already being implemented; calling in consultants to review our structure and make recommendations (when we know perfectly well that painful surgery is needed, but we want them to be the scapegoats, not us). Basically any behaviour that perverts or fudges performance of the primary task of the organisation or is unnecessary for it is likely to have a defensive function.

This is not to suggest that organisational defence mechanisms are inherently wrong or bad. Rituals, for example, may be valuable and necessary as a way of enabling people to manage quite difficult feelings around a retirement or, still more, a death: far from interfering with the task, they enable the work to be resumed. Some decisions are in reality very difficult to confront and it may well be sensible to take time to prepare oneself and others before announcing them. What is important is to try to be aware of these patterns and underlying processes and of one's own contribution to them. This understanding can reduce the unforeseen side effects of our strategies and, beyond that, actually put to positive use some of the potential disruptiveness that the institutionalised defences serve to suppress.

Organisation and Management in a Fluid Environment

Resistance to Change

One perennial problem that managers complain of is resistance to change. Even when the change offers clear advantages, people seem to cling unreasonably to the old ways of doing things. Writers on management offer various solutions, which range from the 'act now, pick up the pieces later' approach to elaborate participative processes, which sometimes seem to assume that individuals, if they go on participating long enough, will gracefully agree to commit suicide for the sake of the wider interests of the organisation.

The obvious question to ask is: what is being preserved and why? In other words, what functions does the existing system fulfil? As a consultant, my analysis usually starts with the manager introducing the new system. Sometimes it also ends there, when I discover that everyone's roles are expected to change but not the role of their immediate manager: that is held to be inviolable. The issue of continuity is nevertheless important. Planning for change needs to include deciding which features of the existing system are to be preserved.

One source of anxiety is disruption or loss of an established structure of dependence. Quite commonly a group's immediate boss attracts a lot of negative projections while the boss's boss is a good figure – a kind of benign 'grandparent'. (This image is not so odd as it might sound because, given the family origins of one's earliest experiences of authority, one can expect them to be replayed in some form within the workplace.) This can be an important asset. One general proposition is that 'individuals and groups most directly affected by [a] change need temporarily to deposit dependency in a leadership that encompasses both the pre-change and post-change configurations' (Miller, 1979, p188). A grandparental figure is well suited to such a role.

Where the immediate boss is respected by the affected group, then it is important not to lose that respect. He/she should be seen as someone equally affected who is working with the group in coping with the implications of the change – part of an 'us' grappling with a change inflicted by 'them'. (Perhaps then a great-grandparental figure will be needed to represent continuity!) Changes of role mean changes in role-relationships and here too the family model is useful in reminding us that roles in a group go way beyond job descriptions. People are readier to make such readjustments if they have some say in designing the new work system. It is the experience of being impotent victims of an imposed reorganisation that will mobilise the strongest resistance: not unnaturally it is felt to deny and devalue all that they did before.

Attention to the underlying dynamics and defences makes it possible to design strategies of change that will generate less resistance, but will not make it go away. Yet the leaders of modern business recognise that survival depends on a capacity for continual – if not continuous – change. Does this mean a continual struggle with the internal forces of resistance?

The proposition advanced here is that resistance is actually built into the conventional paradigms of organisation, which have formed around notions of order, control and predictability. To be successful in the increasingly unpredictable environments of the 1990s and beyond, businesses need a new paradigm, which adds another dimension to the relatedness of the individual to the organisation.

Feudal Organisations and Alienation

In the traditional organisation the individual's position is defined by one work role. Some specialists and a few fast-track managers have a more or less defined progression ahead of them, but they too have only one role at a time. That role locks the individual into a particular set of interpersonal and intergroup relations which acquires its own culture, its own defences. In fact the typical business organisation reproduces fairly accurately the structure of the feudal system in medieval England. This was the intertwining of three hierarchies: governmental, economic and religious. Those at the apex – the king, the barons and the bishops – sometimes collaborated, sometimes squabbled among themselves. The peasants and serfs were kept firmly in their place at the base of all those hierarchies. They had no political power and minimal income, while their religious superiors laid on them the obligation to perform obediently the duties of the station in life to which God had called them. As Dickens put it later, tongue in cheek:

Oh let us love our occupations
Bless the squire and his relations,
Live upon our daily rations,
And always know our proper stations.

Given the intervening technological and social changes, it is somewhat remarkable to find that model substantially unchanged nearly a millennium later. Even some fairly recent innovations, such as Total Quality Management, seemed designed to mobilise the workforce into a quasi-religious movement.

111

Of course, there have been a few modifications. Many employees acquired a second role in trades unions, which had some effect on the absolute power of the monarchs; but, at least in Britain, the membership and power of the unions peaked in the '60s and '70s and declined quite markedly in the '80s, while the industrial democracy movement also died a death in the recession of the early '80s.

Part of the explanation of the long shelf-life of this archaic structure has already been given. It represents a macro-version of the family: the organisation – as mother, perhaps – meets needs for dependency, in return for this employees give their compliance; the structure offers a skeleton on which can be developed elaborate systems to meet people's needs for defences against anxieties; and union membership has provided a safety valve for aggressive and destructive feelings. At the same time, this model has its costs. Resistance to change is only one of them. More serious is alienation, which is as valid a description today of the work experience of many employees as it was a century ago. The individual feels forced to do something that gives him or her little or no satisfaction, by someone else who has coercive powers and steals most of the fruits of the labour. As Miller says:

> The coercive hold that the organization has over the individual, whether 'manager' or 'worker', is that it satisfies his dependent needs and his infantile greed, though it does so indirectly by offering him the pseudo-autonomy of the consumer role. As a consumer, to be sure, he has choices; but the orchestrated pressure to spend and consume is itself a secondary coercion that reinforces dependency on an employing organization, which is to be placated through passivity and compliance . . . The individual's rage and his wishes – not always unconscious – to destroy the organization have to be suppressed or repressed. (1986, pp263–4)

This can lead to the formation of a compliant 'pseudo-self' or 'false-self', which, as Fromm puts it:

> . . . is only an agent who actually represents the role a person is supposed to play but who does so under the name of self. (1941/1960, p177).

Here are two people talking recently about their jobs. Both are managers: the man in a voluntary agency known for the support it gives to its staff, and a woman responsible for a professional service in a health authority. His words were: 'At work, I'm a false self; I take my real self home to my partner.' The woman described having to prepare performance statistics which bore little or no relation to the nature and quality of the work done but were designed to present it in such a way as to attract a bigger budget.

For a business trying to survive and prosper in an unpredictable environment, alienation has serious consequences. The demand for compliance produces a workforce which acts on the belief that its survival is dependent on maintaining the status quo. Any criticisms, reservations and, above all, creative ideas they might have risk threatening the status quo and so it is far safer to take them home or forget about them altogether. Yet these are resources that the business badly needs if it is to engage realistically and effectively with the world outside.

Citizens of the Organisation

One way of inviting these resources to come back in, and also to reduce resistance to change, is actually to legitimate a third role – beyond the regular work role and the union role – through which the individual can relate to the organisation and be a contributor to, rather than a victim of, processes of change. A term that has been used for this is 'citizen of the organisation' (Miller, 1977). Unless you are at or near the level of chief executive, your work role requires you to relate to only a segment of the whole – often a very small segment. Yet your concern is much wider than that. Unofficially and perhaps officially you have information about company-wide issues. In your roles outside the organisation you belong to various networks of relationships through which you pick up soft data from the environment. What you observe and hear on the grapevine outside and inside does not always tally with the official line. Outside, you hear of dissatisfaction with one of the company's products. Inside, you see things going wrong: that new computer system is causing more problems than it solves, but top management is being kept in the dark about it . . . Most employees do have a degree of belonging, commitment and even loyalty: in that sense they are, *de facto*, citizens of the organisation. But they keep their concerns to themselves or share their thoughts with a few mates in the canteen or at the pub after work. To formalise the role of citizen of the organisation is to bring this kind of information into the public domain.

Employee participation has long had its advocates, and 'empowerment' became the flavour of the '80s in many firms. In some settings it has worked quite well in opening up two-way communication and improving work practices. It can be seen as enabling employees to exercise authority based on knowledge and experience in relation to the task, as distinct from conventional managerial authority based on rank. Mutual respect develops as a result. The scope of empowerment, however, is usually limited to the immediate workplace. And too often limits are set on areas that may be discussed. Someone has defined empowerment as 'speaking out without permission', to which should be added, 'and without risk'. That is the power that citizens of the organisation need if they are to feel a sense of responsibility to the enterprise – a psychological 'ownership' – and contribute to it the resources they have to offer.

Some managers find this conception a positive challenge. Those are usually the managers who really do derive their authority from their competence to contribute to the task rather than from the job title that they happen to hold. Even so, it arouses anxiety. It threatens to dismantle the structures that preserve internal order and keep chaos at bay. However, the argument here is that those defensive structures have proved dysfunctional in that they also keep at bay people's potential for contributing to creativity. The essence of creativity, and what the modern business enterprise needs, is to challenge and redefine conventional definitions of 'reality'. Much as we like to believe that 'reality' is permanent, it is no more than a social construct – what we currently believe to be real (Miller, 1983). In a rapidly changing environment, these constructs require continual questioning. That will not happen simply through an orderly rational process: it needs imagination, intuition, fantasy, argument, disagreement, conflict.

What it Means in Practice

Essentially what is required, alongside – or perhaps at right angles to – the existing organisation for the ongoing activities of production, marketing and so forth (the location of work roles), is another form of organisation in which people can assume their roles as 'citizens'. This could take a variety of possible forms. It is necessary, however, that specified periods of time – weekly, fortnightly, monthly – are set aside in which people can explicitly move out of the one role into the other. Various kinds of forum are needed which bring together people from a range of different levels and roles. For members of top management in particular it is a vital opportunity to listen, as well as to speak about, their concerns. The culture is egalitarian: it is citizenship, not the hierarchical role, that confers the right to speak; the common concern is the survival and success of the enterprise.

This is not a version of parliament – a voting or decision-making institution. Decisions continue to be the responsibility of those at the top. But it enables them and everyone else to be reassured that the decisions will be well informed. Experience of versions of this approach is that far from confirming managers' fears that their authority will be undermined, their authority is actually sanctioned more firmly, so long as they are competent: this is a process in which incompetent managers tend to be quickly exposed and weeded out.

It hardly needs saying that such a system is not easily implemented. Much preparation is needed and it will take quite a long time to overcome the suspicion and hesitation that stop a culture of open dialogue being established. But the construction of the parallel organisation offers a means of engaging with the internal world of the organisation in a way that will make engagement with the external world more constructive. One manufacturing unit with just under 1,000 employees began with the salaried bands of 120 managers, supervisors and technical staff. With help from consultants they first met weekly in mixed groups of 15, with the task of exploring how they related to each other. Then there were two week end events, 60 at each, to examine inter-group relations. After that they began to meet in a weekly 'large group' to look at themselves as a total system in relation to their environment. That introductory phase took about six months. The process was then progressively extended to the rest of the site. A culture of open, non-judgmental discussion, with senior managers as co-participants, evolved quite quickly, and with it a great deal of mutual learning. Starting during the introductory phase and continuing afterwards was the spontaneous emergence of task groups, some cross-departmental, to tackle issues that were identified during the group discussions. These fed back into improved performance and over about 18 months there was a striking shift both in the sense of purpose and in the self-confidence of the unit as a whole in relation to the outside world and also in profitability (Miller, 1977).

The effectiveness of such a programme lies in its open-endedness. It is no use trying to pre-ordain how the parallel organisation will evolve and to set limits. It is disturbing to find familiar entrenched patterns of dependency and conflict dislodged, but also rewarding to discover the creative potential when conflicts are relocated and fights are between the right people about the right issues. Moreover, it seems that the effectiveness of the regular work organisation is actually enhanced when the citizens of the organisation have scope for expression.

References

Bion, W R (1961) *Experiences in Groups and Other Papers*, Tavistock Publications, London.

Emery F E and Trist E L (1965) 'The Casual texture of organizational environments', *Human Relations*, pp18, 21–32.

Frankl, V E (1959) *From Death-Camp to Existentialism*, Beacon Press, Boston, Mass.

Fromm, E (1941/1960) *The Fear of Freedom*, Routledge & Kegan Paul, London.

Jaques, E (1953) 'On the dynamics of social structure', *Human Relations*, 4, pp315–40.

Klein, M (1952) 'Some theoretical conclusions regarding the emotional life of the infant', in M Klein *et al* (eds), *Developments in Psychoanalysis*, Hogarth Press, London.

— (1959) 'Our adult world and its roots in infancy', *Human Relations*, 12, pp291–303.

Menzies, I E P (1959) 'A case-study in the functioning of social systems as a defence against anxiety: a report on a study of the nursing service of a general hospital', *Human Relations*, 13, pp95–121.

Miller, E J (1977) 'Organizational development and industrial democracy: a current case-study', in C Cooper (ed), *Organizational Development in the UK and USA: A joint evaluation*, Macmillan, London, pp31–63.

— (1979) 'Autonomy, dependency and organizational change', in D Towell and C Harries (eds), *Innovation in Patient Care: An Action Research Study of Change in a Psychiatric Hospital*, Croom Helm, London, pp172–90.

— (1983) *Work and Creativity*, Occasional Paper No 6, Tavistock Institute of Human Relations, London.

— (1986) 'Making room for individual autonomy', in S Srivastva and Associates, *Executive Power*, Jossey-Bass, San Francisco, pp257–88.

— (1989) 'The 'Leicester' Model: Experiential Study of Group and Organizational Processes', Occasional Paper No 10, Tavistock Institute of Human Relations, London.

— and Rice, A K (1967) *Systems of Organization: Task and Sentient Systems and Their Boundary Control*, Tavistock Publications, London.

Stacey, R (1991) *The Chaos Frontier: Creative Strategic Control for Business*, Butterworth/Heinemann, London.

Turquet, P M (1974) 'Threats to identity in the large group', in L Kreeger (ed), *The Large Group: Therapy and Dynamics*, Constable, London.

Part 3

Strategic Thinking and the Moral Dimension

6

Mission: The Leader's Most Important Task

Andrew Campbell

Introduction

The word mission has come into use in business language since the late 1970s, in the military sense of 'objective': a platoon's mission might be to 'Take hill 49 and hold it until relieved'. 'To be the lowest-cost producer of corrugated packaging materials in Europe', might be the business mission of a manufacturer of corrugated packaging materials.

Corning Glass states, 'We are dedicated to the total success of Corning Glass works as a worldwide competitor. We choose to compete in four business sectors . . .'. Redland's 1988 annual report had the following mission statement on its cover: 'spanning the world with construction materials'.

These examples address two aspects of business mission – the purpose of the organisation, couched in terms of achievement, and the business domain of the organisation, describing what products the company will focus on. In this form a mission statement overlaps with business strategy. Business strategy defines the business domain the company chooses to compete in and the sources of advantage the company is going to exploit in order to outperform its competitors.

Mission statements and business strategy overlap in that they are both concerned with business domain. Both are seen as useful because they take different perspectives. Mission is about purpose: what the organisation's objectives should be. Strategy is about competitive advantage: how the company will outperform other companies with a similar purpose.

But there is also another, growing view of the term mission. Frequently it is used together with words such as philosophy or values to address something much broader than purpose and business domain. Mission statements frequently include sentences about how the organisation is going to achieve its purpose. Mission statements then become much broader, combining thoughts about competitive advantage with ethical principles, organisation beliefs and values.

In his book *A Business and its Beliefs* (1963), Thomas J Watson Jr, son of the founder of IBM, underlined the importance of organisation philosophy: 'The only sacred cow in an organisation should be its basic philosophy of doing business'. Many other leaders support this view, creating statements of mission that are closer to descriptions of business philosophy than to statements of corporate objectives.

The 'HP Way' of Hewlett-Packard (HP) is an example of this broader definition of mission. The HP Way does include a page on corporate objectives, but it also includes a page on 'organisational values' such as 'we achieve our common objectives through team work', and a page on 'strategies and practices', such as the famous MBWA or 'Management by Wandering Around'.

Johnson and Johnson is another famous example of a company that has a combined broad-based statement of mission. 'Our Credo' starts, 'we believe our first responsibility is to the doctors, nurses and patients, to mothers and all others who use our products and services'.

This broad-based concept of organisation mission is one that is critical to the task of leadership. It is a holistic concept that binds together two areas critical to leadership – strategy and culture. This chapter describes this new concept of mission and explains how it fits with the writings of previous academics and consultants.

By taking the reader through a digest of the work of the early leadership theorists, such as Chester Barnard, the culture gurus such as William Ouchi, the general management view provided by the McKinsey 7S model (see page 136), the philosophical and ethical ponderings of authors such as Freeman and Gilbert, the motivation theorists such as Fredrick Herzberg and the modern leadership gurus such as Warren Bennis, I hope to show that the new concept of mission is in fact not new. It is simply a blending of the research, theories and concepts of all these specialist viewpoints.

A New Concept of Mission

The Ashridge mission diamond (see Figure 6.1) contains four elements: values, purpose, strategy and behaviour. These need to link together, resonating and reinforcing each other, giving the organisation an integrity and providing a clear rationale for behaviours and policies.

Purpose

What is the company for? For whose benefit is all the effort being put in? Why should a manager or an employee do more than the minimum required? For a company these questions are the equivalent of a person asking 'Why do I exist?' They are deeply philosophical and can lead boards of directors into heated debate.

First there is the company that exists for the benefit of the shareholders. These companies have the purpose of maximising wealth for their shareholders. All decisions are assessed against a yardstick of shareholder value. Hanson, a conglomerate focused on Britain and the USA, is one example. Lord Hanson repeatedly states: 'The shareholder is king'. Unlike many companies whose chairmen *claim* to be working primarily for the shareholders, Lord Hanson believes what he says and manages the business to that end. Hence Martin Taylor, a director, feels quite free to say: 'All of our businesses are for sale all of the time. If anyone is prepared to pay us more than we think they are worth, we will sell. We have no attachment to any individual business.'

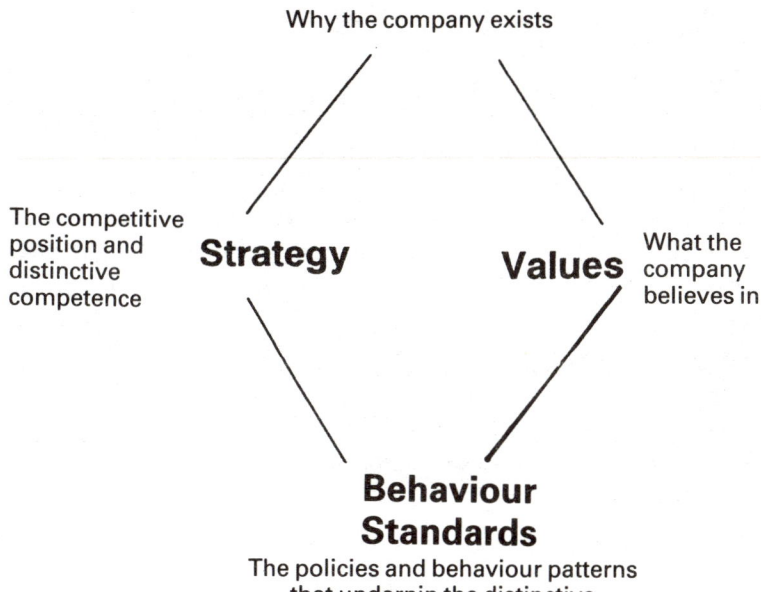

Figure 6.1 *The Ashridge mission model*

Most managers, however, are not as single minded as Lord Hanson. They don't believe that the company's only purpose is to create wealth for shareholders. They acknowledge the claims of other stakeholders such as customers, employees, suppliers and the community. Faced with the question, 'Is your company in business to make money for shareholders, make products for customers or provide rewarding jobs for employees?', they will answer, 'All three'.

The second type of company, therefore, is one that exists to satisfy *all* its stakeholders. In order to articulate their stakeholder-based purpose, many of these companies have written down their responsibility to each stakeholder group. The American electronic equipment manufacturer, Motorola, defines its purpose as:

> . . . to honourably serve the needs of the community by providing products and services of superior quality at a fair price to our customers; to do this so as to earn an adequate profit which is required for the total enterprise to grow; and by so doing provide the opportunity for our employees and shareholders to achieve their reasonable personal objectives.

Similarly, Royal Dutch/Shell, an international energy company, says in its statement of general business principles: 'Four areas of responsibility are recognized: to shareholders . . . to employees . . . to customers . . . to society. These four areas of responsibility are seen as an inseparable whole.'

Managers in the third type of company are dissatisfied with a purpose aimed solely at satisfying stakeholder needs. They have sought to identify a purpose that is greater than the combined needs of the stakeholders, something to which all the stakeholders can feel proud of contributing. In short, they aim towards a higher ideal. The planning director in one company, operating in a depressed region of Britain, explained:

> I don't get excited about making money for shareholders. I like to help businesses succeed. That's something I can get excited about. I believe our future depends on it – I don't just mean this company, it's about the future of the nation, even the international community – it's about world peace and that sort of thing.

At the British retailer Marks and Spencer one manager described the company's purpose as 'raising standards for the working man'. This rings true for many others in the company who felt, particularly in the early days of Marks and Spencer and after the Second World War, that they were improving the standard of clothing available to the average person because they were able to retail high-quality goods at affordable prices. The Japanese clothing and cosmetics company Wacoal has the purpose: 'To promote the creation of feminine beauty and to improve the culture of living'. Such companies have reached beyond the stakeholder definition of purpose and found a higher-level goal that can potentially be supported by all the stakeholders.

Strategy

To achieve a purpose in competition with other organisations, there needs to be a strategy. Strategy provides the commercial logic for the company. If the purpose is to be the best, there must be a strategy explaining the principles around which the company will become the best. If the purpose is to create wealth, there must be a strategy explaining how the company will create wealth in competition with other companies. Strategy will define the business that the company is going to compete in, the position that the company plans to hold in that business and the distinctive competence or competitive advantage that the company has or plans to create.

Egon Zehnder provides an example of a strategy which explains how the firm will achieve its purpose. Egon Zehnder wants to be the most professional, although not necessarily the biggest, international executive search firm. Its competitive advantage comes, it believes, from the methods and systems it uses to carry out search assignments and from the 'one-firm', cooperative culture it has so carefully nurtured.

Marks and Spencer's strategy in textiles is a second example. In its clothes retailing business, Marks and Spencer seeks to offer the best value for money in the high street by providing a broad range of classic, quality clothes. The company's competitive advantage comes from its dedication to quality through managing suppliers, its high levels of service and the low overheads generated by high sales per square foot.

A third example is the US information systems company Hewlett-Packard. Its strategy has been to succeed in high-value niches of the electronics industry and to be better at innovation and product development. It sees its competitive advantage as being in its innovative, high-quality staff and its participative management style.

Behaviour Standards

Purpose and strategy are empty intellectual thoughts unless they can be converted into action, into the policy and behaviour guidelines that help people to decide what to do on a day-to-day basis.

British Airways provides a good example of how to convert purpose and strategy into tangible standards and actions. Its purpose is to be the 'world's favourite airline'. The strategy for achieving this is based on having as good or better in-flight service and comfort, a better on-time record and more friendly and helpful ground services than its competitors. These strategic objectives were then translated into policies such as the need for in-flight services to be at least as good as those of competing airlines on the same route, and the requirement that managers and employees should be helpful and friendly at all times. By translating purpose and strategy into actionable policies and standards, such as 'put people first', senior managers at British Airways have dramatically changed the performance of the airline.

The Body Shop, an international cosmetics retailer, has a purpose of developing cosmetics that don't harm animals or the environment. Its strategy is to be more environmentally conscious than its competitors, hence attracting the 'green' consumer and the 'green' employee. Within the company, environmental consciousness has been translated into policies and behaviour standards, one of which was almost unique when first introduced. All employees have two wastepaper baskets: one for recyclable and one for non-recyclable products. Employees receive training in what can be recycled and what cannot.

Egon Zehnder provides another example of the link between strategy and policies. As we have already said, its strategy is to be more professional than other executive search consultants. Connected with this, it has a set of policies about how consultants should carry out assignments, called the 'systematic consulting approach'. One of the policies is that consultants should not take on a search assignment unless they believe it will benefit the client. Another is that there should be a back-up consultant for every assignment in order to ensure a quality service to the client. Supporting this systematic approach are behaviour standards about cooperation. These are ingrained into the culture rather than written on tablets of stone. An Egon Zehnder consultant willingly helps another consultant within his or her office or from other offices around the world. The firm wants to be the best, which means being better at cooperation than its competitors. As a result it needs a behaviour standard that makes sure consultants help each other.

This commercial logic is the left-brain logic of the firm. Human beings are emotional, however, and are driven more by right-brain motives than left-brain logic. To capture the emotional energy of an organisation the mission needs to provide some philosophical or moral rationale for behaviour to run alongside the commercial rationale. This brings us to the next element of our definition of mission.

Values

Values are the beliefs and moral principles that lie behind the company's culture. Values give meaning to the norms and behaviour standards in the company. In the process of implementing its change in culture, British Airways sent 20,000 of its staff on 'putting people first' training programmes. There is a good commercial reason for 'putting people first' since it will help to retain customers, but there is also a moral reason: we are all people, and life would be better for all of us if we took a little more care of each other. The new behaviours described by the British Airways trainers were presented as a philosophy of life as much as a way of improving the airline. Participants were asked to consider how they greeted their families when arriving home as well as how they handled customers.

Another example of the way in which values can provide an additional logic for behaviour comes from Hewlett-Packard. 'The HP Way' describes the company's famous behaviour standard of Management By Wandering Around (MBWA). To implement its strategy of innovation in high-value areas, HP needs to attract and retain the best engineers and product managers. These high-quality individuals do not like to be closely controlled or hierarchically managed. HP therefore developed the MBWA policy as a management approach suitable for these kinds of high achievers.

The MBWA behaviour standard is based on good commercial logic, but it has also become a crusade of its own. Managers believe it is the right way to manage not only high achievers but all personnel. MBWA is not good behaviour only because it is good strategy but also because it is something everyone should be doing. It acknowledges the innate creativity of individuals and underlines the managers' respect for people. It has become a value. The objective observer can readily identify situations, such as captaining a ship, where MBWA would be totally the wrong style of management. Yet for managers committed to the HP Way it is almost sacrosanct. Like putting people first at British Airways, MBWA in Hewlett-Packard is not only good strategy but the 'right way to behave'.

These two examples show how values can provide a rationale for behaviour that is just as strong as strategy. It is for this reason that Figure 6.1 has a diamond shape. There are two rationales that link purpose with behaviour. The commercial rationale or left-brain reasoning is about strategy and what sort of behaviour will help the company outperform competitors in its chosen arena. The emotional, moral and ethical rationale, or right-brain reasoning, is about values and what sort of behaviour is ethical: the right way to treat people, the right way to behave in our society. My definition of mission includes both these rationales linked together by a common purpose.

Sense of Mission

For a company's leader or management team, the process of achieving intellectual clarity about their mission is a very valuable one. It forces them to face tricky issues of values and strategy head on and can foster greater commitment and understanding within the top team. However, it is not the intellectual understanding of mission that energises the organisation. In companies like Egon Zehnder or Hewlett-Packard, people brim over with enthusiasm for their company. They have a 'sense of mission'.

A sense of mission is an emotional commitment that an individual feels to his or her company's mission. It is evident that some people feel this emotional commitment very strongly. But, even in companies with very strong missions, there are many people who do not feel an emotional commitment. For example, even at the height of Hewlett-Packard's success an employee survey revealed a large minority of employees who did not have a strong belief in the capabilities of the senior management team, implying that they lacked a sense of mission.

A sense of mission occurs when there is a match between the values of an individual and those of an organisation. Because organisation values are rarely explicit, the individual senses them through the company's behaviour standards. For example, if the behaviour standard is about cooperative working, the individual will be able to sense a value associated with helpfulness or a belief in the strength of teamworking. If the individual has a personal value about the importance of being helpful and cooperative, then there is a values match between the individual and the organisation. The greater the link between company policies and individual values, the stronger the individual's sense of mission.

A sense of mission comes from a values match because values engage employees' emotions and it is values that make work worth while (Figure 6.2). Commitment to a company's strategy does not on its own constitute a sense of mission. It is not unusual for groups of managers to discuss their company's purpose and strategy and reach an intellectual agreement. However, the intellectual agreement does not necessarily translate into an emotional commitment. The emotional commitment only comes when the individual can personally identify with the values and behaviours lying behind the plan, turning the strategy into a mission and the intellectual agreement into a sense of mission. Individuals with a sense of mission will find their work satisfying and fulfilling because it has meaning. It is worth while because it corresponds with what they personally feel to be important.

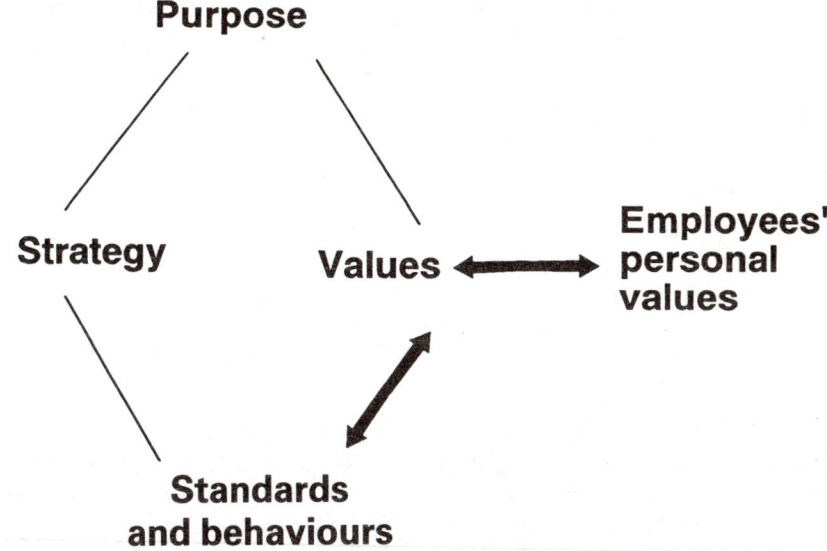

Figure 6.2 *A sense of mission comes from a values match*

Much of this is not new: the importance of values has been underlined in the writings on culture; the role of a clear purpose has been noted by researchers into leadership; the link between strategy and values has been suggested by consultants; and the opportunity to satisfy the spiritual needs of employees through developing a moral rationale for work has been argued for a long time.

This chapter's contribution is to bring all these relationships together into one model around the concept of mission; and to recognise that behaviour standards are most meaningful when they are explained by both a commercial rationale and a moral rationale. The writers whose mental models most closely relate to this are the early leadership theorists such as Chester Barnard and Philip Selznick. Surprisingly it is the motivation theorists Herzberg, McGregor and Maslow whose ideas seem to be furthest away.

Early Leadership Theorists

Chester Barnard is one of the fathers of leadership theory. After a long career in industry culminating in becoming President of the New Jersey Bell Telephone Company and President of the Rockefeller Foundation, he moved to Harvard and wrote a book on *The Functions of the Executive*. Published in 1938, it was the first analytical book on leadership that recognised the non-economic dimensions of managing an organisation. Barnard was among the first writers to acknowledge the importance of what he called organisation philosophy or 'morality'. Two aspects of organisation philosophy need to be managed by the executive: he or she needs to help employees cope with conflicts that arise between their personal morality and the organisation's collective morality; and he or she needs to create an inspiring philosophy or morality to which employees can attach themselves.

In his work, Barnard shows how every individual's behaviour is influenced by several moral codes, such as loyalty to certain religious ethics, a code of family obligations and adherence to professional or work norms and values. Problems arise when these codes conflict in some way. One of three outcomes may occur, says Barnard:

> (1) Either there is paralysis of action, accompanied by emotional tension, and ending in a sense of frustration . . . uncertainty . . . loss of decisiveness and lack of confidence, or (2) there is conformance to one code and violation of the other, resulting in a sense of guilt, discomfort, dissatisfaction or a loss of self respect, or (3) there is found some substitute action which satisfies immediate desire . . . yet conforms to all other codes . . . such a solution frequently requires imaginative and constructive ability.

Business leaders not only have to overcome these conflicts in their own working lives, moral choices becoming increasingly complex as they progress through the organisation, but they also have to help resolve these conflicts for others. Barnard calls this the 'judicial function'. 'There is no escape from the judicial process in the exercise of executive functions. Conflicts of codes in organisations are inevitable,' he says. It is the responsibility of the leader to help employees to find an answer which is acceptable to their personal morality and the morality of the collective whole. Such a task is a 'severe test' of a leader's moral responsibility and ability.

Barnard rates as even more important, the leader's responsibility to create an inspiring philosophy or morality for employees. This should give them 'faith in the ultimate satisfaction of personal motives, faith in the integrity of objective authority, faith in the superiority of common purpose as a personal aim of those who undertake it'. Such a morality will ensure that people subordinate their interests and the 'minor dictates of personal codes' to the good of the cooperative whole.

Barnard calls these two functions of leadership 'moral creativeness', 'the highest expression of responsibility'. He argues that it creates among employees something close to a sense of mission – common meaning, common purpose, personal conviction and 'a spirit that overcomes the centrifugal forces of individual interests or motives'.

Undoubtedly Barnard recognised the need for organisations to provide spiritual fulfilment for employees through a match of the organisation's values and the individual's values, and the advantage for the organisation of having a mission that is inspiring and elevating. However, he did not suggest that leadership is only about creating a morality. Much of his book is devoted to advice on the formulation of objectives, recruitment, motivation and organisation structure. But he distinguished these maintenance roles of the executive from the leadership roles that are concerned with inspiring people. He saw the leadership role as being the creation of moral codes for employees:

> Organizations endure, however, in proportion to the breadth of the morality by which they are governed. This is only to say that foresight, long purposes, high ideals are the basis for the persistence of cooperation.
>
> Executive responsibility, then, is that capacity of leaders by which, reflecting attitudes, ideals, hopes, derived largely from without themselves, they are compelled to bind the wills of men to the accomplishment of purposes beyond their immediate ends. Even when these purposes are lowly . . . the transitory efforts of men become a part of that organization of living forces that transcends man unaided by man; but when these purposes are high and the wills of many men of many generations are bound together they live boundlessly.
>
> So among those who cooperate the things that are seen are moved by the things unseen. Out of the void comes the spirit that shapes the ends of men.

Philip Selznick was a pioneer in the academic study of leadership. He wrote a book called *Leadership in Administration: A Sociological Interpretation*. Published in 1957, it builds on the experience-based insights of Chester Barnard. In Selznick's view, the primary task of leaders is to 'institutionalize' a business so that it becomes infused with values and meaning and becomes a source of fulfilment to its members:

> 'To institutionalize is to *infuse with value* beyond the technical requirements of the job at hand. The prizing of the social machinery beyond its

technical role is largely a reflection of the unique way in which it fulfils personal or group needs . . . From the standpoint of the committed person, the organization is changed from an expendable tool into a valued source of personal satisfaction'.

Selznick bases his theory on a distinction similar to that of Barnard – the distinction between organisations and institutions. Organisations are rational instruments engineered to do specific tasks. Leaders of organisations are mainly concerned with administrative efficiency and policy and procedures which ensure a 'smooth running machine'. Institutions, however, are a product of social needs and are more akin to responsive, adaptive organisms. Institutional leaders are concerned with developing a more comprehensive view of their enterprise. In particular, they want to understand how and why people work *and* have a wider perspective of the organisation itself and its changing aims and abilities.

Institutional leadership is the key to developing both this larger perspective and increasing employee motivation, Selznick believes. The leader can help his or her organisation evolve into an institution through two methods. The first is to define the 'mission of the enterprise', a task which gives a wider perspective of the institution. This involves hard intellectual labour as the leader needs to identify the business's purpose and goals and 'attendant claims and responsibilities'. This process may therefore involve resolving differences of opinion about the business's mission both in and outside the organisation.

The second task of institutional leadership is to infuse values into the institution, thereby giving greater fulfilment to its members. The institutional leader is 'primarily an expert in the promotion and protection of values'. He or she must offer 'a guiding hand to a process that would otherwise occur more haphazardly' and ensure that these values are truly accepted in the institution. When this happens, the organisation begins to symbolise certain values and aspirations of its people and therefore assumes an identity of its own.

Both Selznick and Barnard make a distinction between the task of running an organisation and the task of infusing an organisation with values. In the language developed in this chapter they distinguish between the rational, commercial side of leadership and the emotional, moral side.

The ideas of Barnard and Selznick re-emerged in the 1980s, popularised in books such as *In Search of Excellence* by Tom Peters and Robert Waterman. More recently two academics, Badaracco at Harvard and

Ellsworth at Claremont in the United States, have examined these ideas of leadership and compared them with other theories. They analysed three philosophies of leadership – political leadership, directive leadership and values-driven leadership:

> Each starts with a different view of human nature and these lead to very different patterns of action. Political leadership holds that man is motivated by self-interest and by search for power, wealth and coherence in the face of self-interested behaviour by others. While not rejecting these realities, directive leadership argues that they are too limited for explaining people's motivation. Directive leadership believes that man is also a competitive creature driven to achieve. People want to take personal responsibility for their decisions and have the satisfaction of knowing they have won through their own efforts. Man has a strong, innate drive to realize his own potential or, in psychological terms, to self-actualize. As Maslow has said, 'What man can be, he must be'. As they strive for higher levels of attainment, people meld self-interest with corporate interest.
>
> The values-driven leader takes the directive leader's view one step further and believes that people need to find meaning in life through their work. Meaning is derived from creativity in the service of worthwhile purposes. Creating something of value is the ultimate expression of one's individuality. Values-driven leadership holds that energy, commitment and creativity are unleashed when a company harnesses these motives.

Like Barnard and Selznick before them, Badaracco and Ellsworth recognise the difference between the rational, commercial side of leadership and the emotional, moral side. And they have also concluded that leaders must be involved in both. They must develop their own philosophy that melds the two parts together. Whereas this chapter talks about the need for a leader to have a mission, Badaracco and Ellsworth talk about the need for leaders to develop their own philosophies or 'set of predispositions and prejudices' that meld together the philosophies of leadership and create an 'integrity' for the manager such that 'his behaviour should be consonant with his personality, beliefs and judgments'.

Badaracco and Ellsworth see the leader's personal values as an essential part of his or her personal philosophy. Values-driven leadership is 'not simply an alternative to the other two. Rather it transcends both of them'.

The Importance of Values

The study of values and their role in organisation management has been one of the growth businesses of the 1980s, sparked by three books published in 1981 and 1982.

In *Corporate Cultures* (1982), Terence Deal, a Vanderbilt professor, and Alan Kennedy, a McKinsey & Co consultant, explain the link between values and culture. Like Barmard before them, they are trying to underline the importance of the soft side of management – the emotional dimension. 'Rational managers', they complain, 'rarely pay much attention to the value system of an organization'. Yet 'shaping and enhancing values can become the most important job a manager can do' they believe and: 'In fact we think that often companies succeed because their employees can identify, embrace, and act on the values of the organization'.

Deal and Kennedy have a balanced understanding about the role of values in business. Although much of their analysis is devoted to the benefits of values as a control mechanism – 'In broad terms, they [values] act as an informal control system that tells people what is expected of them', they also recognise that values can be a motivator that gives meaning to work – 'the power of values is that people care about them'.

William Ouchi, a professor at the University of California, Los Angeles, and an equally important author on the subject of values, focuses mainly on the control benefit of values. Coming from an academic background studying control systems, Ouchi published a book in 1981 called *Theory Z*, explaining that some organisations, such as the United States military and IBM, control decisions through a value system or what he calls a 'clan culture'.

The type Z organisation is similar to many Japanese companies. It makes decisions based on values as much as facts. 'In a type Z organization, the explicit and implicit seem to exist in a sense of balance. While decisions weigh the complete analysis of facts, they are also shaped by serious attention to questions of whether or not this decision is suitable, whether it fits the company' (Ouchi, 1981).

To Ouchi, a value system is a governance mechanism. He compares type Z organisations with bureaucracies and with markets. He points out that in type Z organisations and in markets, individuals are encouraged to act selfishly, to do whatever they most want to do. The market mechanism is one way of ensuring that the selfish acts of individuals combine towards a common good. The socialisation of individuals into a value system is the other way of ensuring that 'individuals will naturally seek to do that which is in the common good'. He argues: 'Only the bureaucratic mechanism explicitly says to individuals "Do not do what you want, do what we tell you to do because we pay you for it". The bureaucratic mechanism alone produces alienation, anomie and a lowered sense of autonomy.'

The third influential book published at the beginning of the 1980s is called *The Art of Japanese Management* by Richard Pascale and Anthony Athos (1981). Like Ouchi, they recognised that many Japanese companies have an ingredient that is missing from Western companies. Unlike Ouchi, they examine the benefit these Japanese companies give to their employees – a deeper meaning. Pascale and Athos focus more attention on the way values provide fulfilment for employees than either Ouchi or Deal and Kennedy. Pascale and Athos note that organisation values can become 'superordinate goals [that] tie the purpose of the firm to human values'. They become the 'spiritual fabric' of the organisation and are 'probably the most underpublicized "secret weapon" of great companies'.

The problem with most Western companies is that managers and leaders are shy of the spiritual.

> By an accident of history, we in the West have evolved a culture that separates man's spiritual life from his institutional life. This turn of events has had a far-reaching impact on modern western organizations. Our companies freely lay claim to mind and muscle, but they are culturally discouraged from intruding upon our personal lives and deeper beliefs . . . What is needed in the West is a non-deified, non-religious spiritualism that enables a firm's superordinate goals to respond truly to the inner meanings that many people seek in their work – or, alternatively, seek in their lives and could find in their work if only that were more culturally acceptable.

Pascale and Athos recognise the attention that some companies in the late 1970s were giving to corporate responsibility, mission and mission statements. But they concluded that these efforts were insufficient: 'The trend has been toward expanding the notion of corporate purpose. Nevertheless, recognition of an organisation's role in serving higher-order human values still awaits full-scale acceptance.'

These three books were the beginning of a tidal wave of writings on culture and the importance of values. This has not been limited to academics and consultants: managers of great companies have also been arguing the importance of values. Some of the more telling quotations from chief executives have been captured by Badaracco and Ellsworth. Walter Wriston, one-time chief executive of Citicorp, sees shared values as essential to smooth functioning. He explains:

A lot of leadership is being able to articulate your value system and where you are going in ways people understand. I spend a lot of time trying to hold out before people the concepts of excellence, honesty and integrity.

In the corporation, as in your life, you have to have some benchmarks by which to operate. Whether it is the Boy Scout motto or FASB Rule Number 9, you have to have some framework. A corporation is a collection of individuals. Without a framework, you don't know what you are doing. The only thing that draws our different cultures together is our common value system. For example, collegial management is a value. You have to have trust between people, and that's based on a common set of values and a common set of procedures.

James Burke, chief executive of Johnson & Johnson, sees values as a way of tapping into people's moral yearning:

It is very hard to keep people pulling together if you have a real entrepreneurial environment. The very nature of the people that run our business – as well as the businesses themselves – is to go off on their own. 'To hell with all that crap in New Brunswick [Johnson & Johnson's headquarters]. Who needs the Executive Committee? We know how to do it.' People are also somewhat egocentric.

How do we keep them all together? We try to do it by an overall set of principles and the fundamental moral precepts of the Credo, which everyone buys into and responds to. At some level, everybody is a moral creature, whether they want to admit it or not.

William Weiss, chairman and chief executive officer of Ameritech, writes about the importance of linking employee values and company values. In an article called 'Minerva's Owl: Building a Corporate Value System', Weiss, appeals to Minerva the goddess of wisdom to help him form a value system for Ameritech, which in 1986 had only been set up 18 months earlier to run part of Bell Telephone. He sees a value system as a critical part of leadership:

I am saying that a corporation can create a moral environment, a distinct set of values and standards, to which it holds its people accountable. If a person's individual values are significantly different, he will soon find he is in the wrong place. It is a key responsibility of corporate leadership to set the pattern and tone of this conscience. (Weiss, 1986)

Thomas Watson Jr of IBM was probably first of the leaders of American companies to stress values. He wrote a much-quoted book, *A Business and its Beliefs* (1963), that explains IBM's value system.

It is not only American business leaders who have argued the case for values. Most Japanese leaders consider it such an obvious part of management that it is hard to find quotations that refer explicitly to the management of the value system. Konosuke Matsushita, former chairman of Matsushita Electric, is probably the most outspoken on the subject. Like Thomas Watson Jr he wrote a book about his company's values (*Not for Bread Alone*, 1984).

Even European managers, normally more reserved about the emotional side of management, have been speaking up. Jan Carlsson, chairman of the Swedish airline SAS, wrote about the contribution values-management made to the dramatic change of fortunes at SAS, in a book called *Moments of Truth* (1987). At a recent conference in Chicago he underlined his commitment to emotional management:

> You don't hear much about love in discussions of management philosophy, or human resources for that matter. But if love is defined as the will to nurture growth in other human beings, then it is the appropriate term. Or you can call it respect for the individual, respect for his feeling of responsibility and his desire to do a good job. Allowing an individual to share your vision gives that person greater understanding and motivation. That, to me, is strategic leadership. (Carlson, 1988)

In recognising the importance of values in the model of mission, the chapter so far does no more than acknowledge the weight of academic, consultant and management opinion that values can both motivate employees to behave in a desired way and provide employees with the meaning that can make work fulfilling and worth while.

The Strategy – values Link

Ouchi and others have studied the link between values and behaviours; Deal and Kennedy and also Weiss have commented on the link between corporate values and employees' values; and Pascale and Athos have emphasised the link between values and purpose. Between them these authors have effectively explained the emotional, moral side of our definition of mission.

One area that has received very little attention is the link between strategy and values – the link between commercial logic and moral logic. The consultants McKinsey & Co have the most well-developed understanding of this link. They developed a model of organisation called the 7S model. It has been presented in many formats, but the format in Figure 6.3, with strategy, skills and shared values as the lead Ss, is the one most frequently used by McKinsey in the mid-1980s. Pascale and Athos used an earlier format of the model in their book *The Art of Japanese Management* (1981).

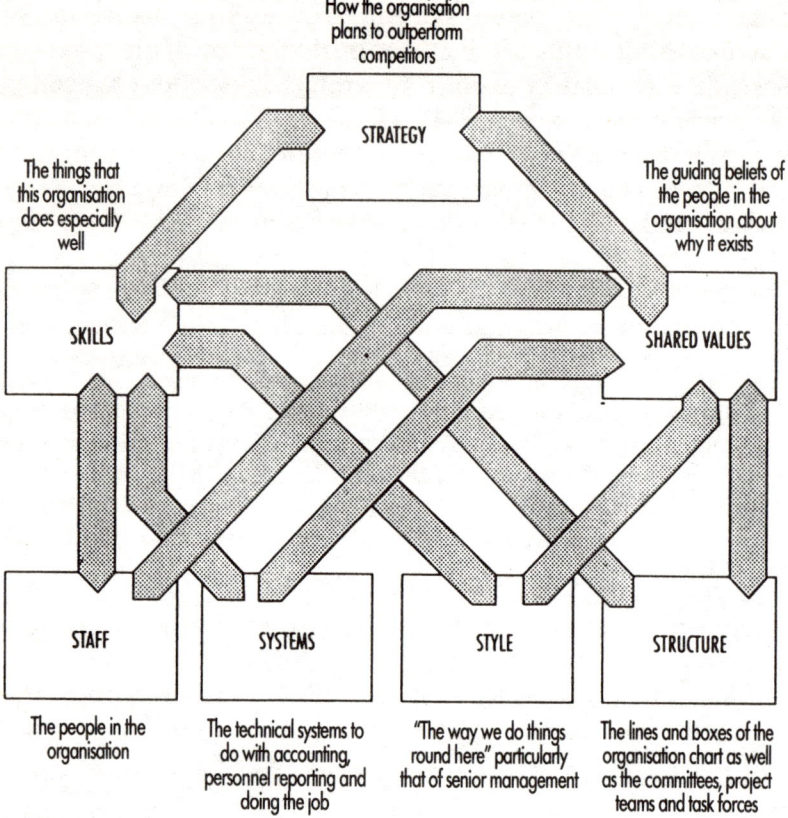

Figure 6.3 *The McKinsey 7S model*

The central message of the 7S model is that organisations are most effective when their seven different elements fit well together: when the strategy fits the values and all the other Ss reinforce the strategy and the values. Consultants at McKinsey use it as a diagnostic tool for understanding organisations that are ineffective, and for managing change. When managing change, the model is useful for ensuring that change is balanced and is aimed at moving towards a future state of 'fit'. The value of the model is that it discourages the belief that organisation is just about structure or management systems. These hard elements of organisation are important, but they are not the whole story. 'Softer' elements such as shared values, management style and skills are also critical to the effective running of an organisation. Managers must act on all Ss in parallel if they want to maintain balance and fit.

With further rearranging it is possible to argue that this chapter's definition of mission is little different from the 7S model. Systems, structure, style, staff and skills can all be viewed as forming part of what we have called policies and behaviour standards (Figure 6.4). With this representation, the only element missing from the 7S model is purpose. Interestingly, in the earlier format used by Pascale and Athos the label superordinate goals was used instead of shared values; and in their discussion of superordinate goals they bring in elements of what we would call purpose. There seems no need to apologise for the overlap between this chapter's definition of mission and the McKinsey 7S model. It is no surprise that there is little in our definition that is dramatically new. What the chapter has done is pulled together previous insights in a new way and drawn out some new implications as a result.

While the 7S model emphasises the need for fit, particularly between strategy and values, it misses the importance of three relationships in the mission model that are vital to a deeper understanding of the nature of organisation management. First, the 7S model does not recognise the importance of the link between the private values of employees and the shared values of the organisation. Through the concept of 'staff' the model acknowledges the need to have people who fit well with the other Ss; but like Ouchi it only sees the control and behaviour benefits for the organisation and misses the fulfilment and feelings of worth that values can ignite in the employee.

Second, the 7S model does not emphasise the importance of behaviour standards. It has been argued here that policies and behaviour standards are the bottom line of mission. By creating some behaviour standards that capture the essence of both the strategic logic and the moral logic in the organisation, leaders can ensure that the values fit the strategy. The behaviour standards are the means of fitting values with strategy. The 7S model has no such powerful integrating thought. It relies on a loose concept of fit that encourages managers to eliminate obviously incongruent elements in their organisation. The Ashridge Mission model is more demanding. It is asking leaders to search for behaviour standards, like British Airways' 'Putting People First' or Hewlett-Packard's Managing by Wandering Around (MBWA), that will act as the integrating mechanism for the mission.

Third, as already pointed out, the 7S model gives little attention to purpose. Purpose is the cornerstone of mission. Forming a purpose is full of pitfalls because managers are trying to sort out the relationship between competing constituencies – shareholders, employees, customers, suppliers and the community. The 7S model sidesteps this area. However, other writers have addressed purpose.

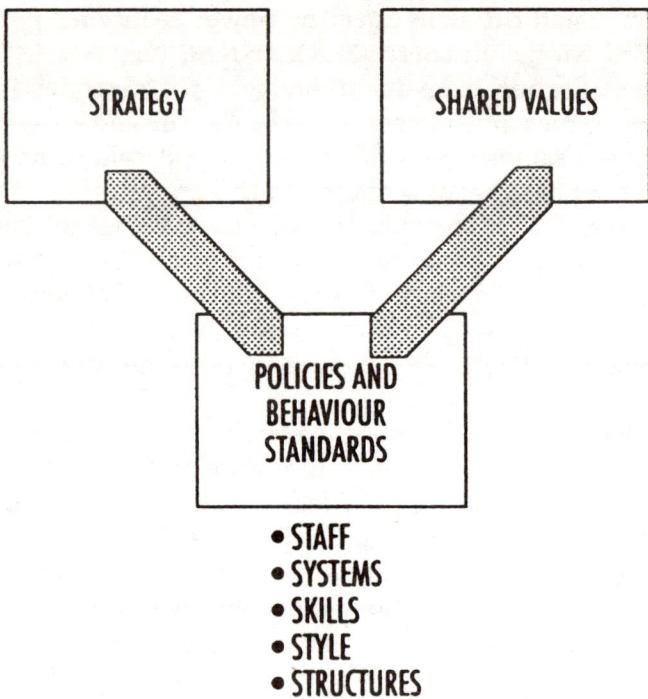

Figure 6.4 *The 7S model rearranged in the format of the model of mission*

Purpose

Philosophers and economists have written at length on the role of business in society. Before the creation of the limited company, the purpose of work and the purpose of an individual's existence were closely connected and closely tied to religion. A Lutheran believed that people had a predetermined fate to which they must submit. Hence work was an act of submission to be borne with a glad heart because it was part of living out the Almighty's wish.

During the Reformation, the Protestant 'work ethic' was born. In Weber's words: 'For everyone, without exception, God's Providence has prepared a calling, which he should profess and in which he should labour' (1930). Humankind was seen to be working for the 'divine glory', using its talents to the maximum. Like the parable of the talents, the individual was expected to work to maximise his or her contribution to the world.

During the Industrial Revolution, capitalists built companies. It became hard to view these industrial capitalists of the late eighteenth and early nineteenth centuries as leaders of a divine calling. The religious connection with work became less relevant and was replaced by work as a social duty. The individual worked to contribute to the well-being of society. Business was also seen in this context: business's purpose was to produce goods to help society.

In the years since the Industrial Revolution the role of work and the purpose of business have become much less clear. Work has become for many a way of achieving success, of accumulating wealth and gaining independence. For others it has become a creative activity. Like the artist, the employee is fulfilling some inner need to express himself or herself. Work has become a much more selfish activity, connected with personal gratification. This has left a philosophical void. The role of business in society has become unclear. If businesses contain groups of people pursuing selfish ends, then what is the role of business in society?

Three views of business have evolved. The first is that business is an association of stakeholders each pursuing selfish ends and joining together in an association purely because they find it easier to achieve their ends through business. Each stakeholder group – shareholders, employees, suppliers, customers – has equal importance in the association. Each has the right to bargain for the maximum split of the cake that can be made available to them without unbalancing the established relationships. The company is a vehicle of convenience for self-interested groups. It is a form of controlled marketplace.

The second view of business that has developed is associated with Milton Friedman (1962). Railing against the mood in business for what was called in the 1970s 'corporate social responsibility', the need to do charitable deeds for the benefit of the community, Friedman argues that the purpose of business is to create wealth and this can best be done by maximising profits. The capitalist system is designed so that the unremitting pursuit of profits by business will result in the greatest overall contribution to the system.

The third view of the role of business is that it should maximise the public good and promote social harmony. This is a particularly Japanese view promoted by leaders such as Konosuke Matsushita of Matsushita Electric. Companies make products for the public good. The public rewards the company with loyalty and support, making sure that all the stakeholders are well rewarded for their efforts.

Edward Freeman and Daniel Gilbert, professors at the University of Virginia and Bucknell University in the US, have captured much of the confusion about the role of business in their book *Corporate Strategy and the Search for Ethics* (1988). They define seven possible purposes for business:

1. The 'stockholder strategy' based on the property rights of stockholders
2. The 'managerial strategy' recognising that managers have the power to pursue their own ends
3. The 'limited stakeholder strategy' that focuses on satisfying the needs of two or three stakeholder groups
4. The 'unrestricted stakeholder strategy' recognising that all claimants on the business need satisfying
5. The 'social harmony strategy' based on a positive view of the public good rather than a satisfactory view
6. The 'Rawlsian strategy' that argues for equality among social groups unless inequality helps to raise the level of the worst off
7. The 'personal projects strategy' that views business as a vehicle for all stakeholders to pursue their personal projects.

Choosing between these purposes is obviously an important management task. Moreover, linking purpose with strategy and with values is also important. The authors conclude a chapter entitled 'The Revolution in Management' with the words:

> Corporate strategy is about purpose and so is ethics. Purpose is a person-based justification for action, shaped through interdependent bargaining among multiple parties. Ethics not only parallels strategy, through a common concern with purpose, but also provides a framework for reasoning through the thornier aspects of strategy as purpose. By explicitly acknowledging the connection, we can make some real intellectual and practical progress in the study of corporate strategy.

And, the authors could have added, in the study of mission.

The importance of purpose has also been documented by the leadership theorists. We mention only the work of Warren Bennis and Burt Nanus, who wrote a book entitled *Leaders: The Strategies for Taking Charge* (1985). They argue that one of the most important roles of the leader is to grab the attention of the organisation by creating a vision of the future that can serve as a motivating purpose. Bennis and Nanus were not concerned about the philosophical issues underlying purpose. They had recognised the link between purpose and motivated behaviour. A clear purpose is one of the tools leaders can use to energise the organisation:

> When the organization has a clear sense of purpose, direction and desired future state and when this image is widely shared, individuals are able to

find their own roles both in the organization and in the larger society . . . This empowers individuals and confers status upon them because they see themselves as part of a worthwhile enterprise. They gain a sense of importance, as they are transformed from robots blindly following instructions to human beings engaged in a creative and purposeful venture. (Bennis and Nanus, 1985)

In other words, people gain a sense of purpose if they can see that they are building a cathedral rather than carrying bricks. The authors also recognise the linking role of values. Values act to bind the emotions of employees to the purpose. By articulating a purpose:

the leader operates on the emotional and spiritual resources of the organization, on its values, commitment and aspirations . . . Great leaders often inspire their followers to high levels of achievement by showing them how their work contributes to worthwhile ends. It is an emotional appeal to some of the most fundamental of human needs – the need to be important, to make a difference, to feel useful, to be part of a worthwhile enterprise.

Motivation Theory

Throughout this chapter, it has been shown that the definition of mission includes little that is completely new. All the relationships within the definition have been explored by other authors. Finally we turn to the motivation theorists. Employees develop an emotional attachment to their work and their organisation when their values match the values of the organisation. Surprisingly, almost no acknowledgment of this relationship exists among the early motivation theorists. The motivation giants such as Herzberg, Maslow and McGregor say little about people's search for meaning and the potential of finding meaning and fulfilment through commitment to an organisation. We have to examine the work of organisation psychologists like Edgar Schein to find the search for meaning identified as a powerful source of motivation.

Frederick Herzberg, professor of management at the University of Utah in the US, is one of the best-known professors of motivation theory. His status was reinforced a few years ago by the republication as a *Harvard Business Review* classic of an article titled 'One more time: how do you motivate employees?' (1986). In the article Herzberg addresses the perennial problem of management: 'How do I get an employee to do what I want him or her to do?'. He points out that many of the traditional methods of getting things done fail to motivate employees.

He illustrates this well: 'I have a year-old Schnauzer. When it was a small puppy and I wanted it to move I kicked it in the rear and it moved. Now that I have finished its obedience training, I hold up a dog biscuit when I want the Schnauzer to move.' In both cases, Herzberg points out, it is him who is motivated, not the dog. The Schnauzer does not want to move, it is purely responding to a stimulus given by Herzberg. So how does a manager get an employee to want to do something?

Herzberg distinguishes between intrinsic and extrinsic motivators. Extrinsic motivators are those he used to get his dog to move. Intrinsic motivators, such as 'achievement, recognition for achievement, the work itself, responsibility, growth and advancement', give employees the internal desire to do something.

The solution to the original question of how to get employees to do what is required is, in Herzberg's view, job enrichment. By 'bringing the job up to the level of challenge commensurate with the skill that was hired', managers can reap a 'return in human satisfaction and economic gain that would be one of the largest dividends that industry and society have ever achieved through better personnel management'. Herzberg says nothing about values or about sense of mission as a motivator.

Dr Abraham Maslow is another Titan in the motivation field, with his hierarchy of needs theory. In *Motivation and Personality* (1970) he describes a model which charts the progression from basic physiological needs, such as food and shelter; to social needs, such as safety and self-esteem; to the highest need, the search for self-actualisation. The latter is 'the desire for self-fulfilment, namely the tendency for [the individual] to become actualised in what he is potentially'. Such an individual has satisfied his or her basic needs, has achieved social stability and has a healthy measure of self-esteem. He or she does not feel 'the pangs of loneliness, of ostracism, of rejection, of friendlessness, of rootlessness'.

Maslow's assertion that every person seeks 'self-actualisation' has powerful implications for motivation at work. Maslow clearly states that fulfilling the highest human need yields powerful results: people live healthier and more stress-free lives and achieve 'more profound happiness, serenity, and richness of the inner life'. Self-actualisation also enables people to develop their individuality and enjoy better relationships with others. Because 'the higher the need the less selfish it must be', people who achieve self-actualisation are more likely to work towards an unselfish cause.

Maslow's self-actualisation only touches on the motivation that can come from a sense of mission. He recognises that people search for meaning, 'for knowledge, for understanding, for a life philosophy, for a theoretical frame of reference, for a value system'. But he does not translate this into a concept that is equivalent to a sense of mission. The mission model implies that there is a need at a higher level than self-actualisation – a need to contribute to something worth while, a need for a sense of mission.

Edgar Schein, professor of organisation psychology and management at the Massachussetts Institute of Technology (MIT), does recognise the importance of mission in employee motivation. He recognises that academics have not yet developed a complete theory of human behaviour, particularly behaviour at work. He suggests that behaviour is dependent on inherited traits, learned routines and perception of the situation. Values are important because they influence perception.

Referring to the work of Etzioni and others, Schein describes a number of perceived relationships or psychological contracts between individuals and organisations. The coercive relationship such as custodial institutions; the utilitarian relationship where the individual is involved to the extent of doing a fair day's work for a fair day's pay; and the normative relationship 'which means that the person intrinsically values the mission of the organization and his or her job is personally involved and identified with the organization' (Schein, 1980).

Unfortunately even Schein does not recognise the implication that this categorisation has for business. He does not challenge Etzioni's original assumption that business organisations will inevitably have utilitarian relationships with their employees. Organisations with normative relationships are deemed to be non-commercial such as hospitals, religious groups and voluntary organisations.

It is this blindness to the opportunity for business organisations to develop missions that are intrinsically valued that has left a hole in motivation theory. The culture writers, such as Pascale and Athos, recognise the opportunity from studying Japanese companies and some American companies such as IBM. The reason motivation theorists have given so little attention to this area is that so few of their ideas have been based on empirical fieldwork. Motivation studies are so frequently carried out in the sterile atmosphere of the laboratory, an environment where sense of mission is absent by definition.

Review

This chapter has attempted to show that none of the relationships central to its definition of mission is new. All of them have been exposed by other writers, some of the wisest of whom were writing as long ago as the 1930s. One book has been deliberately left out of our analysis, *In Search of Excellence* by Tom Peters and Robert Waterman (1982). It became the best-selling business book of all time because of its gleeful recognition of the emotional side of organisations. It champions the human being in organisations, arguing that people are the difference between good and bad organisations.

In a chapter of the book entitled 'Man Waiting for Motivation', Peters and Waterman carry out a review of the literature in a similar fashion to this chapter. They point out that the individual is 'quite strikingly irrational. He reasons by stories, assumes himself to be in the top 10 percent judged by any good trait, and needs to stick out and find meaning simultaneously'. They examine psychologists, philosophers and many of the practical studies of behaviour and conclude that people yearn for transcendence:

> Perhaps transcendence is too grand a term for the business world, but the love of product at Cat, Bechtel and J&J comes very close to meriting it. Whatever the case, we find it compelling that so many thinkers from so many fields agree on the dominating need of human beings to find meaning and transcend mundane things. (Peters and Waterman, 1982)

It is this observation that makes it possible for a leader to help an employee develop a sense of mission. And it is the opportunity to create employees with a sense of mission that makes mission the leader's most important task.

References

This chapter is drawn from two of the author's previous publications: *A Sense of Mission*, Economist Hutchinson (1990), and *Do You Need A Mission Statement?*, Economist Publications (1990).

Badaracco, Joseph L Jr and Ellsworth, Richard R (1989) *Leadership and the Quest for Integrity*, Harvard Business School Press, Cambridge, Mass.

Barnard, Chester I (1938/1968) *The Functions of the Executive*, Harvard University Press, Cambridge, Mass.

Bennis, Warren and Nanus, Burt (1985) *Leaders: The Strategies for Taking Charge*, Harper & Row, New York.

Carlsson, Jan (1987) *Moments of Truth*, Ballinger.

— (1988), *Speech given at AMA Human Resources Conference*, Chicago, Ill, 20 Apr.

Freeman, Edward and Gilbert, Daniel (1988) *Corporate Strategy and the Search for Ethics*, Prentice-Hall, Englewood Cliffs, NJ.

Friedman, M (1962) *Capitalism and Freedom*, University of Chicago Press, Chicago, Ill.

Herzberg, Frederick (1968) 'One more time: how do you motivate employees?', *Harvard Business Review*, Jan/Feb.

Maslow, Abraham H (1970) *Motivation and Personality*, Harper & Row, New York.

Matsushita, Konosuke (1984) *Not for Bread Alone: A Business Ethos, A Management Ethic*, PHP Institute Inc.

McGregor, D M (1960) *The Human side of Enterprise* McGraw-Hill, New York.

McGregor, D M (1967) *The Professional Manager*, McGraw-Hill, New York.

Ouchi, William (1981) *Theory Z: How American Business Can Meet the Japanese Challenge*, Addison-Wesley, Reading, Mass.

Pascale, Richard Tanner and Athos, Anthony G (1981) *The Art of Japanese Management*, Simon & Schuster, New York.

Peters, Thomas J and Waterman, Robert H (1982) *In Search of Excellence: Lessons from America's Best Run Companies*, Harper & Row, New York.

Schein, Edgar H (1980) *Organizational Psychology*, Prentice-Hall, Englewood Cliffs, NJ.

Selznick, Philip (1957) *Leadership in Administration: A Sociological Interpretation*, University of California Press, Berkeley.

Watson, Thomas J Jr (1963) *A Business and its Beliefs: The Ideas that Helped Build IBM*, McGraw-Hill, New York.

Weber, Max (1930) *The Protestant Ethic and the Spirit of Capitalism*, Allen & Unwin, London.

Weiss, William I (1986) 'Minerva's Owl: Building a Corporate Value System', *Journal of Business Ethics*, 5, Kluwer Academic Publishers.

7

Business and Ethics

Midi Berry and William Keyser

Introduction

Imagine the following situations:

You are a senior research scientist in a cross-functional team charged with bringing to market a new pharmaceutical product for treating the common cold. You have only been with the team for three months but in reviewing files on the project, you became concerned that the tests may not all have been carried out in a sufficiently rigorous manner. You even suspect that certain recent test results have been falsified, under pressure of getting the product to market before a competitor's product. You expressed your concerns to the project director; when you pressed your case, he became aggressive, warning you to 'stop trying to rock the boat'. You feel caught: on the one hand, you do not have sufficient evidence to prove your case beyond dispute; on the other, all your instincts and professional judgment tell you that things are not right. What can you do?

You are corporate training manager for an oil company, and have been faxed by one of the company's African subsidiaries to send them photocopies of the materials from your recent course on the management of change. You explain that, since many are protected by copyright, they will need to order these direct from the publishers. Your colleagues reply: budgets are tight, and orders take months to arrive. Moreover, ignoring copyright law is accepted practice in their country. Will you let them have the photocopies?

You are production director of a British electronics firm taken over by a German owned multinational. A supplier has sent you a dozen bottles of vintage port – he has done this each Christmas for years. Under the

146

former ownership, it was common practice at work to give and receive presents at Christmas. The marketing director, just back from head office, mentions that your new parent company prohibits the giving and receiving of any gifts. She laughs when you tell her about your port and suggests that you had better 'drink the evidence quickly'. What will you do?

You are part of a top management group that recently developed a draft statement of corporate values. One item with which everyone seemed satisfied was 'We will conduct ourselves according to the highest standards of honesty and integrity'. The statement was shared with all managers in the company, in a series of meetings intended to stimulate discussion: reactions have varied from mild enthusiasm to cynicism. A senior accountant in your division, your direct report, with a dotted line relationship to the finance director, tells you her concerns about the way in which certain corporate accounting practices are being conducted. She says it is common knowledge in finance that the company sails close to the wind, and describes specific examples of sharp practice in which she was pressured to collude. She feels this doesn't square with the newly espoused statement on honesty and integrity. She had been wanting to speak out before, but was afraid. Now she feels, in the wake of the statement of corporate values, that people can't ignore what's going on. She anticipates that raising these issues with the finance director would be 'like talking to a brick wall'. What action will you take?

Managers working at all levels in business today face difficult calls on their judgment. The way in which they respond – their processes of decision making and the actual decisions made – can be influenced by many factors:

- The national or international legal context and culture in which they work;
- explicit ethical guidelines and principles published by their employer;
- views of colleagues and other stakeholders in the business;
- family, school and other formative influences in their upbringing;
- their inherent preferences in decision-making style and personal code of ethics.

If, in trying to maintain personal integrity and collective justice, managers find themselves perplexed and challenged to reconcile apparently contradictory viewpoints, they are not alone. They, their fellow managers, employees, customers and society at large have the doubtful privilege of living in interesting times. Many traditional collective standards are being questioned; and moral compasses have to cover terrain subject to unusual magnetic disturbances. Increasingly people can find themselves wondering 'Which way *is* north?'

Ethical choice usually seems most difficult when made at the operational level – when one can see and touch the people whose lives are affected by the decisions. When taking a strategic view, distance may appear to offer detachment and objectivity. We can decide whether to trade with a country known to operate an oppressive political regime, from a stance of principle or pragmatism, without having to visualise the people suffering under that regime. We can make choices about market positioning with regard to product and service quality without ever meeting a customer. True, the factors involved may be complex, but we can adopt a cost-benefit approach. Analytical decision making holds sway in most strategic planning meetings, while intuition, emotion and gut-feel are rarely acknowledged explicitly.

Yet, as understanding about the dynamics of organisations evolves and develops, there is increasing pressure to view businesses in their totality and this is as true for ethics as, say, for, 'total quality'. What occurs, intentionally or otherwise, at one level in an organisation has an effect upon other levels; short-term decision making impacts the long term and vice versa. Any ethical decisions made at the strategic level should therefore support and inform operational choice: misalignment between the strategic intent of the company and the attitudes and actions of people working at the 'ethical coalface' at best provokes uncomfortable tension and dissent, at worst poor economic performance and a discredited reputation.

Moreover, in examining ethical choice closely, a sense of integrity and authenticity appear to be fundamental to its effective practice. This suggests that the whole person needs to be congruently involved in making ethical decisions or mixed messages may be received. That in turn may require the inclusion of instinct and heart as well as head, whether the focus is on the long term and strategic or the short term and operational.

We cannot pretend that this chapter will reduce, much less remove, magnetic disturbances from the path of managerial decision making, at strategic or operational levels. We hope that it may help managers to make more sense of their compass reading in this time of changing paradigms.

We start with a historical perspective: by rooting ourselves in the past, we may better understand the present and possibly anticipate the future. We also consider why 'business and ethics' should be included in a book providing guidelines for strategic thinking.

Some conceptual models are offered to aid managers when thinking strategically about ethical policy combined with examples of ways in which different companies have approached their ethical practice.

The chapter ends by providing a possible process and a checklist of ethical issues for businesses to consider. These are intended less as a definitive list of the 'whats and hows' and more as a stimulus to further exploration, to be visited at times when the compass seems to swing particularly violently or if its face becomes scratched and hard to read.

We do not intend to exhort readers to follow one type of ethical policy-making procedure or even to extol particular ethical positions. Inevitably, we have our own moral codes and viewpoints, some of which we are conscious, others of which may be perceived more easily by the reader than by ourselves. One deliberate assumption is that we are addressing an audience reared in and managing from a predominantly Western experience of the world. Another is that managers reading this book know more about their own business than we will ever know. We believe that they and their colleagues have the right and responsibility to determine the ethical position appropriate to their company. We hope that this chapter may assist them in fulfilling that right and discharging that responsibility.

Ethics in History

Ethics, most simply defined, are the choice between good and evil, between right and wrong action. They involve a process of evaluating what is good and what is bad, whether this is undertaken individually or collectively, and their primary function is the regulation of human relations

When we look back along the path taken by humanity there is danger of oversimplifying the past – just as when looking backwards through a telescope the image is small and detail obscured. Nonetheless, analyses by historians, anthropologists and psychologists suggest that, for pre-patriarchal societies (early hunting, herding and planting communities), ethics were not a conscious issue. Their prime orientation was to the survival of the community and its members; their basic criterion was practical rather than moral, and the primary regulating mechanism was taboo. The individual was a member of a herd and as such part of a non-personal group-patterned process. Activities were coordinated by instinct, the will was the will of the group. What today we might call 'right' would then have been characterised as that which benefits and supports the life of the group, or that which appeases fear and eliminates danger.

Ethics come into consciousness at that time in history when the individual becomes aware of himself or herself as a separate entity, with some sense of personal responsibility for the relationship with other individuals or the community:

> Ethics . . . arose with the ego. For a sense of individual responsibility presupposes the sense of 'I'. (Whitmont, 1983)

As patriarchy succeeded matriarchy in the Western world, from antiquity through the Middle Ages and well into the Renaissance, the trend was for the increasing differentiation of individual consciousness from that of the group. But the primary definition of individuals lay in their relationship and utility to the collective. People were valued as doers of deeds, and as controllers of the external world. If actions were socially useful, they were deemed to be good; if not they were bad.

Moreover, the belief (common to the religions of Judaism, Christianity and Islam) was of one supreme God: God the Creator, with a Divine Plan. Belief in the existence of an external God entailed belief in the existence of a single, absolute code of ethics. Heroic individuals, such as Moses, Mohammed and Jesus, fulfilled the function of informing humankind what that code was. People were then judged in terms of their readiness and ability to interpret and apply this externally derived code of ethics. Reasoned and disciplined obedience was the required response of the individual; personal feelings and emotions were appropriate only if they supported and toed the collective line. Indeed, they were frequently suspect, since they could and occasionally did interfere with reasonable behaviour.

The rise and achievements of modern Cartesian/Newtonian man, with a continuing stress on the discipline of will and reason, have their antecedents in the patriarchy of Western religions. The increasing belief that, through his mental development and technological achievements, man could even take over God's role in controlling the universe led to the progressive secularisation of matter. Work and achievement themselves became, for many, effective substitutes for the Divine Plan and encouraged the growth of the 'Puritan work ethic', which still dominates much of the Western business world today.

Individual consciousness and differentiation were emphasised further by the rise of entrepreneurialism and the development of business empires. Yet individualism was still subject to collective judgment and discipline: indeed the only individuals given value in this system were the group's special heroes – those leaders who fulfilled society's collective ideals through outstanding performance. One of the bywords for many Western businesses, 'Excellence', comes from the Latin *'excelere'*, which means to outrun others. Striving for excellence and the competitive spirit were highly valued. The hero as conqueror developed and exerted his willpower and, in so doing, often needed to repress individual emotions and feelings, desires and hurts. His goodness was based upon training his will to comply with a collective law which deified the patriarchal ideals: efficiency ('I can'); possession ('I own') and honour ('I am respected in the community').

Of course, even the conquering hero needed regulation with respect to his relations with others. 'Love thy neighbour as thyself', a cornerstone of the Christian ethical code, has probably been the primary 'litmus paper' for assessing the ethical stance of business in the West. We can distinguish, albeit simplistically, between two dominant types of business activity from the seventeenth century onward: one, personified by certain dynastic business families, whose moral code was plain for all the world to see and for whom 'Love thy neighbour as thyself' could well have been the family motto; the other, a rapacious and evil Dickensian-style employer, who was only 'in it for what he could get' and who ruthlessly exploited child and adult alike in the pursuit of personal wealth and aggrandisement.

Most businesses probably fell somewhere between these two poles, yet extremes make a point. Almost certainly, ethical decision making during the Industrial Revolution and well into the twentieth century was a simple matter, by comparison with some of the choices facing modern management. Essentially one external code still ruled society. The choice was that of keep it or break it. Risks to the individual and to businesses, such as they were, involved the possible economic dis-benefits of doing right, or the results of being found out in wrong-doing.

Ethics in our Changing World

As we conduct our business lives now on the eve of the third millennium, many factors combine to present a world in which goalposts seem to be moving much of the time. It is often difficult to see where they are today, much less predict where they will be tomorrow. The forces underlying change and instability are various. Following our historical theme, though, it is possible to see the way in which patriarchy has been found to have reached its useful limits, and even to be revealed as increasingly inadequate as the sole organising ethos for our times.

A new paradigm, ushered in by modern physics, biology, systems thinking and depth psychology, suggests that the dynamics of our world are poorly described if we continue to think in terms of a Creator who manipulates it from outside, like an object. We borrow as much from the ancient Eastern religions as we do from quantum physics when we conceive rather of the world as a continuous flux of process, in some remarkable and profound way inner directed – an enfolded immanence flowing towards external realisation and manifestation.

The dualistic notion of absolute good and evil, so appropriate to the world view which conceived of an external Maker, loses its potency in this paradigm. Thus, we find:

> We stand in need of a re-orientation, a *metanioa* . . . we must beware of thinking of good and evil as absolute opposites . . . In practical terms, this means that good and evil are no longer so self-evident. We have to realise that each represents a *judgment* . . . Moral evaluation is always founded upon the apparent certitudes of a moral code which pretends to know precisely what is good and what is evil. But once we know how uncertain the foundation is, ethical decision becomes a subjective, creative act. (Jung, 1963)

In the holistic world view, humankind becomes just one interconnected part of a unitary cosmic organism, and energy is contained as much within the flow, the relationship between the parts, as within the parts themselves. 'Love thy neighbour as thyself' changes to 'Love thy neighbour – he or she is part of thyself'! And the function of ethics is extended from the regulation of human relations to the regulation of relations between all parts of the organism – which encompasses humanity's relationship to its whole universe.

Moreover, it seems that the function of humanity within the web may hold a particular significance for the whole in ethical decision making: the unique power of reflective thought endows us with the role of consciousness and possibly, thereby, of conscience for the whole. If so, this is a weighty responsibility, and one which, at least in terms of our relationship to the environment, many ecologists and scientists would say we are currently showing ourselves ill equipped to fulfil (Lovelock, 1983).

What this changing world view also suggests is that an inner-directed conscience becomes as much a matter for the individual as for the collective. In a world where good and bad are relative, people need to look inside themselves as much as to the outer world for guidance: to be open to what seems to be seeking to manifest. They need to attune themselves in an experiential, intuitive and felt sense as well as to apply their will, mental discipline and powers of analysis to ethical choice. Moreover, they need to sustain the tensions that arise from finding themselves in new ethical positions which may confront and challenge long-held collective beliefs.

In the emerging world view, business is an integral part of society and cannot be viewed as some discrete area of activity with laws unto itself – it can no longer (if it ever did) concern itself with the material world alone, leaving matters of conscience to the church. And as if this did not provide enough complexity in the business executive's life, consider the issues arising from the trends towards globalisation.

As long as patriarchy ruled, and with it an accompanying colonising approach to business expansion around the world, it was possible to take a 'one external code' view of the universe, irrespective of the indigenous cultures in which expanding businesses might find themselves. Currently, a key business phrase, from America to Europe to Africa, is 'learning to manage diversity'. We are still at an early stage of understanding what this may mean for business in the future. What we do know is that such aspirations are far from being realised. To take them seriously demands that we be open to the exploration *on equal terms* of many different external ethical codes from many different cultures. And this in an era when the balance between collective perspectives and individual codes is also up for re-evaluation.

A holistic paradigm also challenges us to be willing to confront the problem of ethical garbage within ourselves and within our organisations. It seems a natural human tendency to want to think well of oneself and relatively few people identify themselves comfortably as capable of unethical thoughts and deeds. It seems easier by far to project 'bad motive and evil deeds' on to others than to risk facing our own personal and organisational shadows. The dilemma in the new world view is that, if we project all our repressed thoughts and deeds on to convenient scapegoats and allow them to carry the ethical can, they remain part of the total system. We may sack a thief but, our neighbour is still ourself. If we seek constantly to hold the ethical high ground, it can result in painful polarisation and stagnation for all. The pluralistic challenge of this new paradigm for business managers is significant.

We learn from the Greek myths what a difficult time it can be for mortals when different gods and goddesses battle for supremacy. As we look around the world at apparently chaotic local, national and international affairs, it may seem like a re-run of the Battles of the Titans and the Giants. The promise, or at least opportunity, offered by certain thinkers of our times is for humanity to move beyond this and evolve in consciousness: to the point where instinct (so highly developed in primitive communities), mind (so superbly refined in recent millennia), and heart (yet to receive much official share of the decision-making stage) learn to work in harmony and take us to new levels of ethical awareness. The threat, or at least fear, expressed by many is that we 'can't get there from here': that nuclear annihilation, global warming, AIDS, or some combination of these and other horrors will consign us to oblivion.

In the midst of all this, managers have a job to do. The 'wash still has to be got out' if customers' needs are to be met, employees paid and shareholder expectations fulfilled. One fundamental question is whether devoting time and energy to ethical considerations at a strategic level offers any real advantage, by comparison with the head, heart and stomach aches it can engender.

What has Ethics to do with Strategy?

Ethics have nothing or everything to do with strategy. On the one hand, strategy is about intent, while ethical considerations can be addressed on an ad hoc basis. On the other hand, ethics exist in an organisation whether or not it does any strategic thinking. Either way, ethical dilemmas arise in organisational life, whether given prior thought or not, and whether they are tackled by individuals or collectively.

An American chainstore group, Nordstrom, welcomes its new staff, by conferring power on the individual:

> We're glad to have you with our Company. Our number one goal is to provide **outstanding customer service**. Set both your personal and professional goals high. We have great confidence in your ability to achieve them. Nordstrom Rules: Rule No.1: **Use your good judgment in all situations**. There will be no additional rules. Please feel free to ask your department manager, store manager or division general manager any question at any time.'

East Midlands Electricity, a British utility, defines its values collectively, by saying:

> The Company operates by a set of values and ethics which include:

> 1. Adherence not only to the letter but also to the spirit of the law, and accepted standards of behaviour.

2. Integrity and honesty in all our dealings.
3. Respect for the individual.
4. Innovation, the seeking and acceptance of change, and the prompt adoption of relevant new techniques.
5. The expectation of high performance standards from all its employees and a willingness to recognise and reward achievement.
6. Courtesy, concern and quality in personal presentation, language and appearance.
7. Concern for the environment.

This statement is accompanied by a twelve-point statement of strategy, which also includes behavioural ambitions like, 'Setting and delivering exceptionally high standards of customer service'.

Both these organisations have chosen in different ways to think about strategy and ethics as part of an integrated activity. However, there are many who choose not to do so. The question for organisations seems to be whether there is corporate advantage to be gained or a moral imperative to be fulfilled from devoting prior thought to the issues and seeking to arrive at an ethical view through the strategic thinking process. The need for judgment will remain. If strategic thinking about ethics is undertaken in a business context without explicit attention being devoted to ethical issues, implicit ethical assumptions will nonetheless be there. The corollary is also true.

Much will depend on management's perspective of the role and purpose of organisations. There are many who think of an organisation simply as a rational entity in pursuit of goals. In this case, thinking about ethics is only appropriate in so far as ethical considerations may affect the achievement of those goals. One risk of this perspective is that the organisation may adapt poorly, because it rationalises away any issues that get in its way. If the organisation is defined as being merely about survival – a significant reason for thinking strategically in the first place – it may also lessen its ability to create its own future through its own ethical standards.

When managed from the perspective of culture, an organisation is seen as a reflection of knowledge, ideology, values, norms and rituals. These may be codified, in explicit statements of corporate values. Such a perspective attributes value to the integrative benefits of socialisation. It can also run the risk of people feeling manipulated – leading to resentment and mistrust – with culture controlling rather than expressing human character (Morgan, 1986). If the organisation is perceived as being part of the cosmic unitary organism, influencing and adapting to the conditions that surround it, we can also expect attitudes which tend towards democracy and a lesser willingness to prescribe ethical choice for its members.

Thinking about strategy *implies* thinking about ethics. What happens in strategic thinking when there is no conscious attention paid to ethics, is that the basic assumptions and beliefs derive from a 'taken for granted' view of the organisation. We can infer these assumptions and beliefs from the 'artifacts' we see around us in organisational life (such as in technology or behaviour patterns), but they are based on invisible ideas about the nature of human relationships or our relationship to the environment, for example.

Organisation strategy suggests that we want to see an outcome that is different from today. The ability to see a need for change and the ability to make it happen is central to leadership (Schein, 1985). Leadership is central to strategic thinking and strategic thinking entails ethical choice, by intent or default. It feels easy to go round in circles and still wonder 'Which way is north?'.

What is – or What Ought To Be?

If we decide to break into the circle and think explicitly about our ethical position, it may be helpful to decide whether we intend to describe what is – descriptive – or what ought to be – normative (Brown, 1990).

A clear example of the *descriptive* mode of thinking is expressed in Ericsson's 'Our Values' statement:

Operations
Ericsson is an international company and we focus on its totality when performing our tasks and satisfying customers' needs

Customers
A customer is a partner in co-operation with whom we establish long-term customer relations

The individual
We stimulate the creation of an open, straightforward and instructive working climate

Leadership
Our leaders inspire us with team-spirit and create positive relations

Organization
Our organization allows profit responsibility to be decentralised in operations managed by objectives.

(Note: each of these statements is accompanied by sub-statements.)

On the other hand, a *normative* example is the 'Aspirations' Statement of Levi's:

We all want a company that our people are proud of and committed to, where all employees have an opportunity to contribute, learn, grow, and advance based on merit, not politics or background. We want our people to feel respected, treated fairly, listened to, and involved. Above all, we want satisfaction from accomplishments and friendships, balanced personal and professional lives, and to have fun in our endeavors.

When we describe the kind of Levi Strauss & Co we want in the future, what we are talking about is building on the foundation we have inherited: affirming the best of our company's traditions, closing gaps that may exist between principles and practices, and updating some of our values to reflect contemporary circumstances.

The statement continues by describing the type of leadership necessary to make the aspirations a reality and includes discussion of: new behaviours; diversity; recognition; ethical management practices; communications and empowerment.

An example which encompasses both *descriptive* and *normative* ethics is contained in a memo to 3M management from William McKnight, the president – in 1948. The memo, known as the 'Challenge of Management', says:

As our business grows, it becomes increasingly necessary to delegate responsibility and to encourage people to exercise their initiative. This requires considerable tolerance.

Those people to whom we delegate authority and responsibility, if they are good people, are going to want to do their jobs in their own way. These are characteristics we want, and people should be encouraged as long as their way conforms to our general pattern of operations.

Mistakes will be made, but if a person is essentially right, the mistakes made are not as serious in the long run as the mistakes management will make if it is dictatorial and undertakes to tell those under its authority exactly how to do their jobs.

Management that is destructively critical when mistakes are made kills initiative, and it is essential that we have many people with initiative if we are to continue to grow.

The 3M example also serves to illustrate Schein's point that 'the only thing of real importance that leaders do is to create and manage culture', but Schein also stresses that 'a company must analyze its culture and learn to manage within its boundaries, or if necessary change it' (Schein, 1985). Hence 3M has been doing that ever since, noting both how the world and it, like other companies, is changing. It enshrines its (ethical) principles as:

1. The promotion of entrepreneurship and insistence upon freedom in the workplace to pursue innovative ideas. 2. The adherence to uncompromising honesty and integrity. 3. The preservation of individual

identity in an organisational structure which embraces widely diverse businesses and operates in different political and economic systems throughout the world.

The global corporation, and its parts such as 3M Europe or its subsidiary 3M UK, establish goals and strategies designed to fit with the principles and objectives.

Descriptive and normative statements each carry risk: if a company describes what is, and its subsequent actions are found to be at a variance, it is open to the charge of hypocrisy and likely to engender cynicism among customers, employees and the community at large. If it talks about what should be and acknowledges that it is not there yet, it may thereby ensure that the new age will never dawn – that it will remain in the future, and that the obstacles which prevent people behaving now as they believe they should will continue to manifest one way or another', 'I will be good – tomorrow'.

One of the strongest recent examples of an ethics statement being fulfilled is the Johnson & Johnson 'Credo'. It may be argued as to whether it is descriptive normative, or both, but it contains phrases like:

> . . . We are responsible to our employees, the men and women who work with us throughout the world. Everyone must be considered as an individual. We must respect their dignity and recognise their merit . . .
> We are responsible to the communities in which we live and work and to the world community as well. . .

The 'Credo' is so deeply a part of the company's culture that when their product Tylenol was maliciously tampered with, the company did not hesitate about its duty – immediately to remove the product from public sale and ensure that no product was on any store shelves or in the distribution system, no matter what the cost.

Good and Bad Ethics – Good and Bad Business

Difficulties in organisational life arise when there is a conflict between self and collective interest at any level and also from differences in perspective about what constitutes good and bad. A simple model offered by Bellingham and Cohen (1990) helps to organise thinking around the link between business and ethical good/bad decisions (Figure 7.1). They suggest that decisions or strategies that fall into the good/good or the bad/bad cell are relatively easy to make. Bellingham and Cohen go on to suggest that more opportunities exist in the good/good cell than many business people realise; that few companies

Ethics

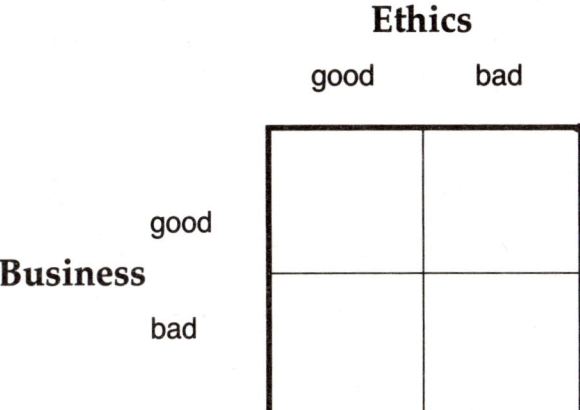

Figure 7.1 *Bellingham and Cohen's model*

succeed in the long term if they consistently operate in the good business/bad ethics quadrant and that more understanding is needed for the hard choices that exist in the good ethics/bad business mode.

'Why can't we do good works at work?' asked Edward Simon, president of Herman Miller. 'Business is the only institution that has a chance, as far as I can see, to fundamentally improve the injustice that exists in the world. But first, we shall have to move through the barriers that are keeping us from being truly vision-led and capable of learning.'

Bellingham and Cohen's model can also act as a useful template if enquiry is extended to considering the perspective of different stakeholders. Each stakeholder can claim some accountabilities from the organisation. Many of these are now becoming established in law at local, national and international levels. Others are appearing in codes of conduct appropriate to particular interest groups, for example investors or consumers, and in codes of practice for industrial relations or sectoral activity.

Integrating the 'Hard' and the 'Soft'

Another way of thinking about ethical aspects of strategy and the process of moving from purpose (intent) to implementation (behaviour), is offered by considering both what is traditionally referred to as the 'hard' and the 'soft' in business (Figure 7.2). The process of integrating the two may be difficult but ultimately less likely to produce strategies which have in-built conflicts.

left brained logic   *right brained intuition*

rational   emotional

commercial   moral

Figure 7.2 *Integration of 'hard' and 'soft'*

The Ashridge Strategic Management Centre work on mission describes how strategy and values constitute the 'left and right brain' of companies (Campbell *et al*, 1990). In Chapter 6 of this volume Andrew Campbell describes the Ashridge diamond model for developing mission and how it links to the McKinsey 7S model for developing strategy.

In this left and right brain perspective, we may see echoes of the psychological type model offered by Jung as long ago as the 1920s (Jung 1923). He distinguished between two types of decision making – the thinking function which uses impersonal, objective and logical analysis to make a choice and a feeling function which is personal, subjective and makes decisions on the basis of what feels right and wrong. Jung characterised each function as rational but each as very different in style. Studies using an instrument designed to enable people to assess their stylistic preferences reveal that most people in Western businesses report a preference for using a thinking style of decision making. It is not surprising, therefore, that the left-hand side of the model has tended to be addressed more consistently than the right. At the same time, ethical choice is a process of evaluation and ultimately requires the exercise of the feeling function.

Encompassing all these structures and models is the premise that managers operate within an overall system. If we can learn to understand the system and develop beyond trial and error or simple linear thinking, feeling part of something larger than ourselves, we may perhaps achieve something of the 'metanoia', or shift in mind, referred to earlier. If not, the suggestion is that: 'Learning disabilities are tragic in children, but they are fatal in organizations' (Senge, 1990).

Manifestations of Ethical Thinking

As an organisation goes about its business it may manifest one or a number of the ethical activities shown below:

- making public the organisation's ethical stance
- publishing codes of ethics
- auditing ethical performance
- management making explicitly ethical decisions
- providing ethics workshops
- soliciting stakeholder ethical opinions
- writing ethical rules and sanctions
- responding to ethical challenges ad hoc
- complying with the spirit of the law
- complying with the letter of the law
- taking steps to minimise ethical exposure
- challenging the status quo.

The activities which are taking place provide clues not just about the state of ethical thinking, but also about the whole way in which the business perceives itself. Levels of consciousness within the organisation are likely to determine the nature of ethical thinking and action that contribute to strategy. They may also be significant in determining the extent to which any ethical positions stated by the organisation are sufficiently internalised by its members to result in congruent action.

Ethics and Organisational Consciousness

Roger Harrison (1991) has described three levels of consciousness and calls them *'transactional'*, *'self-expression'* and *'mutuality.'*

In a *transactional* culture, people who tend to do well are those whose primary concern is to please people with more power and authority; managers and supervisors are expected to be strong, directive and politically astute, with conflicts resolved by the use of rules, authority and/or political clout. The dominant orientation of the organisation is materialistic and the achievement of maximum profit or gain.

In such an organisation, a published statement of values might not be appropriate, whereas a codified set of rules, for example relating to the giving or receiving gifts, might. The integrity of accounting may be above reproach, while the way information is presented and handled may be tightly controlled. In an organisation manifesting a transactional culture, communication patterns between people are mostly up and down the hierarchy – the chimney syndrome. A survey of staff opinion would almost certainly have poor communication high on its list of findings. And yet curiously, this very fact may go hand in hand with the importance of roles and functions producing an organisation which is very secure, if somewhat overstaffed and inefficient.

In a bank, for example, whose systems and procedures have historically been laid down in part to protect depositors' money, the integrity of bank managers has had much to do with ensuring that the chances of fraud, insecure loans, or openness to illegitimate persuasion by clients were minimised. As long as its stakeholders are all in alignment, the transactional level can be both congruent and highly ethical, in its own terms. A problem arises when the expectations and requirements change: when, for example, in the case of the bank, customers require that their manager 'be flexible and bend the rules a little because this is a special situation'; 'be quick because I won't be able to do this deal if I have to wait while your machine goes through the motions of security and levels of authority – trust me'; 'be friendly every day when I come into the branch, even if your bosses are on your back about getting the paperwork done'. And the problem is exacerbated if society's mores shift to value initiative and enterprise more highly than security, and then expect its banking sector to be open to risk sharing too. The view of 'right action' may shift, at both the individual customer and the collective level, and suddenly the security-conscious bank manager finds himself or herself out of step.

In a *self-expression* organisation, people who do well tend to be those who are ambitious and energetic and they are valued for their competence and contribution. The rules, systems and procedures for making decisions and coordinating work are flexible; people are empowered to modify the established rules and procedures to cope with unusual circumstances, not least because the organisation's attitude to the outside world is expansive/competitive. Nordstrom, the company quoted earlier (p 154), exhorts individuals to use their good judgment, thereby giving a strong message that individual competence will be a yardstick of successful performance.

The results orientation will mean that the organisation will wish to be characterised as customer driven and will probably use participative styles. It may, however, have some difficulties in resolving internal conflicts, since work groups may tend to be egoistic and competitive Corporate values statements may be developed and involve lots of corporate 'hoopla'; but they may also tend to have face value only.

Chances are that all the latest management techniques will be tried – value analysis, portfolio management, cycle time reduction. Such initiatives, taken on by managers with missionary zeal and with high currency, may obscure some more fundamental human values.

Tensions can arise, for example between functions each displaying the highest individual integrity: finance doing battle for results, because of a preoccupation with the delivery of shareholder value, with personnel holding out for continuation of a high spend on personal development. Both may claim 'ownership' of the ethical high ground. This may be the very time to appeal to an ethically driven strategy to clarify the superordinate goals and seek to reconcile conflicting interests. Or it may be that the battle between the opposing factions will itself reveal basic assumptions that have previously been implicit and that, once better understood, will inform future ethical debate.

In a *mutuality* organisation, the people who flourish are those whose primary concern is for people, with managers oriented towards the development of others. The dominant orientation of the organisation is towards service outside and relationships inside; words with which it is familiar include: caring, cooperation, cohesion, contribution, sharing and process. In these cases, the word 'ethics' is probably common in the organisation's vocabulary and as of much concern as questions of economic performance. The organisation's prevailing attitude internally and externally is cooperative and contributive: its aim is to develop relationships of harmony and mutual benefit with its suppliers, customers and other stakeholders, through processes of partnership and trust. A mutuality perspective seems to fit the needs of the new paradigm.

For companies whose path has taken them, for example, far along the 'total quality' trail, such a mutuality level of consciousness seems to become a *sine qua non* and yet, in practice, many still find themselves rooted in belief systems which have more to do with self-expression and competitive advantage than sharing and harmony. And in times of crisis and stress, businesses will often tend to become transactional, with an orientation to the short-term, whatever their normal focus.

Thus, none of these levels is likely absolutely to preclude one or another. Indeed there are plenty of organisations where a mixture is to be seen. 3M, already referred to (p. 157), is probably one such case. Another may be Mars Incorporated: one of its 'Five Principles' of business is 'mutuality of benefit', but this does not prevent a strong focus on market share and personal competence. As part of its continuing process of 'bringing the challenge of business ethics back to work', the president, Forest Mars, recently initiated a series of workshops for senior people across the company worldwide. As well as reminding participants of the company's business ethics and standards, the workshops are intended to enable them to realise their value to the company and to understand ethics in business more generally. Perhaps most significantly, the objectives of the workshops are to challenge and debate business ethics versus personal values in practical application and to create an environment where business ethics can be discussed and *challenged*. In 3M too, the recent 'Growing Together' initiative has been intended 'to reinforce the need for a consistent approach to the human aspects of business management' while at the same time stimulating a process of two-way dialogue, so that 'not only is information issued, advice handed out and expectations set, but that in return views and opinions are sought, suggestions encouraged and discussed'.

Harrison's model of organisational levels is particularly useful in our pluralistic times, since it reinforces the theme that no one way of approaching the issue of business and ethics can be said to be right. His framework also reveals that many of those companies 'feeling the heat' in ethical terms are ones who, whether from internal or external pressures, seek to move from one level to another. In this situation, ethical standards which have been the order of the day are being challenged by new ones. Harrison makes it plain that any change interventions in an organisation need to be matched to organisational realities:

> The key to designing effective interventions is not to disrupt the organisation's functioning any more than is required to improve its external performance and its internal health.' (Harrison, 1991)

Shifts in level may sometimes be conscious in intent and at other times seem to emerge for unlikely reasons. A company rooted in a transactional level undertakes a 'defining our Vision and values' exercise because it seeks the security of doing what everyone else in the trade is doing. Suddenly it seems to have got more than it bargained for: employees demand the right of self-expression and customers band together to exert pressure for change. 'Beware of invoking new gods. You might just get what you asked for'. Then, looking back some years later, it is possible to see how an apparently unintentional act drove change; managerial attitudes themselves have undergone a perceptible shift and self-expression has become the order of the day. Whether intentional or not, the discomforts and stresses of level shift can be painful, both individually and collectively.

Where to Break into the Circle of Thinking about Ethics in Business

As we have seen, ethics *are*. We can opt to think about them before or after the event. We can involve the individual, the collective or both. The point in the circle where it is most appropriate to break in depends upon the nature of the organisation and its 'ethical history'. We offer the model in Figure 7.3 as a way of considering the ethical development process.

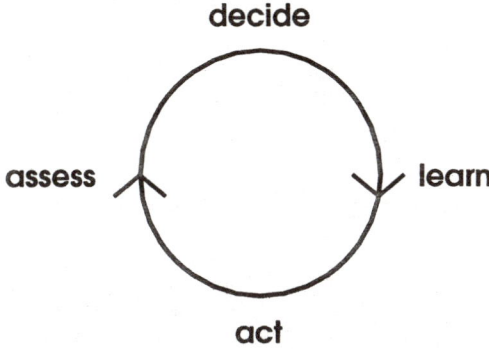

Figure 7.3 *Implementing ethical strategy*

At the stage of determining what the ethical policies might be, there are a number of ways this might be done:

- the chief executive on his or her own
- senior management/committee of the board
- informal discussions
- a participative or consultative process involving some or all of the staff
- opinion surveys
- an ethics audit.

Any of these processes may involve any of the stakeholders and different kinds of feedback loops may be involved. It may be that there is an established process habitually used for establishing consensus in the organisation or it may be seen very much as a prerogative of one or more special parties, such as the quality council, the public affairs committee or the human resources group.

Once through the initial determination, the results may be codified in a document, video or other more informal medium of communication. The manner of communication also depends on the culture and management style of the organisation. As we have seen earlier in the chapter, 3M and Mars use such a document as a vehicle to help in the learning process, seeing the document as a key component of sharing and debate as well as of policy definition.

A part of the learning stage will be the process of testing how far any statements on ethics are born out in practice, as well as the extent to which they can be challenged and how safe it is to blow the whistle if alleged transgressions occur. What procedures will be established for resolving conflict and how are the stresses and strains of ethical development to be addressed? What recognition and reward is appropriate for ethical behaviour and what happens about transgressions? A directive approach will probably have made initial decisions, but a more consultative style may allow the emergence of appropriate procedures through the dialogue and process of learning.

During the action phase (deciding and acting on operational dilemmas such as those described at the start of this chapter), the process may well require ongoing monitoring and feedback of the practical implications of earlier decisions. Do aspirations get trampled by expediency or is the organisation able to live up to its ideals? The most telling pieces of ethical evidence can be the behaviour and actions of senior management and informal leaders.

The assessment stage of the circle of thinking may include a formal audit – just as at the determination stage. Several instruments exist in the public domain or organisations may design their own. These may form part of a regular assessment or survey of staff attitudes or a review procedure of the board, if they are internal. Today, there are also more and more institutional checks on organisational behaviour, ranging from surveys of the best organisations for whom to work to watchdog bodies serving the public interest in fields such as the environment, consumer affairs, equal opportunities or health and safety.

Ethical Issues Checklist

- Employees
  - personal health, welfare, safety and development
  - respect for difference, discrimination and management style
  - recruitment, pay, conditions, performance and recognition
  - honesty, privacy and fairness
  - giving and receiving gifts or inducements
  - rights, responsibilities and sanctions.

- Customers
  - contractual commitment – letter and spirit
  - product and service safety and quality
  - pricing and value for money
  - sales and promotion practices
  - data protection, restrictive practices and anti-trust
  - responsibilities and relationships.

- Shareholders and finance sources
  - fiduciary duties and regulations
  - provision of information
  - investment protection
  - rewards for risk
  - shareholders and stakeholders
  - conflict of interest and privileged information.

- Suppliers and competitors
  - terms and conditions
  - purchasing position and bias
  - settlement and financial power
  - piracy and espionage
  - fair trading and competition
  - disclosure and confidentiality

- Government and community
  - compliance, dissent and lobbying
  - regulators and the law – obligations and intent
  - locus of responsibility in the community
  - extent of civic commitment
  - abuse of economic power and affirmative action
  - corporate giving and sponsorship.
- Environment
  - protection of the biosphere
  - use of natural resources
  - reduction and disposal of waste
  - use of energy
  - risk and accident reduction
  - environmental impact of products and services.

References

Bellingham, Richard and Cohen, Barry (1990) *Ethical Leadership: A Competitive Edge*, HRD Press.

Brown, Marvin (1990) *Working Ethics*, Jossey-Bass, San Francisco.

Campbell, Andrew, Devine, Marion and Young, David (1990) *A Sense of Mission*, Hutchinson, London 1990.

Harrison, Roger (1991) *Humanizing Change*, Harrison Associates.

Jung C G (1923) *Psychological Types*, Harcourt Brace, New York.

Jung C G (1963) *Memories, Dreams, Reflections*, Collins, Routledge and Kegan Paul, London.

Lovelock, James E (1979) *Gaig – A New Look at Life on Earth*. Oxford University Press, Oxford.

Morgan, Gareth (1986) *Images of Organization*, Sage, Newbury Park, California.

Schein, Edgar (1985) *Organizational Culture*, Jossey-Bass, San Francisco.

Senge, Peter (1990) *The Fifth Discipline*, Doubleday, New York.

Whitmont, Edward C (1983) *Return of the Goddess*, Arkana (Penguin), Harmondsworth, Middlesex.

8

Business and Discrimination

Geraldine Healy

Introduction

Issues of discrimination and disadvantage may not be considered part of the language of business strategists, but national and multinational organisations are now investing resources in the development of managing diversity and equal opportunities. What is it that has spurred such household names as, for example, the British Broadcasting Corporation, Grand Metropolitan, Littlewoods, the Midland Bank and British Petroleum to invest in the promotion of equal opportunities? The triggers for action are various, but the organisations all share the belief that strategic action in this area is good for business.

Grand Metropolitan, a multinational company with fairly auto-nomous subsidiaries, state that:

> . . . cultural diversity creates an environment in which individual differences are evident, different means to an end are respected, and the talents and attributes of people from different backgrounds and heritages are fully valued, utilised and developed. Such an environment, we believe, can achieve superior business results.

Their goals may be summarised as follows:

- to create an organisation where cultural diversity is a driving force, making us more effective with each other and with our customers
- to improve our competitiveness by reflecting in our employee population the diversity that exists in the marketplace
- to enhance . . . management and human resource systems and practices to support the development of all employees. (Greenslade, 1991)

Grand Metropolitan's approach is long term. To achieve its objectives the following are regarded as key: executive responsibility and commitment, education and training, individual accountability, and monitoring.

Grand Metropolitan is only one of many organisations whose anti-discrimination initiatives are driven from a business perspective. Such organisations are aware of the consequences of not taking these issues seriously:

> . . . feelings of inadequacy, powerlessness and hopelessness culminate in the alienation of the black labour force. This alienation manifests itself in increased sickness and absence, apathy, anger, indifference and diminished output. These symptoms are often cited as the cause rather than the effect of racist employment practices. Every employer . . . seeking to maximise the performance of its labour force, should adopt fair and equitable employment practices. If nothing else, it makes good economic sense to ensure that the labour force feels, and is seen to be, fairly treated. (Agbolegbe, 1984)

The precise business case for attending to discrimination in organisations such as Grand Metropolitan, the BBC and Littlewoods is organisationally specific; but they all invest in managing diversity and equal opportunities because:

- women and ethnic minorities are important customer groups
- women and ethnic minorities are an under-represented and under-utilised human resource
- legislation requires it
- it is a factor in maintaining competitive advantage.

These points are the key factors in ensuring that strategic thinkers over the next decade will not be able to ignore questions of discrimination and disadvantage. To explore these questions, this chapter focuses on discrimination and disadvantage in relation to gender and ethnicity, those groups most directly affected by legislation; this is a limitation, in that many measures adopted by organisations cover a wider range of groups than space allows for here. The chapter firstly considers the extent of the problem, then what triggers action, and finally the steps organisations take to manage diversity and equal opportunities issues.

The Extent of the Problem – How Discrimination is Institutionalised

Discrimination is built into organisational life at key stages in the employment process: recruitment and selection, reward systems, working time, equal treatment, training, promotion, redundancy. Personnel systems and procedures, as well as other structures and practices within organisations, embed barriers to the creation of equal opportunities.

Recruitment and Selection Processes

Good practice is first to produce a *job description* from an analysis of the requirements of a job. The job description should be used to produce a *person specification* identifying the qualifications, skills and experience which indicates a person's *suitability*. Jenkins (1985) distinguishes between *suitability*, the technical ability to do the job, and *acceptability*, the likelihood that the person will fit into the organisation without creating problems. If the criterion used is that of *acceptability*, then discrimination is more likely to arise, thus leading to a perpetuation of the existing horizontal and vertical occupational segregation.

Many employers do use the criterion of acceptability and thus reduce the chances of ethnic minority members: 'We are high class store and it may affect the selling'; 'I'd like to take him but what would my customers think?' Work experience providers stipulate that they only want a white trainee, or they refuse to interview a youngster with an Asian name. One study showed that at least one-third of private employers discriminated against Asian applicants, Afro-Caribbean applicants or both and found that figures for employer discrimination were no lower than in 1973 and 1974 (Brown and Gay, 1985). The Commission for Racial Equality (CRE) has carried out studies in accountancy, graduate employment, journalism and law, where they found that both direct and indirect discrimination still operate both at the point of entry and in progression (Brown, 1992). Where organisations allow acceptability to take precedence over suitability, they allow discriminatory practices to be perpetuated.

The extension of the internal labour market via 'word of mouth' recruitment methods is likely to discriminate indirectly against under-represented groups. Where ethnic minority workers or women are under-represented in the workforce, this method of recruitment will perpetuate the existing composition of the workforce, and may be unlawful. Moves towards greater informality in recruitment will perpetuate such practices.

Recent studies (Collinson, Knights and Collinson, 1990) have shown how sex-typing is still prevalent. One argument runs that it is not so much that women are rejected, rather that they are recruited for specific work tasks offering few career opportunities. This fails to recognise that sex-typing and rejection go hand in hand. This is indicated in the following quotes: 'Men could do the job but the starting salary is too low. You'd never get a bloke to do it'; 'There's girls out there who are more intelligent than anyone in the branch . . . but they've no drive, which suits us fine. We rely on people's inertia since our salaries are not very attractive'. Women's perceived lack of ambition and higher turnover in clerical work was explained not as a consequence of the rates of pay, low status, tiered recruitment, tight supervision, mundane work, and limited autonomy and career opportunities, but because they were women. Thus by focusing solely on the consequences of the vicious circles of job segregation, namely female turnover rates, selectors' rationalisation drew on 'partial truths' that sought to deny their own and the company's part in reinforcing these vicious circles.

Agencies are often used by organisations to carry out initial sifting of applications and they may also be agents of discrimination. The instructions received by agencies may not reflect the criteria of *suitability* through the use of appropriate job descriptions and person specifications, rather agencies may act on instructions which may be potentially discriminatory. The CRE regularly receives evidence of employers applying pressure and giving instructions to discriminate to private sector recruitment agencies. Racial discrimination by employers and training providers was also experienced by careers staff when trying to place ethnic minority young people in jobs and training schemes.

Personnel/human resource managers might reasonably be considered the guardians of the recruitment process. Yet a number of studies have shown that their lack of influence may put women, ethnic minorities and people with disabilities at a disadvantage. A study of 45 companies revealed the frequent failure of personnel managers to ensure implementation of formalised practices because they were either too remote at corporate level or confined to the subordinate service role at operational level. The way that discriminatory practices of line managers are ignored is illustrated by a corporate personnel manager: 'I can honestly say that if women have the right drive and ambition, there really shouldn't be anything to stop them. I'd be the first to say if I thought there was any sort of discrimination . . . of course we have individuals who are prejudiced against women or colour, but we can't do anything about that.' A more senior colleague elaborated the passive policy of the head office (of an insurance company), 'There are quite patently one or two of the bigger branches . . . where I think the manager isn't quite so keen on training female sales inspectors. But I wouldn't be looking to press because if the manager's not committed I don't feel it's the right environment for a young lady to succeed' (Collinson *et al*, 1990). Such paternalism is frequently used as a reason not to face up to discriminatory practices and is indicative of both managerial weakness and lack of motivation to tackle the underlying problem. Decentralisation, devolvement and deformalisation is likely to perpetuate the condoning of bad practices.

Rewards Systems

Differential pay rates for men and women and the vertical segregation which affects both women and members of ethnic minority groups mean that the patterns of segregation build in financial disadvantage. Typically, pay systems for women contain shorter grading structures so ensuring that women do not have the same earning potential as men, and concentrate them at the bottom of scales. In the public services, for example, fewer additional payments are added to basic pay when women are the majority of the labour force, and even where equally eligible, women do not receive payments to the same extent as men. Legal pressures to combat non-discriminatory pay systems are permeating managerial consciousness very slowly.

The secrecy and informality which characterise the methods used for assessing performance and of deciding pay increases encourage notions of *acceptability* to come to the fore in such an informal context and disadvantage both women and members of ethnic minority groups. Industrial relations and organisational change, such as the shift to decentralised bargaining and the increasing adoption of merit pay would seem to bode ill for women's opportunities.

Working Time

Working time is one of the key barriers to women. Research indicates that established patterns of working time might act to inhibit processes of desegregation (Horrell and Rubery, 1991). If women are to be encouraged to return to the labour market once they have had children, then working time patterns may have to be adjusted; for example, flexi-time and mornings only are some of the preferred patterns of working for women returners (Healy and Kraithman, 1989 and 1992). But in the United Kingdom, the 'long-hours culture' links commitment with the numbers of hours that an employee is present. There is an uneven fit with such cultures and the need for flexibility of a person with family responsibilities, resulting in conflict between the organisation's policies and practices and the employees' personal needs. In these circumstances, it is clearly men who will reach higher positions. But Britain tends to be unique in that men work very long hours; this experience is not common in Europe, as can be seen in Table 8.1. The regulation of hours worked may be the single most effective means of promoting equality at the workplace; the Maastricht Treaty's proposed 48-hour maximum working week is a first step.

Table 8.1 *Men working long and women working short hours in Europe 1988*

	Men working 46+ hours %	Women working part time %
Luxembourg	10.7	15.3
Netherlands	12.5	57.5
Federal Republic of Germany	14.6	30.6
Denmark	16.5	41.4
Belgium	14.2	23.4
France	19.6	23.7
Italy	20.3	10.4
Spain	19.4	13.0
Portugal	24.0	10.5
Ireland	33.2	17.1
Greece	39.3	10.3
United Kingdom	41.8	44.0
Europe as whole	23.1	28.0

Source Eurostat 1990

Equal Treatment

On a day-to-day basis, the attitudes outlined above translate into managerial style: it is difficult to overestimate the depth and complexity of the ways in which the dominant forms of sexuality and race are produced and reproduced, not just in the broad structuring of organisations, but also in their minutiae. Equal treatment is in many ways problematic to handle as organisational social behaviour has a nebulous quality that is hard to pin down into procedures; it is also linked to the contradictory position in which women, ethnic minority groups and people with disabilities find themselves, of being both highly *visible* and *invisible* at the same time.

Humour

The notion of humour is a critical dimension in the way people are

174

treated at work. Humour is used to form relationships, trust and contact. It may also, however, be used as a way of widening the differences in the working relationship between men and women and between white people and minorities. Humour has within it a power dimension which, when used in a racist and/or sexist way, can not only undermine recipients, but also make it difficult for them to defend themselves without appearing humourless and, worse, confirming that they are not 'one of us'.

Harassment
The outcome of visibility may have negative consequences. There is now an increasing awareness that certain kinds of behaviour are unacceptable and may be deemed racial or sexual harassment. The quality of individuals' working lives is affected by the treatment they receive at work from their superiors and their co-workers. If that treatment involves racist jokes, name calling and bullying, or unwelcome sexual attention, insults or ridicule of a sexual nature, then the quality of working life is inevitably degraded and this may lead to stress, absence, or quitting the firm. Worse, the victims may feel that to be accepted they have to condone this kind of behaviour.

Tolerance by employers of racist and sexist behaviour has led to its perpetuation. This has made it difficult for victims of such behaviour to be sure that the reporting of incidents would be taken seriously. Effective policy development on racial and sexual harassment is a step towards ensuring that the dominant culture is shifted to make clear the unacceptability of such treatment. Good practice is to set guidelines that inform staff on the unacceptability of both racial and sexual harassment and indicate the kind of steps that must be taken if incidents occur. But, procedures setting out what racial or sexual behaviour is and linking these with disciplinary procedures, are only a minimum requirement. Racist and sexist behaviour may be so much a part of the institutional value system that attempts to change it may meet with hostile or indifferent responses that undermine the formal systems for producing equality. Training and education programmes on the nature of racist or sexist behaviour are required to enable an understanding of the kind of behaviour which is unacceptable to an organisation.

Invisibility
The invisibility of potentially disadvantaged groups is complex. Women and people from ethnic minorities may not be actively involved in the white, male culture. Lunch-time activities may centre on the bar

or male sporting activities when only the dominant group will be invited. Organisational politicking may be done here or after hours, at a time when those with family responsibilities may not be present. Their invisibility threads through the social intercourse of the organisation; views may not be asked, or when proffered may not be heard, as they are expected to be of little value. The dominant prejudices in our society act as listening screens and filters so that the views of women or minorities apparently may not be heard, but the views may then be repeated, unattributed, by a white male and given value by dominant group members.

Language

Language is an important reflection of invisibility. Some organisations still adopt a style of communication, both written and verbal, which implies that its audience is male. The male 'he' may be used as a generic term to cover he and she without an understanding that the message of this exclusive style of communication is one that marginalises part of the workforce. Similarly, in training exercises, language and imagery may serve to marginalise women, members of minority ethnic groups and people with disabilities. They may be excluded from examples or included only in stereotypical roles. Lack of sensitivity may be at the heart of discriminatory language practices, and with only a little thought this can be effectively eradicated. An example of the use of language as symptomatic of a wider pattern of discrimination was shown in the 14-month sex discrimination case brought against British Gas by Hilary Williams. Ms Williams was demoted from her £45,000 a year post following privatisation and restructuring. She was the only woman at her level and the only person to be demoted, despite the fact that the job had not substantially changed, and when the news was broken to Ms Williams by her superior, he said, 'Thank God you've taken it like a man, even though you are the wrong shape'. Ms Williams received aggravated damages and British Gas was ordered to reinstate her.

Double-speak

Cockburn (1991) argues that men engage in a coherent and consistent discourse of gender differentiation:

> On the one hand, women were described as more diligent and industrious: 'you can rely on the girls, they work harder', they were *nicer* than men in middle management, women were less autocratic, gave orders more 'sweetly', 'they charm the birds out of the bloody trees', they had

more sympathy with staff feelings and related better to the public. Men also indicated a repertoire of negative representations of women and, significantly, they were criticism of women *only* in relation to authority. Two themes emerge, firstly that women are not capable of authority and secondly, that they turn into nasty people when in authority. On the first count, women 'lack a bit of judgment, and get a bit emotional', 'are not cut out for it', find it difficult to be ruthless enough and so on. On the second count, women in top jobs are 'bossy', 'pushy', 'absolute bastards'.

Cockburn showed how the mythology perpetuates itself by the view among junior men that certain women managers (with whom they had no direct contact) were 'tartars', 'ferocious', 'got a kick out of lording it over men'. Such views are not covert and as such may indirectly prevent women putting themselves forward. Or they may directly be discouraged by such attitudes as, 'you wouldn't want to change your nice little personality, would you?' The cost of career development therefore, it is implied, is no less than a fundamental personality change.

To overcome such entrenched patterns of behaviour is a considerable challenge since attitudes are the product of experiences both inside and outside the workforce. An organisation's decision to deal with discrimination is the outcome of the impact of certain triggers.

The Triggers for Action

Organisations are provoked into installing policies to deal with discrimination by: legislation, changes in the labour market, pressure from employees, management initiatives and organisational change.

Legislation

Legislation is a key reason for developing a policy on discrimination. In the UK the Race Relations Act, the Sex Discrimination Act, the Equal Pay Act, and their accompanying Codes of Practice must all be complied with. In 1989 the CRE conducted a survey on the extent of compliance with the Code of Practice for the elimination of racial discrimination and the promotion of equality of opportunity in employment. Their findings were that the level of awareness of the Code was relatively low. Of a sample of 899 employers, only 18 per cent had actually read through the Code. As might be expected, size of the organisation was a significant variable; the large organisations had a greater level of awareness than the medium and small.

The extent to which the law is a trigger for change is variable. The discussion on compliance and awareness of the Codes of Practice, suggests these may be less than intended. The inadequacies of the existing statutes are recognised by the Equal Opportunities Commission (EOC) and the CRE and they are campaigning for their strengthening. Nevertheless, it was found that the law is a significant moral and instrumental pressure on management thinking and policy; even where there had been minimal movement, there appeared to be calculations about the potential costs of non-compliance (Jewson *et al*, 1990).

Decisions from the European Court have also influenced the priority given to equal opportunities issues, for example the Equal Pay (Equal Value Amendment) and the Barber case on pensions have had far-reaching effects on British equality legislation and practice.

Labour Market

It might be argued that the labour market is a stronger trigger for change – where firms experience a labour or skills shortage, they may turn to equal opportunities practices in order to resolve the shortages. The 'demographic time-bomb', the decline in the number of young people coming on to the labour market, became part of the human resource vocabulary in the late 1980s, and it turned attention to the potentially under-utilised resource of women returners. The service sector of the economy has been most progressive in introducing equal opportunities policies; in fact it is those organisations which already employ large numbers of women and tend to see such policies as a significant contribution to tackling labour shortages and to human resource planning. Industrial employers are reported to be lagging behind in their commitment to equal opportunities, although US-owned companies were reported to be ahead of comparable UK-based companies (Cockman, Bacon and Woodrow 1989).

Apart from active measures by some firms to recruit younger people, most small and medium-sized enterprises take their labour supply as they find it; there is limited experimentation with alternative sources of labour and a general lack of overt equal opportunities policies.

Pressure from Employees

Pressure from trade unions and employees influences the direction of equal opportunities policies and the extent to which equal opportunities reach the bargaining agenda. On average, the three critical aspects of policies – monitoring, positive action and discipline – were four times more likely to occur in union-agreed policies than in those which had been arbitrarily imposed by an employer; also, where equal opportunities committees were established there appeared to be markedly more discussion of equality issues than in other unionised companies where no such committee existed. Furthermore, when workplace representatives are trained in equal opportunities matters, there is a positive effect on the 'equality process' (Ball, 1990).

However, the level of resistance within organisations to taking equal opportunities issues seriously is evident throughout an organisation and does not exclude trade unionists. Male shop stewards as individuals may not believe in equal pay or equal opportunities and may act against the interests of women on specific issues, whatever their union's policy on equality might be. To quote a female officer: 'Sometimes I'm completely amazed at the level of ignorance amongst male trade unionists. You tend to think that the women's movement has been going a long time and a lot of issues have had media attention – issues that strike you as crucial, that have been really well aired. They haven't even thought about them. You need to sit down and rationally talk things through – go round and educate branch officials, showing how certain things affect women. Then they might just see' (Watson, 1988). This also highlights the significance of involving those most likely to benefit from the policies. In fact, where there are female or black trade union officials, equality bargaining will make the greatest progress (*Labour Research*, 1990; Heery and Kelly, 1988).

Management Initiatives

Organisational initiatives often follow from an interaction of the above three factors, together with a belief in the commercial benefits to be gained from being an equal opportunity employer.

The need to be seen to be representative by customers (for both commercial and political reasons) also may trigger proactive approaches. The power relationship between buyer and supplier may be the spur for suppliers to take equal opportunities more seriously, through a form of contract compliance (see p184). The need for such initiatives becomes clear when it is realised that profit margins may be cut to the bone at the bottom of the subcontracting chain; in the clothing industry, for example, many entrepreneurs have dispensed with all or have kept only a core of factory-based workers, preferring to shift the risks of subcontracted orders on to the shoulders of a home-working labour force (often female and minority).

A more public approach has been adopted by the signatories to Opportunity 2000, a 'Business in the Community' initiative in the UK.

This aims to increase opportunities for women, is funded by industry and is grounded in business rather than social arguments for increased equality. Opportunity 2000 recognises the role of the expert in heightening opportunities and offers information and assistance to bring about more opportunities for women. By becoming an Opportunity 2000 employer, an organisation agrees to:

- Develop 'challenging but achievable goals' based on an assessment of each organisation's current situation and future needs
- Make a public statement of commitment to the organisation's specific Opportunity 2000 goals
- Publish progress at agreed intervals.

Already a large number (over 100 in May 1992) of organisations are signatories to this initiative, and in many ways it is an ambitious and far-reaching approach to the problem of women's lack of opportunities. The contention is that the success of the initiative will depend on four key issues:

1. The demonstration of commitment from the top
2. Behaviour change
3. Building ownership
4. Making the investment.

Opportunity 2000 is partly predicated on the notion of labour shortages; its initiative may need to be strengthened to cope with economic downturns.

The early stages of Opportunity 2000 indicated that the campaign had developed a more strategic approach and had raised awareness of best practices in organisations. Despite the recession, organisations like the National Westminster Bank and Rank Xerox have increased their proportion of women managers since Opportunity 2000. National Westminster's increase is from 16.3 per cent to 18.1 per cent and they are aiming for 33 per cent by the year 2000; Rank Xerox have increased their 10 per cent of women in senior management in 1990 to 15 per cent in 1992 and have a target of 25 per cent by 1995. The goals that organisations set themselves was the aspect of the initiative which perhaps most encouraged confidence yet, despite the above examples, these goals often lacked rigour and detail.

Organisational Change

Organisational restructuring in the 1980s and '90s has been characterised by various forms of decentralisation: the adoption of tight-loose, multi-divisional forms; opted out schools; hospital trusts; privatisation; competitive tendering. These moves create greater autonomy for line managers and a greater role for line management in human resource management. In the 1970s the emphasis of human resource management was on 'consistency', 'set procedures', 'rules and regulations', and these are all important aspects of good practice in equal opportunities. However, by the late '80s the emphasis was on 'our organisational culture', 'mission', 'customer requirements', and 'commitment'.

The tendency toward deformalisation, decentralisation and the devolution of management responsibilities can run counter to equal opportunities developments, which often rest on principles of formalisation and centralisation. The down-sizing that accompanies much restructuring also does not provide a climate conducive to raising equal opportunities in the organisation's strategic priorities.

The globalisation of markets has been one factor forcing organisational change and it also has an impact on human resource management. Thus, US-based multinational companies may take equal opportunities more seriously than their UK-based competitors; and European social action programmes, despite Britain's opting out at Maastricht, are influencing human resource strategies of international companies. Where organisations are not convinced, trade unions will be putting social chapter 'rights' (relating to equal benefits to part-timers, maximum working hours and further maternity provisions) on to the bargaining agenda.

The above discussion indicates the triggers for change and the impact of restructuring and globalisation. Before turning to the actions organisations can take to develop equal opportunities, organisations should recognise their current approach to managing equal opportunities.

Analysing the Organisation's Current Position

An organisation can analyse its current position by auditing its existing practices in order to find out what needs to be done in its own organisational context. Here an equal opportunities typology is presented in order to help readers classify their own or others' organisations. This is an analytical construct to enhance understanding; it is not a set of inevitable stages through which an organisation must move in order to develop. It enables an organisation to distinguish between the different approaches to equal opportunities and to distinguish between approaches that aim to *reduce* levels of discrimination and those which aim to *solve* particular recruitment problems. The typology is useful as a snapshot at a moment in time. The four types of equal opportunity organisation are set out below.

1. Negative Organisation

A negative organisation will not have an equal opportunities policy nor will it have knowledge of legislative requirements; it will make no claims to provide equal opportunities and the institutional belief will tend to be that they are not necessary as discrimination is not practised. Alternatively, the negative organisation makes a conscious choice *to* discriminate. Such choices may relate to employer taste or to a particular perception of reality; for example, where an employer believes that women have lower productivity than men, they will only hire them at a lower wage.

2. Minimalist/partial Organisation

A minimalist organisation will have an espoused equal opportunities policy. It will tend to focus on informality as the method of management. Its recruitment methods will emphasise *acceptability* rather than *suitability*, and equal opportunities will have a low priority and profile. There is no attempt to assess outcomes in this kind of organisation.

3. Compliant Organisation

The compliant organisation will take a more self-conscious and professional approach to equal opportunities. It will be careful that it fulfils its legal obligations; it will have developed a formal approach backed by training. Policies and procedures will reflect 'good practice' as set out by the statutory agencies and will focus particularly on recruitment. Assessment of outcomes will be partial. Equal opportunities take their place alongside other strategic developments and their level of priority will depend on their significance to the organisation at a particular moment. The focus is likely to be on the contribution equal opportunities principles make to solving labour shortage problems rather than on resolving problems of discrimination.

4. Comprehensive Proactive Organisation

The proactive organisation will have a dynamic approach to equal opportunities. It will have many of the characteristics of the compliant organisation. The proactive organisation will carefully assess outcomes in relation to a workforce audit and develop future strategies accordingly. Positive action approaches will be a feature of the proactive organisation. Equal opportunities retain a high priority alongside other strategic developments. Resolving problems of discrimination will be of equal importance as the labour market dimension of equal opportunities. The implementation of equal opportunities practices will be 'with enthusiasm'. The organisation will be able to measure the outputs of its equal opportunities policies both quantitatively and qualitatively.

Removing the Obstacles to Fair Treatment

The proactive organisation first aims to remove the obstacles to fair treatment – the points at which discrimination is institutionalised, as outlined earlier in the chapter – and it will consider the role of training and development, and other positive action strategies, such as child-care, contract compliance (see below), special provisions and targets as a means of assessing progress.

Training and Development

The Development Dimension
Development is one of the key processes that can be used to dent the entrenched vertical segregation of women and minorities. Women receive less training than men. This is partly related to the negative consequences of horizontal segregation for women; since female dominated occupational groups are less likely to be offered employer-sponsored training than male groups, women are more likely than men to finance their own training in order to enter particular occupations. In the UK this leads to a significant gender gap in access to training for 16–19 year old employees (Clarke, 1991) and it has been shown that discriminatory practices on the grounds of race also operate for this age group (Cross *et al*, 1990). Training for adult employees is very unevenly distributed over the workforce – highly qualified full-time employees in high-level, non-manual occupations in large workplaces are much more likely to have received recent job-related training than poorly qualified, part-time manual employees in small workplaces. Although women are more likely than men to be employed in non-manual occupations, and therefore have been given access to job-related training, a number of

other factors mean that within a given occupation they are generally at a disadvantage relative to men. The key factor identified by Clarke (1991) is part-time employment.

In considering the 'development dimension', it is important to confront the views already paraphrased that women are not career oriented, that they do not want to 'get on'. One of the dominant outcomes of studies of women returners in the UK is the very high expressed demand for training (Healy and Kraithman, 1989 and 1992; Hardill and Green, 1990). These studies also indicated a high level of preparedness of the samples to retrain and a strong belief that employers should provide training. For women returners, there were anticipated constraints in relation to taking up training provision; predictably, these centred on childcare facilities and costs, hours of training and geographical location. The recession of the early '90s is not conducive to a reappraisal of training provision for all but the most visionary of employers.

The Awareness Dimension

This dimension of training can also be used as part of an organisation's wider corporate strategy for equality. Training cannot prevent employees from acting unlawfully, but it can raise their awareness of the issues and enable them to recognise unacceptable behaviour and understand their role in change. The danger is that an organisation may introduce equal opportunities training, and then feel that they have 'done equal opportunities' rather than recognising the limitations and ongoing nature of the training role. Nevertheless, training is an important change agent and, used as part of a strategic approach, it can be very powerful.

The compliant organisation will ensure such training takes place, if only to ensure that its practices are in line with legal requirements. Much equal opportunities training centres on legal requirements and the main focus is recruitment and selection. The proactive organisation will take into account equal treatment in the way that people are employed; so that anti-harassment and anti-racist training are increasingly forming part of the agenda.

The Positive Action Dimension

This dimension of training and development tackles segregation more overtly, which enables an organisation to identify an under-repre-sented group and provide training to enable the group to develop within the organisation. For example, women are sent on management courses, courses are provided for black journalists. So, in Britain it is lawful to take positive action to improve the selection chances of under-represented groups. However, unlike the US, it is unlawful in Britain to practice positive discrimination at the point of selection: for example it is unlawful to specify that a post is to be filled by a woman unless genuine occupational qualifications require it.

Positive Action

Positive action is wider than training and refers to efforts to remove obstacles to the free operation of the labour market. It aims to promote free and equal competition among individuals; for example, crèche facilities at the workplace, language training, extended leave arrangements, targets, and advertising campaigns designed to reassure candidates from disadvantaged groups that their applications will be judged on their merits.

Childcare Provision
This has received much attention in recent years. Evidence suggests that where workplace childcare facilities exist, women will increase their participation in the labour market (Healy and Kraithman, 1989).

Special Provisions
In relation to the personal and religious needs of people from ethnic minorities, these are important aspects of positive action. Good practices includes provision for extended leave, time for religious observances, sensitivity at times of Christian celebration and the provision of alternatives.

Images
Organisations are learning the value of directly addressing the diversity of people who make up their customer base and their potential employees. The multi-ethnic base of advertisements for British Airways, Benneton and Burger King are good examples of customer-directed advertisements. The images presented in a number of recruiting adverts directly target particular sectors of the population. British Rail begins a recruiting advertisement for trackwork with the slogan, 'It's only man's work because women rarely apply', and the advertisement includes a photograph of four women on trackwork. The Metropolitan Police have used positive images in an attempt to increase the proportion of ethnic minorities in the Force. By adopting a business-

driven positive action approach in their advertising policy, the organisations are trying to widen their customer base and the pool from which they recruit, and further they are avoiding the alienation and anger of the targeted groups.

Contract Compliance
This is also used by buyers to ensure certain standards of behaviour from their suppliers. Contracts frequently include a clause binding suppliers to comply with all statutory regulations. In equal opportunities this form of negative compliance may be considered of little value, since statutes are not mentioned; even 'negative organisations' may believe they are complying with statutory duties since they know no better. A more interesting opportunity lies in the 'quality movement'. Many companies will only deal with suppliers which meet specified standards, and there is no reason why these should not include equal opportunities compliance. Contract compliance can form an important part of a proactive approach to equal opportunities either as part of, or apart from, the quality approach. Littlewoods, for example, has adopted this approach and argues that it has enhanced its standing with customers and workforce.

Targets and Objective Setting
These are increasingly seen as an important part of positive action. An example of *targeting* is the case of a high street retail store which set percentage targets by grade for the proportion of women and black people. Cockburn describes the steps taken to achieve these targets:

> First, the recruitment process was to be rid of bias. Second, some practical impediments to women's advancement were removed, for instance the 'geographical mobility' requirement for store managers. New criteria were inserted into job appraisal. Women were boldly made 50 per cent of trainees for store manager posts. But above all managers with responsibility for recruitment and promotion were instructed to 'think women'. It was emphasised that women had all the competence of male colleagues . . . Besides, and here a sort of positive sex-stereotyping was introduced, women were now represented as bringing much needed feminine qualities to business. Positive action was agreed by the chief executive and some influential personnel managers. (Cockburn, 1991)

Whilst the targeting policy did show benefits for high-ranking white women, other groups benefited less.

An alternative to targets, is individual *objective setting*. Grand Metropolitan is making equal opportunities a cash-linked objective for every senior manager on a worldwide basis. Individual objectives are set by the organisation which include appropriate departmental representation for people of colour, the attendance of at least one training event on the issue and the arrangement and sponsoring of an educational event to promote cultural diversity. Making equal opportunities part of an appraisal or merit pay system is a powerful incentive for ensuring the matter gets more than mere lip-service.

Monitoring and Review of Positive Action Programmes

Monitoring and reviewing progress is an essential aspect of good practice. A one-off launch of an equal opportunities policy is not sufficient. Second- and third-phase developments are crucial to build on early success and to review the groups who may not have benefited. Recent developments at British Gas (perhaps influenced by the Williams case, see p.174) illustrate the importance of the second wave. Despite existing policies, such as career break schemes, flexible working, enhanced maternity leave and pay, and a 30 per cent childcare allowance, British Gas were concerned that women made up only 10 per cent of their management grades compared with the 28 per cent in the total workforce. 'The culture was seen by women as strongly male, sexual harassment was identified as a problem by some women employees, many managers failed to see women as equally promotable as men' (*Equal Opportunities Review*, 1992). The measures which British Gas have adopted include the appointment of a director of equal opportunities, a new policy and procedure to eliminate harassment, a training package for all managers to improve equal opportunities awareness, and equal opportunities performance objectives for managers. The example is interesting in that it shows how certain measures may facilitate women's entry and retention in the labour market, whereas different measures are needed to ensure their development.

Reviews of equal opportunities developments need to be made in the context of general strategic developments, and need to assess honestly the influence of the barriers to recruitment, development and equal treatment within an organisation. Such reviews also need to take account of the impact of changing strategies elsewhere in the business.

Conclusions

What does all this mean to the business strategist? It indicates that the high level of competitiveness which management is actively seeking may be impaired by the inefficient use of its human resource and by ignoring its customer base. Inefficiency and unfairness operate at the point of recruitment, in the way that people are treated, in working practices, and in opportunities for promotion. This chapter has shown how discrimination and disadvantage can permeate the whole of an organisation and that it is far from a marginal issue. Current organisational trends may act to the detriment of disadvantaged groups, but not inevitably. International influence may act as a positive force to good practice; and far-sighted dynamic management working with trade unions and equal opportunities specialists can ensure that their existing and future labour force is not restricted by unfair notions of acceptability.

The production of equal opportunities policies is not sufficient to move towards eliminating discrimination and disadvantage. The developments that have been made have often been the outcome of external pressures, such as legislation but more forcible has been the labour shortage argument. At a time of recession, this argument loses its persuasiveness, and the developments cease or slow down. The affected parties watch, and not without cynicism, as their interests move down the organisation's priorities. It is important that equal opportunity issues are seen as part of the dynamic context of the organisation's business objectives and that policy development is sufficiently flexible to shift and adapt its structures to organisational change. The business arguments outlined in this paper become more pertinent during a recession. Efforts to gain employee commitment and to enhance customer base will look empty if issues of discrimination and disadvantage are not given some constancy in a perpetually changing environment.

References

Agbolegbe, G (1984) 'The Experience of Black Nurses in the UK', *Race and Employment in the NHS*, Kings Fund, London.

Ball, C (1990) *Trade Unions and Equal Opportunities Employers*, Manufacturing, Science and Finance Union, London.

Brown, C (1992) 'Racial Disadvantage in the Employment Market', in P Braham, A Rattansi and R Skellington, *Racism and Antiracism – inequalities, opportunities and policies*, pp 46–63, Sage/Open University, London.

— and Gay, P (1985) *Racial Discrimination – 17 years after the Act*, quoted in Brown C *op cit*.

Clarke, K (1991) *Women and Training: A Review*, Equal Opportunities Commission Research Unit, Manchester.

Cockburn, C (1991) *In the Way of Women – Men's resistance to sex equality in organisations*, Macmillan, London.

Cockman, Bacon and Woodrow (1989) *Report on an equal opportunities policy and practice survey*, London.

Collinson, D, Knights, D and Collinson, M (1990) *Managing to Discriminate*, Routledge, London.

Cross, M, Wrench, J and Barnett, S (1990) *Ethnic Minorities and the Careers Service – An investigation into processes of assessment and placement*, Report for the Department of Employment by the Centre for Research in Ethnic Relations, University of Warwick, DE Research Paper No 73, London.

Equal Opportunities Review (1992) No 42.

Greenslade, M 'Managing Diversity: Lessons from the United States', *Personnel Management*, Dec 1991, pp 28–32.

Hardill, I and Green, A (1990) *An Examination of Women Returners in Newcastle*, Training Agency, Newcastle.

Healy, G and Kraithman, D (1989) *Women Returners in the North Hertfordshire Labour Market*, Training Agency, Local Economy Research Unit, Hatfield Polytechnic, Hertford.

— (1992) 'Human Resource in Utilisation in the United Kingdom: Forces and Constraints in Relation to Gender', *Paper presented to the 3rd international Human Resource Conference*, Ashridge.

Heery, E and Kelly, J (1988) 'Do Female Representatives Make a Difference?' *Work, Employment and Society*, Vol 3 No 4.

Horrell, S and Rubery, J (1991) 'Gender and Working Time', *Cambridge Journal of Economics*, No 15 (4), Dec.

Jewson, N and Mason, D (1990) *Ethnic Minorities and Employment Practice*, DE Research Paper No 76, HMSO, London.

Labour Research (1990) Dec.

Watson, D (1988) *Managers of Discontent*, Routledge, London.

Part 4

Strategic Thinking and International Developments

9

Competitive Advantage on a Global Scale

John Sykes

Introduction

By now, most senior managers are familiar with what has become the standard way of thinking about competitive advantage. If we apply the standard approach to the clothing industry in the United Kingdom, for example, we come up with an analysis along the following lines. Savile Row tailors, such as Gieves & Hawkes, produce and sell the highest-quality menswear, both made to measure and off the peg, to high-income males at premium prices. Next, the retail chain founded by George Davies, on the other hand, sells fashionable clothes for men and women, mostly bought in from external suppliers, to people in the 25–45 age bracket at specially designed shops throughout the United Kingdom. Gieves & Hawkes sales staff are middle aged and very conservatively dressed, while Next has young staff dressed in a casual style. Both operate within the clothing industry but are positioned very differently within that industry, just as Daimler-Benz and Fiat are, in the car industry. Gieves & Hawkes seeks to achieve and sustain competitive advantage through product, location and service exclusivity in a narrow target market. This enables Gieves & Hawkes to charge premium prices, so achieving very high mark-ups on relatively low sales volumes and hence high levels of profit. Next, on the other hand, aims at a wider market and offers a well-designed fashionable product in a boutique-style ambience with helpful but low-pressure service and displays of merchandise that change frequently. The result was – before Next over extended itself – large sales volumes at reasonable margins and hence high levels of profit. For Next, competitive advantage lies not in exclusivity over a narrow range but in wider coverage and lower costs.

According to this standard approach to analysing competitive advantage, a firm will succeed if its managers build sustainable competitive advantage. The prescriptions are for managers to identify the 'critical success factors' leading to sustainable competitive advantage and then put them in place to succeed. This way of thinking strategically frames the opportunities and the problems that managers have to deal with in such a manner that an individual company is at the centre of attention. Its managers are assumed to have the power to determine its market position, provided that those managers have a realistic understanding of the structure of their market and the kind of competitive advantage that this creates. This way of thinking sounds obvious and convincing, but it is built on a number of assumptions that need to be questioned.

The purpose of this chapter is to surface the assumptions we make when we analyse competitive advantage and derive strategies from such analyses. The chapter begins by refreshing our memories on what the notions of industry structure, competitive advantage, value chains and generic business strategies mean. As we do that we will see how trying to apply these analytical tools turns out to be a tricky business. Things become even trickier when we move the idea of competitive advantage into the international arena. The second section of the chapter examines the underlying reasons for competitiveness at the level of nations rather than individual companies. The implications for companies are examined and the conclusion we reach is that strategic thinking is defective when it frames opportunities and problems with the individual firm at the centre. Every firm is a part of a system or cluster of others and it cannot determine its strategy in isolation from the behaviour of the dynamic system of which it is a part. The third section of this chapter considers the meaning of expressions such as 'global competition' and 'global industries' and explores the implications of globalisation for corporate strategy development.

Formulating a Competitive Strategy

The standardised approach to determining competitive strategy which has become so widespread among Western managers is based on Michael Porter's models of competitive forces, value chains and generic strategies (Porter, 1980 and 1985). Those models prescribe a sequence of steps that lead up to the selection and implementation of a competitive strategy.

Defining the Industry

The first step managers are supposed to take in analysing competitive advantage is that of defining the industry that their firm operates in. An industry or market segment consists of groupings of customers with common requirements and a distinct grouping of competitors supplying products or services that compete directly with each other to meet customer requirements. A distinct industry or market segment is one where rivals must compete for similar kinds of competitive advantage (Porter, 1980).

There is for example a photocopying machine industry where Xerox tries to defend a position of market dominance and Cannon and other mainly Japanese competitors try to erode that position. Some analysts argue, however, that there is no longer a strategically distinct photocopying industry: since photocopying machines have become components in total office reprographic and information storage systems, the more useful industry definition may be 'electronic information and reprographic equipment'.

Thus, drawing boundaries around an industry or segment is a matter of judgement subject to change as technologies and customer requirements alter. Right at the start of the procedure for formulating a competitive strategy we come up against a problem – the basic unit of analysis is a shifting and uncertain one. Suppose, however, that we are able to come up with an acceptable definition of an industry, then the next step in developing a competitive strategy is to analyse the five competitive forces in that industry.

Identifying the Five Competitive Forces

The structure of an industry determines the nature of the competition and the form that sustainable competitive advantage takes. Analysis of current industry structure and identification of how it is changing is therefore vital. And, according to Porter, industry structure is determined by the five competitive forces illustrated in Figure 9.1 (Porter, 1980).

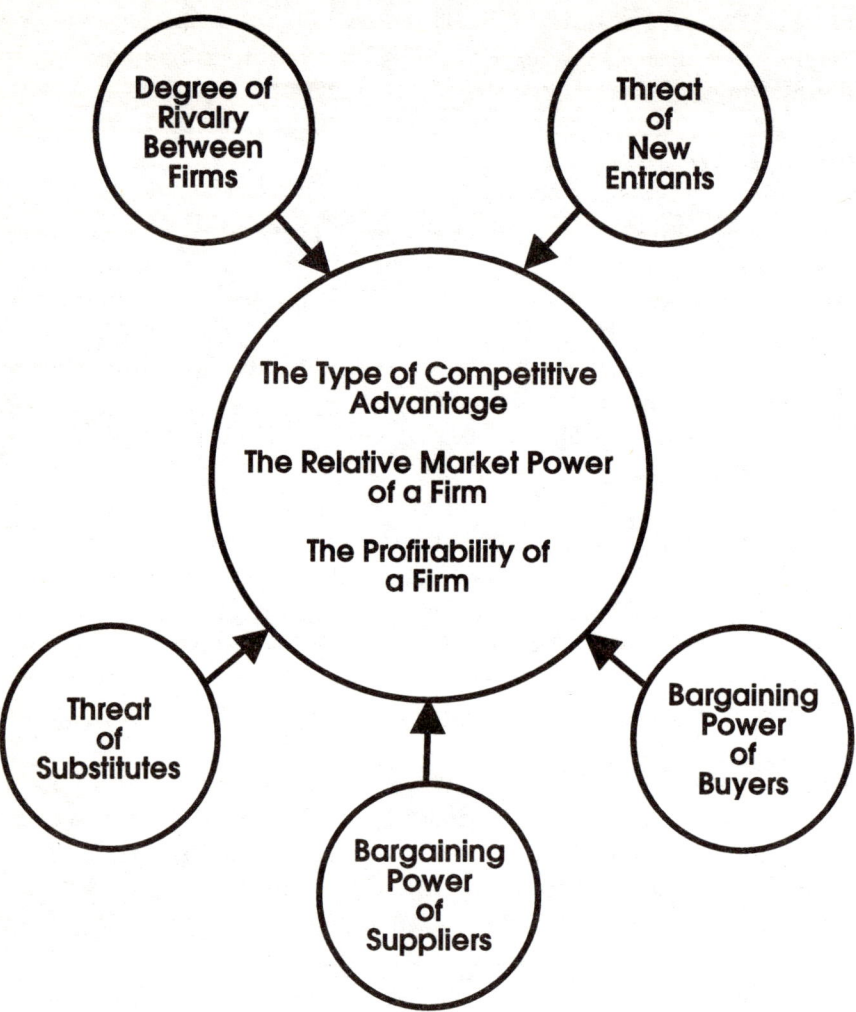

Figure 9.1 *Porter's five market forces*

The profit potential of an industry is limited when:

- New entrants expand the capacity of an industry and through their striving for market share push down margins
- Powerful buyers put pressure on prices, so bargaining away profits
- Powerful suppliers put pressure on costs, so eating up profits
- Fierce competitive rivalry erodes profits by pushing down prices or creating the need for costly advertising or R&D
- Close-substitute products limit the prices that can be charged.

The competitive forces are therefore clearly important because their configuration determines the long-term profitability of an industry and the potential sustainability of the profits of companies operating within that industry. In other words, an understanding of the five forces should help strategists to work out whether an industry is attractive or not, either as a place to be now or as a proposition for the future. The analysis of the five competitive forces is also supposed to indicate how managers may best respond to them and also how they might try to influence those forces in a favourable way.

This reasoning is convincing until confronted by a live example. In the 1980s, Burger King was the butt of many in-jokes among franchised food chain operators. Its outlets, particularly in New York, were poorly managed, profits were reputedly low and although the business was for sale no one wanted to buy it. An analysis of the five competitive forces would have indicated little problem in terms of the bargaining power of buyers or suppliers; new entrants were not likely and there was no immediate threat of substitute products. The main competitive force determining profitability was, therefore, the strength of the market leader, McDonalds. In terms of image and perceived management strength relative to McDonalds, Burger King was simply rated a loser and the five competitive forces analysis would have confirmed its unattractiveness both current and potential. However, Burger King was snapped up by the UK multinational Grand Metropolitan and since that takeover it has performed remarkably well: morale is high and profits are up. The analysis would have led to the conclusion that Burger King was not an attractive business to acquire, but in fact it turned out to be attractive; other factors led to a different outcome.

The problem is that the five forces model is a dangerously static way of understanding how markets work. It may help to describe what the current situation is, but it is of little use in understanding how that situation changes, because it assumes cause and effect links that run in one direction only. To see this, consider an example that Porter gives:

> Industry attractiveness and competitive position can be shaped by a firm. Successful firms not only respond to their environment but also attempt to shape it in their favor. Indeed it is changes in industry structure, or the emergence of new bases for competitive advantage that underlie substantial shifts in competitive position. Japanese firms became international leaders in television sets, for example, on the strength of a shift toward compact, portable sets and the replacement of vacuum tubes with semiconductor technology. One nation's firms supplant another's in international competition when they are in a better position to perceive and respond to such changes. (Porter, 1990, p34)

But, did an interpretation of current industry structure lead to the Japanese shift toward compact television sets? Or did Japanese companies happen to be strong in compacts because of domestic consumers' preference for small sets, at a time when the US market was moving toward two- and three-set households, and new microchip technology was making it possible to produce lighter, more attractive and better-quality sets? If US television manufacturers had been operating in the Japanese market at the time might they have been able to react more quickly to market developments? Cause and effect could run in either direction and in fact could be circular.

To summarise, the model of five competitive forces determining industrial structure may provide a useful way of describing the current state of an industry and it may perhaps give some indication of the current attractiveness of that industry, but as a predictive tool to help companies cope with change, its usefulness is highly questionable.

Selecting the Generic Strategy

Continuing with the standard approach, the analysis of the structure of an industry is said to enable managers to identify the nature of that sustainable competitive advantage which will allow them to cope better than their competitors with the five forces and so achieve above-average profitability. According to Porter there are just two routes to choose from to achieve sustainable competitive advantage: low cost and differentiation. When combined with the scope or range of a firm's chosen activities these lead to four generic strategies:

- Broad low cost across a whole industry
- Focus low cost in some industry niche
- Broad differentiation across a whole industry
- Focus differentiation in some industry niche.

The low-cost strategies are based on efficiency – the ability to design, produce and market a given product with fewer resources than the competitors. Differentiation, on the other hand, is more about effectiveness – providing a unique product or service, superior to that of the competitors in terms of quality, special features or after-sales service. Lower cost translates into higher returns at the same price as the competitors, while differentiation allows a firm to command a premium price that leads to higher profits on the same cost base as competitors. Porter's advice on generic strategies is very precise – successful firms are those that make a clear choice. They choose either low cost or differentiation and they avoid getting stuck in the middle – success flows from an 'either/or' choice.

But, getting stuck in the middle in this sense, is exactly what Japanese manufacturing companies have been doing for some years now, much to the dismay of their international rivals. They make attractive, differentiated products and manage at the same time to be the lowest-cost operators. In most industries, firms will not survive unless they are able to combine the skills of differentiation with the ability to keep costs to the levels of industry leaders (Hendry, 1990). The simplicity of the 'either/or' choice of a standardised generic strategy is appealing but it really does not help managers very much to be advised to go for low cost or differentiation when both are necessary for survival.

Returning to the procedure for formulating competitive strategy, once managers have identified the right generic strategy, they must then identify where costs should be cut, how products should be differentiated, or how markets should be better targeted. For this purpose, Porter has developed the simple but powerful concept of the value chain.

Specifying the Value Chain

The value chain (see Figure 9.2) groups a company's activities so that managers can identify:

- Where they can most effectively reduce costs; and
- How each activity can contribute effectively to differentiated needs.

Figure 9.2 shows how inputs flow through a firm, how value is added at each stage, and how outputs and profits finally emerge. Those activities that build up buyer value can be divided into:

- Primary activities of production, marketing, delivery and servicing of the product
- Support activities of providing purchased inputs, human resources and some combination of technologies
- Activities that constitute the firm's infrastructure such as general management and finance.

While all these activities add value, some are likely to be more critical than others. If managers analyse the flows through their firm in this way, they should be able to identify where the critical links are and operate on those. Furthermore, managers need to ensure not only that each link in the chain is making a full contribution, but that linkages

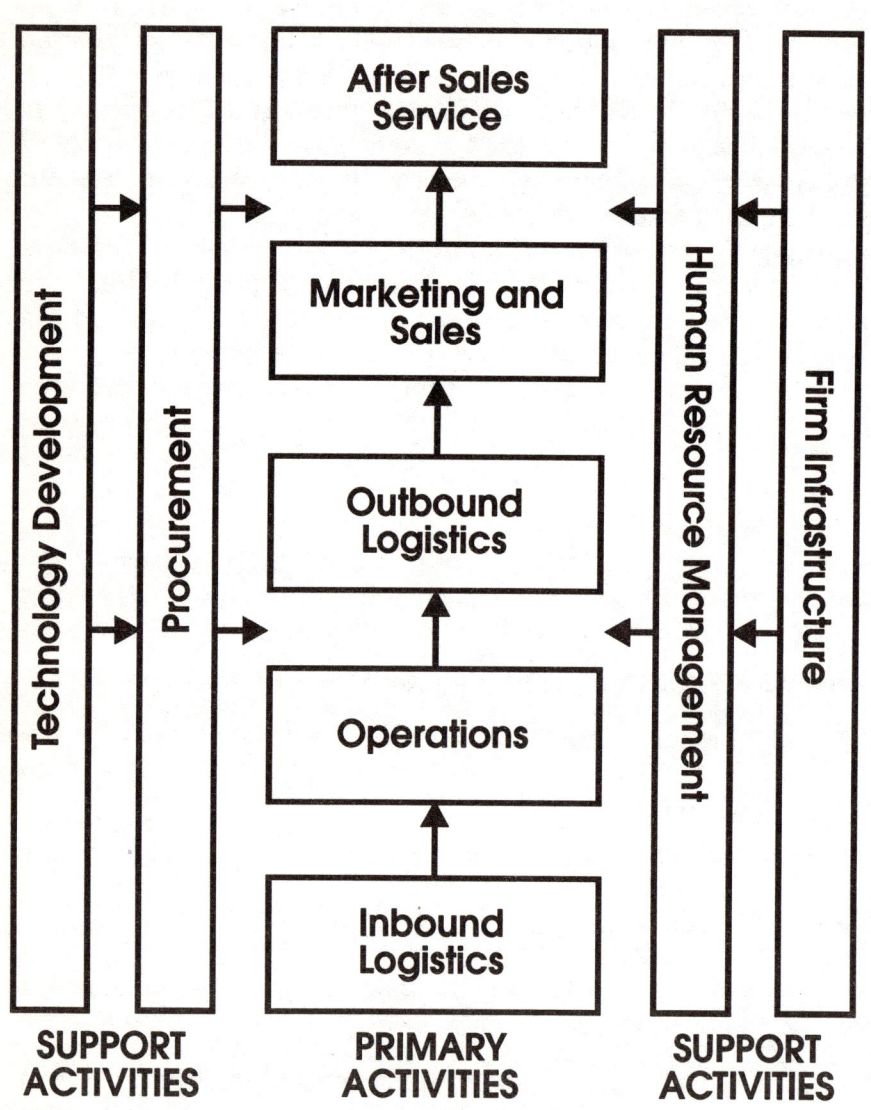

Figure 9.2 *The firm's value chain*

between each activity are working in the best interests of customers and of the whole organisation. This kind of thinking is at the heart of quality management and internal marketing programmes.

In highly competitive industries where product differences are slight, cost control is paramount and the value chain is best defined in terms of each activity's contribution to total cost. It is not too difficult to compare costs broken down in this way either with competitors' costs or with the costs of external providers of such products or services. The purpose of this analysis is to identify the critical success factors at each link in the chain to be addressed, in order to reap low-cost advantage. The analysis might lead to a decision to divest or to acquire new technologies in particular links.

In those industries where strategy is driven more by product differentiation than by cost, the value chain is best defined in terms of each activity's contribution to customer conversion and retention. The analysis here is more dependent upon subjective judgement than that described above but is crucial if a firm's activities are really to reflect its strategic intent. Market research, formal or informal, will help to reveal the product or service attributes a firm must deliver to customers and potential customers in the target market. Managers must examine each activity in the value chain and assess the contribution which each activity can or does make to creating value in the customer's eyes.

The notion of the value chain can be extended beyond the boundaries of an individual firm to trace the path a product or service follows right from the raw material stage through production and distribution to the final customer. As products or services travel along this chain, value is added at each point, accumulating into the combination of values that the customer is looking for. The total value chain therefore consists of a number of firms, as illustrated in Figure 9.3.

When managers see their firm in the context of the total value chain, they may be able to identify which links in the chain are the crucial ones for achieving low cost or differentiation. It is these links that will control the whole chain and therefore provide the most attractive opportunities. The kinds of strategy a firm will be able to follow will depend upon the links of the value chain it covers – strategy will have to fit the location in the total value chain. By understanding the value chain, managers may be able to change it to the benefit of their company.

Throughout, managers must remain aware of the true sources of competitive advantage for the firm. Strategy is not just about responding to market research information and selecting what seems to be the most profitable product markets; it is also about creating competitive

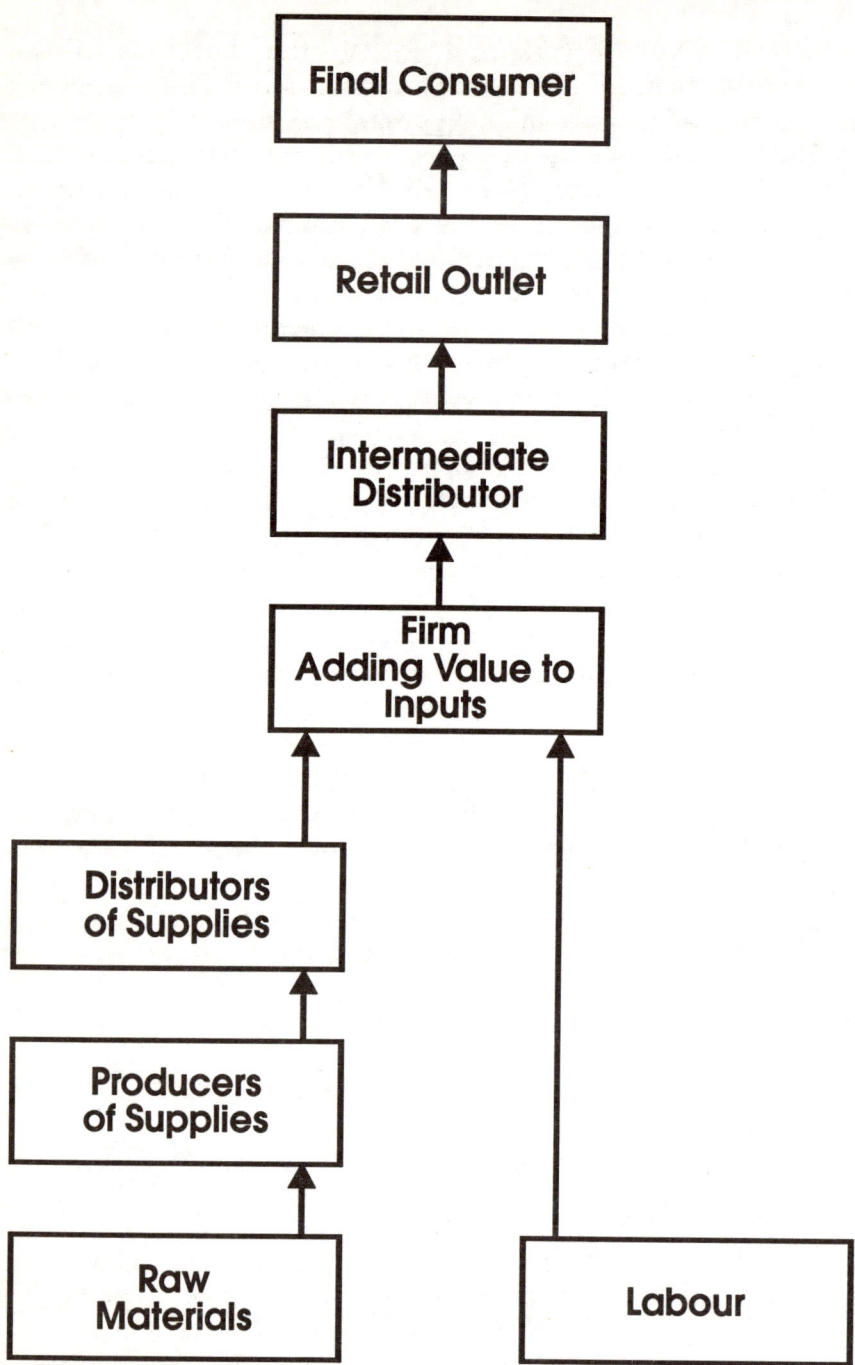

Figure 9.3 *The industry value chain*

advantage. And this may require investing in links that generate product attributes most strongly demanded by customers and that also match the firm's distinctive competence compared with its competitors.

An illustration of these points is provided by different approaches taken by Panasonic and Tandy to consumer electronics. Panasonic appears to have made the strategic decision to invest heavily in R&D and production, in the belief that independent wholesalers and retailers would readily accept their excellent product, particularly if it was supported by heavy advertising. Tandy, on the other hand, decided to develop its competitive advantage in the 'upstream' part of the industry through sourcing components from the most competitive suppliers and controlling the retail part of the business through its own franchised outlets. As the competitive situation changes and customers develop new requirements, the companies may decide to redeploy assets to focus on other parts of the value chain, or to continue reinforcing current strengths. At present, however, Panasonic and Tandy see the crucial links in the value chain and their respective 'critical success factors' very differently.

Managing the value chain effectively is not a question of examining each link in isolation and maximising the contribution of each as a discrete entity. Coordination has a vital role to play. The value chain must be managed as a system rather than a collection of separate parts. Strategic management then becomes a matter of reconfiguring the whole system, by regrouping, adding and subtracting individual activities, always in relation to the whole. For example, Japanese car manufacturers have very successfully coordinated the R&D and production functions to improve quality and to reduce design-to-delivery cycles. General Motors in the United States, on the other hand, has suffered from having functional activities in the chain which communicate poorly and unwillingly. The results are clear: declining sales, declining profits and an organisational system that is simply not working.

At this point we have to conclude that developing competitive strategies is a complex ambiguous task surrounded by uncertainty. Right at the start of any logical procedure we may try to follow, we find that the industry or market segment, the basic unit of analysis, is a slippery concept, the creation and alteration of which might turn out to be the key element of the competitive strategy. Then, simply identifying the existing competitive forces and trying to predict how they will change does not allow us to identify clear-cut 'either/or' choices of a generic kind. Instead, to succeed, we have to develop unique patterns of action that represent 'both/and' choices – some arrangement or configuration of opposites such as low cost and high quality at the same time. And to make matters more complicated, when we try to identify in general terms where and how to intervene to develop these factors that combine low cost and differentiation, we find that a firm is a complex interlinked system, or value chain, that is in turn a part of an even bigger interlinked complex system – the industry's value chain. As we think in these terms we begin to frame opportunities and problems in such a way that an industrial system rather than an individual firm is at the centre of attention. Success comes from playing a part in a complex system.

This insight into the importance of systems thinking in developing competitive strategy has recently been taken much further by Michael Porter in his latest book, *The Competitive Advantage of Nations* (1990), and we go on to explore his ideas in the next section. Essentially Porter is now saying that you need to take account, not simply of the vertical industrial value chain, but of the wider system, or national context, within which that chain operates.

Putting Competitive Strategy into an International Perspective

It is striking how some companies in one country exercise worldwide domination in a particular industry and yet other companies in that same country perform poorly in international markets. For example, the Italian shoe industry displays a clear competitive advantage on an international scale while its consumer electronics firms yield to the dominance of Japanese companies. Porter concludes that this occurs because there are specific national factors that shape a supportive environment for firms in one industry but not for others: conditions combine to form a system that enables national domination of certain international industries. Porter identifies four broad categories of such conditions which form a system that he calls the 'national diamond'.

The Diamond: Determinants of National Competitive Advantage

The national diamond is made up of the four categories depicted in Figure 9.4:

1. *Factor conditions*. This defines a nation's position in terms of those factors of production which are necessary to compete effectively in a particular industry; for example skilled labour or good road and rail systems.

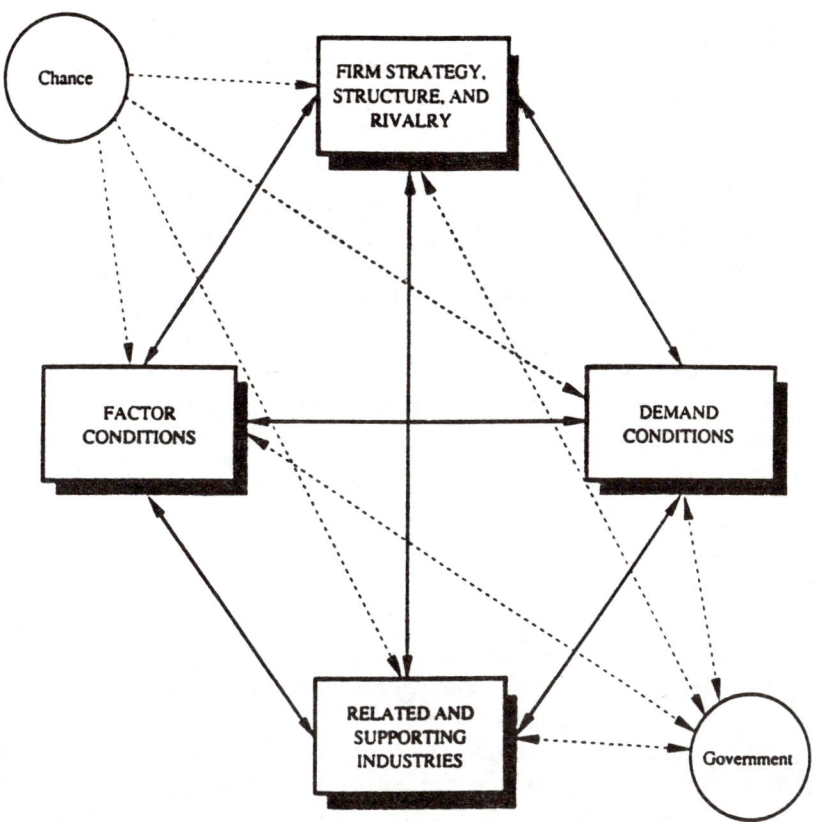

Source: Porter, 1990

Figure 9.4 *The national diamond*

2. *Demand conditions.* This category covers the nature of home demand for an industry's product or service; for example whether demand is highly sophisticated or not, whether customers accept what is provided or insist on high levels of service.

3. *Related and supporting industries.* This is concerned with the presence or absence in a nation of supplier industries and related industries which are intentionally competitive. For example the Italian shoe industry is backed by leather manufacturing and design industries.

4. *Firm strategy, structure and rivalry.* This set of conditions has to do with the factors governing how companies are created, organised and managed, and the nature of domestic rivalry.

The manner in which a particular industry develops in a country will also depend upon the policies of that country's government. And finally there is luck and chance. For example, a few electronics firms were set up to take advantage of the scientific expertise of Berkley and Stanford Universities. These few firms attracted other firms – competitors, suppliers, customers – and in this way 'Silicon Valley' emerged.

The point being made in Figure 9.4 is that a firm cannot simply, on its own, decide that it is going to pursue one strategy rather than another in a particular industry. Instead, the success of a firm's strategy will depend on the nature of the national diamond of which that firm is a part, and on the impact that firm has on the diamond and the diamond has on the firm in a circular feedback process. Thinking strategically means understanding how this complex interconnected international system is evolving, and understanding what part might be played in it.

An individual company will succeed, therefore, only if the industry or segment national diamond is favourable. Porter concludes:

Firms gain competitive advantage:

- where their home base allows and supports the most rapid accumulation of specialised assets and skills . . .
- in industries when their home base affords better ongoing information and insight into product and process needs . . .
- when the goals of owners, managers and employees support intense commitment and sustained investment . . .
- when their home environment is the most dynamic and the most challenging and stimulates and prods firms to upgrade and widen their advantages over time. (Porter, 1990, p71)

The national diamond is a self-reinforcing system where the effect of one particular element of the diamond is dependent on the state of the others. The necessary consequence of the interaction of the diamond's elements for a nation's firms is that they can only succeed if they are part of a cluster of industries that support each other because they are connected through vertical and horizontal relationships. (In Chapter 3 of this book, Bengt Johannisson explores how such networks of enterprises foster innovation.) Examples of what is being talked about are provided by the manner in which robotics firms in Japan reinforce each other, while in Germany this happens in the printing press industries and in the United States it can be seen in those industries related to the design and manufacture of medical patient-monitoring equipment. In all these industries, the firms of a nation have managed to retain competitive advantage internationally over a considerable period of time.

However, favourable national circumstances, taking the form of mutually reinforcing diamonds, are not on their own sufficient for the development of the globally competitive firm. In addition, firms must seize the opportunities provided by a favourable environment and attain competitive advantage through their own persistence.

Global Competitive Advantage

Given a favourable national diamond, management initiative and persistence can reap competitive advantage through:

- improvement, innovation and change
- reconfiguring entire value systems
- a global approach to strategy
- seeking out and selling to the most demanding and sophisticated buyers and sellers
- seeking out those buyers who have the most difficult needs to meet
- aiming to exceed the highest regulatory and product standard hurdles
- sourcing from the most advanced and international home-based suppliers
- treating employees as permanent
- establishing outstanding competitors as motivators.

The importance of being part of a self-reinforcing cluster of firms leads to the conclusion that a global firm's home base is crucial to its success:

> A firm can only have one true home base for each distinct business or segment. If it attempts to have several it will divide strategic authority, fragment technology development and forego the synergistic benefits of concentrating the key skills. Most importantly, it will sacrifice the dynamism that arises from true integration in a national 'diamond'. The goal of a company should not be to replicate the home-base advantages of other nations. This will require moving its home base. Instead the goal is to tap selectively into sources of advantage in other national 'diamonds' to supplement its own. (Porter, 1990, p606)

Firms which retain their base in a cosy, protected home environment will perish as their markets open up to international competition when barriers are dismantled, as for example in Europe.

We started thinking about competitive strategy from the perspective of an individual firm and pretty soon discovered that this would not take us very far. We discovered that we need to think about strategy in the context of the industrial value chain of which it is a part. That too was limiting and so we broadened the frame of reference into a national system and considered the part this plays in international success. The next section looks more closely at the international global aspect.

Understanding Globalisation

Early in the 1980s it became fashionable to predict the demise of the multinational corporation as markets globalised and the global corporation took over (Levitt, 1983). The global corporation is one that operates as if the entire world, or major regions of it, are a single entity: it sells the same thing in the same way everywhere. Competition becomes globalised when the major suppliers to a particular world market take an integrated approach to that market. They no longer manage each country's market as an autonomous unit but organise their activities along the value chain in order to reap maximum gain from their worldwide operations.

This approach contrasts with that of the multinational corporation which operates in a number of countries and adjusts its products and practices to each. The global corporation does not adapt to differences within and between nations, but forces suitably standardised products and practices on the entire globe. Such standardisation leads to low prices, high quality and greater reliability, and this persuades people to abandon their requirement for difference.

So, international competition may be 'multi-domestic' when competition in each country is independent, or competition may be global when the competitive position of a firm in one country affects and is affected by its position in another. Global corporations were succeeding at the expense of those operating on a multi-domestic basis, it was held, because markets were globalising; that is, customers were becoming similar no matter what nation they came from. This has happened in the fashion goods, cars, domestic appliances and capital equipment industries, particularly in the developed world. Customers have become global in that they:

- are aware of what is available in other countries
- want the best that is available, now, irrespective of country of manufacture or supply.

Where markets and competition have become truly global, companies must standardise their approach or die. The traditional 'marketing-led' approach of adapting to customer needs in each country will no longer work because:

- So long as the price is low and the quality good, customers will buy a product even if they have told market researchers that they want something else

- The economies of scale from the standardisation of production and other elements in the value chain, can reduce costs dramatically.

However, there are dangers in this kind of strategy. Products that aim for some average of national preferences can end up as something that no one wants. Parker Pen made this expensive mistake in the 1980s when its managers tried to move away from a wide, nationally differentiated product range to a globally standardised range. The customers did not buy and the previously independent country units were totally demoralised as a result of having decision-making power taken away from them.

There is a contradiction then: some forces pull toward globalisation while others pull toward the maintenance of difference. One way of dealing with this is to 'think globally, act locally'.

> Imagine you are the CEO of a major automobile company reviewing your product plans for the years ahead. Your market data tell you that you need to develop four dozen different models if you want to design separate cars for each distinct segment of the Triad market. But you do not have enough world-class engineers to design so many models. You don't have enough managerial talent or enough money. No one does. Worse, there is no single 'global' car that will solve your problems for you. America, Europe and Japan are quite different markets with quite different mixes of needs and preferences. Worse still, as head of a worldwide company you cannot write off any of these Triad markets. You have to be in each one of them – and with first-rate successful products. What do you do?
>
> If you are the CEO of Nissan you first look at the Triad region by region and identify each market's dominant requirements. In the UK for example tax policies make it essential that you develop a car suitable for corporate fleet sales. In the US you need a sporty 'Z' model as well as a four-wheel drive family vehicle. Each of these categories is what Nissan president, Yatake Kume, calls a 'lead country' model – a product carefully tailored to the dominant and distinct needs of individual national markets. Once you have your short-list of 'lead country' models in hand you can ask your top managers in other parts of Triad whether minor changes can make any of them suitable for local sales. But you start with the lead country model. (Ohmae, 1989, p 155)

The crucial consideration for Nissan, therefore, is not how they got their customers and country managers to accept a standardised global product – as the proponents of globalisation would have it. Rather, they work at keeping customers in the main developed markets of the world happy and at the same time keep worldwide costs of R&D, production and marketing to competitive levels. Nissan think global in that they see their worldwide activities as an integrated whole, where coordination and leveraging of activities can reduce overall costs or create added value. They act locally, however, in that they recognise the particular requirements of local customers and managers and do their utmost to meet those requirements.

Ohmae has coined the term 'equidistant' to describe this way of thinking about global markets (Ohmae, 1989). He contrasts the perspective of most managers today with this notion of an equidistant perspective. Most managers focus on their home country markets and the organisational units that serve them. They see everyone and everything else as a rather peripheral part of the 'rest of the world'. The equidistant perspective however sets plans and builds organisations in which all key customers are seen as equidistant from the corporate centre.

Asea Brown Boveri, ABB, is a good example of an organisation which is clearly trying very hard to foster an 'equidistant' philosophy:

> ABB is a company with no geographic center, no national axe to grind. We are a federation of national companies with a global coordination center. Are we a Swiss company? Our headquarters is in Zurich, but only 100 professionals work at headquarters and we will not increase that number. Are we a Swedish company? I'm the CEO [Percy Barnevik] and I was born and educated in Sweden. But our headquarters is not in Sweden and only two of our board directors are Swedes. Perhaps we are an American company. We report our financial results in US dollars and English is ABB's official language. We conduct all high level meetings in English. My point is that ABB is none of these things – and all of these things. We are not homeless. We are a company with many homes. (Taylor, 1991)

There are probably no more than a handful of companies in the world who could claim to have a management team at the top which operates with a genuine equidistance of perspective and yet it would seem to lie at the very heart of what globalisation is about and, from a more parochial perspective, at the very heart of what the Single Market in Europe is supposed to be about.

Conclusion

This chapter has sought to describe how strategic thinking about the concept of competitive advantage has been evolving. In the early 1980s the focus was on a relatively static analysis of how to position a firm, in a standardised way, in a given environment, albeit one that a firm might be able to shape. Strategic thinking meant identifying the state of the five forces that determine the form of competitive advantage. The next step in strategic thinking was to identify which of the tailor-made low-cost/differentiation strategies was appropriate to secure and sustain that advantage. And this was competitive strategy. Opportunities and problems were framed in terms of a firm adapting to its environment.

We then saw how sophisticated strategic thinking involved understanding how a firm operated as a value system interconnected with an industry value system. This kind of thinking leads managers to perceive greater variety in the strategic choices open to them. Strategic thinking is not simply about cost and differentiation, but about moulding and changing links that connect parts of a system to each other and that connect the firm to others in the vertical chain that runs from raw material suppliers to customers.

Strategic thinking takes a further leap when we perceive a competitive strategy to be one that flows from the interconnection between a firm and the cluster – horizontal and vertical – of industries and customers it is part of. This is a perception of an evolving interconnected self-reinforcing system in which chance plays a part. And we also saw that strategic thinking cannot stop at the boundaries of the nation but needs to put competitive strategy into a paradoxical global context in which some forces pull to uniformity and others to difference.

References

Hendry, John (1990) 'The Problem with Porter's Generic Strategies', *European Management Journal*, Vol 8, No 4, Dec.

Levitt, Theodore (1983) 'The Globalization of Markets', *Harvard Business Review*, May–June.

Ohmae, Kenichi (1989) 'Managing in a Borderless World', *Harvard Business Review*, May–June.

Porter, Michael E (1980) *Competitive Strategy: Techniques for Analyzing Industries and Competitors*, The Free Press, New York.

— (1985) *Competitive Advantage: Creating and Sustaining Superior Performance*, The Free Press, New York.

— (1990) *The Competitive Advantage of Nations*, Macmillan, London.

Taylor, William (1991) 'The Logic of Global Business', An Interview with ABB's Percy Barnevik, *Harvard Business Review*, Mar–Apr.

European Integration

Roger Bennett

Introduction

Accommodating the effects of West European economic integration is arguably the dominant issue currently facing British business. Laws and practices that regulated UK commercial activity for generations are rapidly changing. UK company law has had to be altered to comply with EC Directives, as have: technical product standards; industrial health and safety requirements; the law on intellectual property; public procurement arrangements; laws on advertising, marketing and sales promotion; agency law; consumer protection regulations; and the law on competition, mergers and company acquisitions. Progress towards a common currency in the core Continental EC nations and (post-Maastricht) a greatly expanded Community role in labour relations and employment protection, moreover, are seemingly inevitable. Clearly, *every* UK firm is affected directly or indirectly by the completion of the European Single Market.

Maastricht, the European Union (EU) and the European Economic Area (EEA)

The 1991 Maastricht Agreement has enormous implications for European business. The majority of EC member countries are now committed to the creation of a common currency by the end of the century (possibly beginning in 1996) and, independent of EC institutions, to the adoption of key elements of the European Social Charter.

A single European currency will require firms to quote prices in a common unit and will enable consumers readily to compare the prices of similar items sold in various EC countries. It means pan-European price labelling and packaging, easier product positioning in national markets, and the absence of currency conversion costs for businesses in nations that are members of the common currency area (CCA). Firms outside the CCA, conversely, will need separate prices, packaging and labelling for domestic and European markets, and must incur the (substantial) expense of currency conversion. A common currency removes *entirely* the currency exchange risk associated with international transactions. However, such risks – and the consequent need to hedge against them via the forward currency exchange markets – will continue to apply to non-CCA enterprises. Share prices in European companies will be quoted in the same currency units everywhere, facilitating pan-European share trading and enabling immediate access to all European stock exchanges by investors and companies throughout the Community: a major advantage to businesses seeking finance from external sources. Also, a common currency will expedite intra-EC cash transfers, leading perhaps to far wider *pan-European* ownership of company shares than previously. Note however the increased volatility in share prices likely to occur as funds move without hindrance across national EC frontiers.

The other important treaty signed in 1991 concerned the formation of the European Economic Area whereby the entire European Free Trade Area (EFTA) – including Switzerland, as the Swiss government had not conducted a referendum at that time – agreed to adopt all major EC legislation concerning: business methods; technical standards; public procurement; competition; freedom of establishment for businesses; the free movement of goods, services, capital and labour etc. All tariffs are to be removed among EC and EFTA countries that participate in the EEA scheme, creating thereby the largest unified market in the developed world. The EC itself is to be known as the 'Economic Union' once the EEA and a common currency are in place.

Strategies for Europe

The new situation necessitates fresh thinking about business strategy and, importantly, demands the incorporation of a European dimension into all the sub-systems of a firm. A wide range of products is becoming available to domestic customers, who may choose to purchase items supplied from other EC countries. Community product standards could compel alterations in the sizes, shapes, ingredients, safety features and other characteristics of a company's output; local authority and central government supply contracts might be lost to European rivals. And no business can afford to ignore the possibility of obtaining cheaper and better-quality material, component and other inputs from abroad. Also, of course, the *competitors* of firms will themselves probably wish to undertake business in the Community, and the contacts and experiences they acquire while doing this might help them develop a competitive edge in the domestic market.

Accordingly, all businesses require corporate plans for coping with the Single Market. Plans should itemise the management skills required for successful entry to European markets, (eg language skills, export documentation, trading in foreign currency, familiarity with foreign advertising media etc); must review the firm's outputs to make them appeal to wider European audiences; re-examine existing advertising and other promotional strategies; identify locations suitable for establishing administrative offices abroad; and assess the changes in operating costs expected to result from new transport and distribution procedures.

Need For a Flexible Approach
The Single Market is dynamic, sophisticated, complex, and altering more rapidly and extensively than any other trading area. National Markets are liable to fragment into many more sub-units than at present, with intense rivalry for domination of these smaller markets from efficient, low-price and aggressive foreign firms. To succeed in this environment a firm must be adaptable, immediately aware of fresh opportunities and, importantly, *able to learn from and instantly rectify its mistakes*. Volatility and the numerous uncertainties connected with the new situation establish a need for policies, management styles and organisational frameworks that are flexible and quickly able to respond to fast-changing conditions. Practical manifestations of response flexibility include:

- Action-orientated strategies which suggest *general directions* for the enterprise rather that 'tablets of stone' quantitative objectives. Strategies should be seen as a sort of route map for guiding the enterprise towards the attainment of its mission, not as a collection of rigid rules.
- The alignment of internal systems (organisational, procurement, staffing, budgeting, marketing, quality control etc) to meet *pan-European* operational requirements.

- Ensuring that the company's core businesses can cope with environmental turbulence.

Contingency plans must be drafted and (wherever possible) substantial reserves maintained. It may be appropriate to buy in management expertise from outside, and it is certainly necessary to promote within the business a *culture* that is relevant to the demands of the new situation. Also essential is the installation of a first-class management information system capable of identifying the threats and opportunities arising from the completion of the Single Market and the firm's involvement in pan-European trade.

Note moreover the need for a genuinely holistic approach. Single Market strategies affect the firm *in its entirety*, cutting across functional and departmental divisions and thus needing to be implemented *as a whole*.

The Strategy Mix

A combination of defensive and offensive strategies is required. Offensive strategies are necessary for assaulting new markets; for improving, altering and developing products; for obtaining European public sector contracts; entering strategic alliances with European firms. Defensive measures might be appropriate in order to retain domestic market share, cut costs and maintain the keenest local prices, protect know-how and intellectual property, and to avoid being taken over by a foreign EC company. Mergers and/or collaborative ventures with other domestic businesses may be essential to develop a critical mass sufficient to fight off increased competition from EC rivals; or to operate joint procurement, research or distribution services.

Free trade in combination with the harmonisation of product standards means that no manufacturing business can afford stockholdings, labour retention, or machine under-utilisation higher than *pan-European* (not just domestic) industry norms, implying the removal of excess capacity (previously made possible by lack of foreign European competition) in *all* manufacturing firms. Soaking up internal spare capacity necessitates the redefinition of target markets; diversification (possibly) into new product lines; and the initiation of comprehensive and ongoing audits of existing just-in-time procurement and inventory systems, production scheduling and control arrangements.

Financing the Business

The European Commission has for many years sought to create and impose uniform standards and practices on company management and business finance. Specific measures have included the following:

- Guaranteeing freedom of establishment and operation for financial services providers anywhere in the EC. Firms and individuals may borrow in any Community state and engage in transactions on any EC stock exchange.
- The imposition of management procedures within financial services firms; including the maintenance of certain minimum levels of reserves; directors' qualifications; rules concerning the format and publication of share issue prospectuses; and the extent of the information to be given in brochures, financial services advertisements and other publicity materials.
- Specification of financial requirements for public companies; for example minimum subscribed share capital, contents of consolidated company accounts, the nature of the data to be issued prior to a share issue, thresholds for shareholding disclosures.
- Minimum qualifications for company auditors.
- Company liquidation.

European integration greatly extends the availability of financial services to European businesses (which collectively absorb 60 per cent of the total 'outputs' of EC financial services firms), and intense competition and improved efficiency in this sector is sure to have a major impact on the profitabilities of EC companies. The expansion of the financial services sector is being facilitated by the massive improvement currently occurring in the EC telecommunications industry, which is making available an extensive and responsive financial information 'nervous system' capable of instantly transmitting changes in share prices, trading conditions, and finance costs and availabilities throughout the EC. As the European financial information system improves and consolidates, so it becomes easier for businesses to comb the Community for different sources of capital and meaningfully to compare their costs. Indeed, there is no theoretical reason why future Community share markets should not operate jointly; linked by cable, satellite and open systems computer interchange.

Accounting Standards

Community rules require that public companies listed on the stock exchange of any one EC country be able to raise money on the stock exchanges of others, on equal terms with local firms. Unfortunately for the suppliers of company finance, however, accounting practices differ considerably among Community states, although moves are afoot to harmonise national procedures. Already, standard formats have been prescribed (*via* Company Law Directives IV and VII) for balance sheets and other published accounts; for the valuation of assets (which must now be valued on a going-concern basis rather than on historical cost) in all EC nations; and for the structure of consolidated accounts issued by groups of companies based in EC territory. Nevertheless, accounting conventions will continue to differ for several years (particularly *vis-à-vis* the assessment of goodwill, valuation of brands, and the definition of a 'subsidiary' company) making it difficult for investors to compare the financial performances of companies resident in various EC nations.

A major consequence of disparate national accounting systems is that the book profits of British companies are sometimes reported as being higher than in comparable Continental enterprises. Writing-down allowances are more generous in several EC nations (especially Germany) than in the UK, reserves are frequently more substantial (in some countries a certain percentage of each year's profits must, by law, be kept in reserve) and Continental European businesses generally are inclined to calculate their profits in an extremely conservative manner.

New Perspectives on European Business Finance

As well as creating a wider choice of financing options for companies, pan-European freedom of establishment for banks and other financial service providers could extend Continental financing *cultures* to British business. There is far less bank, debenture and family financing of medium to large firms in Britain than in the rest of the Community. All EC countries have a stock exchange but, compared with the UK, they have insubstantial share markets: fewer companies are listed on Continental exchanges, and turnover is low. For example, less than 650 German companies are quoted on the Frankfurt Stock Exchange; in contrast to about 2,600 UK companies quoted in London. Italy has just 200 firms listed on its stock exchange, with only two of these having more than half their share capitals in the hands of the general public. In both Spain and France, around 50 per cent of the top 200 companies are family owned. The London Stock Exchange has a market capitalisation more than double that of the German, Italian and French exchanges combined.

Equity issues by Continental businesses typically involve private placings with large investors, especially banks – which in many EC states invest directly and heavily in companies, occupying seats on company boards and helping with overall strategy formulation. Hence, shares become locked into family and institutional investors, making it difficult to acquire companies on the open market. Arguably, this enables Continental businesses to adopt long-term perspectives, plough back profits, expand and diversify without having to worry about hostile takeover attempts by other firms.

The UK approach is quite different. In Britain, companies are regarded as commodities to be traded in exactly the same way as any other marketable item, leading – so advocates of the UK system allege – to optimum efficiency as supply and demand inexorably direct scarce resources towards the most efficient businesses. Also, the existence of an active share market creates an objective means of valuing companies. Note how the differences between the two systems create major problems for UK companies, which have to compete on an uneven playing field in relation to mergers and takeovers. Arguably, UK short-termism causes British firms frequently to lack cash and immediately realisable assets, placing them at a disadvantage compared with Continental rivals that possess extensive reserves accumulated over many years.

A further problem for British businesses is that the high proportion of Continental firms owned by private families and/or that have large blocks of their shares in the hands of large banks or other institutional investors means a shortage of companies available for sale in certain EC countries. Corporate cultures in the European Community outside Britain are not attuned to the cut and thrust of hostile acquisitions, and shareholders often have to be cajoled and seduced into parting with their shares. Contrast this with the UK situation, where shares in listed companies are freely available, where companies can be valued instantly, and where there exists a well-established company research system adept at identifying vulnerable enterprises. Normally, Continental interest rates are lower than in Britain, so that funds for financing acquisitions can be borrowed less expensively. Past profit-retention policies among Continental businesses, moreover, have resulted in a large number of cash-rich predator companies.

The depressing consequence of all this is that British firms increasingly require strategies for avoiding being taken over by EC rivals; causing them perhaps to be overgeared, to distort their market share prices to take on obligations that will make them unattractive to predators, and to sell off valuable assets when they should instead be concentrating on attaining their missions.

Venture Capital

In Britain, venture capital has long provided medium-term equity developmental finance for young high-risk businesses. Whether UK-style venture capital financing will spread to the Continent (at present it remains an essentially Anglo-American phenomenon), or whether Continental approaches to funding the expansion of recently established enterprises will become commonplace in Britain, is a vexed question. On the Continent, families, banks and industrial companies frequently invest long term in risky small businesses, but *without* attaching the strings that UK venture-capital providers often impose on client companies. Typically, moreover, the Continental investor becomes directly involved with the recipient firm's strategic planning. France has an active venture-capital industry, as (to much lesser extents) do Germany and Spain. Other Continental countries, however, have negligible venture-capital markets.

Nevertheless, the European Commission is actively promoting the extension of venture-capital financing among EC businesses. Support is available *via* the 'Venture Consort Scheme' (which is seeking to establish pan-European syndicates of venture-capital providers) and through 'Eurotech Capital', a scheme intended to promote high-technology projects in small to medium-sized enterprises. Under the Venture Consort Scheme the European Commission provides capital jointly with private EC companies, sharing the profits (hopefully) resulting from the project.

Management Buy-outs

In the 1980s there were approximately 3,000 management buy-outs (MBOs) in the UK, compared with 430 in France, 240 in Italy, and barely 100 in Germany. Spain had 35 MBOs, Denmark 63 and Belgium 52. UK buy-outs accounted for 75 per cent of the total value of all European (EC and EFTA) MBO transactions over the period. It seems, therefore, that Continental Europe is generally unenthusiastic about MBOs.

Militating against a significant increase in non-UK Community management buy-outs are: the high levels of financial reserves held within many Continental companies (which enable them to survive recessions and hence retain divisions and subsidiaries); the absence of Continental equity markets capable of providing the capital for buy-out activity; and the high salaries and occupational status frequently enjoyed by executives in large Continental companies (making them reluctant to take on the risks attached to a voluntary buy-out). Another factor is the close long-term relationship between firms and their banks common in Continental nations, since banks (in contrast to venture-capital providers) are normally averse to the uncertainties that arise when carving up companies in which they have a substantial financial interest. This is especially true of Germany where, according to OECD estimates, only 19 per cent of the total assets of firms are represented by equity capital (compared to over 50 per cent in Britain), the rest being contributed by banks and families. Also, the commercial laws and tax regimes of most EC countries (Britain and the Netherlands excepted) are not conducive to MBO activity.

Nevertheless, the venture-capital industry itself predicts significant increases in the volume of Continental MBOs over the next few years. This forecast is based: on the large rise in Continental company rationalisations and mergers that is resulting from the completion of the Single Market; on the numerous business closures and shake-outs caused by recessionary conditions in certain EC states; and on the continuing increase in the age structure of the European population. The latter will cause many founders of successful post-War Continental family businesses to retire over the next decade, and MBOs represent a convenient way for firms to acquire an independent legal form.

Financing Research and Development

In 1991 the European Community launched its biggest ever programme for funding company R&D. About six billion ECU became available for industrial research; one billion ECU for human resources development; 400 million to assist industrial development in rural areas; and 200 million for European media. Most of the funding involved scientific and technological R&D under the Community's 'Framework Programme'. Grants from this can be a major source of income for EC firms, possibly altering their core strategies and policies: market shares may be affected; competitive advantages gained or forfeited. High-risk projects that otherwise could not be considered can suddenly fall within a company's grasp. Note moreover that the 1991 programme only covered 1991 and 1992. The 1993 programme is even bigger.

To qualify for funding, a project must seek to attain one or more of the following objectives:

- Promotion of the harmonisation of EC technical standards
- Improvement of the competitiveness of European industry

- Enhancement of social cohesion within the Community
- Improvement of EC technical and scientific training.

Proposals are required to include a statement of exactly *how* the results of the research are to be implemented.

Clearly, every business concerned with technical research needs continuously to search for EC grant opportunities and to develop expertise in formulating and progressing applications (Collins, 1991). Additionally, they must monitor competitors' successes in attracting research awards, and know where to look for potential partners for cross-border collaborative research projects.

Large and Small Firms
In principle, funding is available to *any* Community business, regardless of its industry or size. In practice, however, larger firms obtain the majority of grants – particularly for long-term basic research or work likely to affect industry standards. Such research is known as 'pre-competitive' or 'pre-normative'. It is funded with the specific intention of altering the *strategic orientations* of large companies.

Critics have alleged that grant-assisted R&D conducted by large organisations have failed to achieve reasonable results, notably in the field of information technology. In recognition of this, the EC is increasingly directing funds towards small to medium-sized enterprises (hopefully capable of *exploiting* developments) rather than to big businesses conducting fundamental research. It is essential, therefore, for smaller research-orientated companies to become competent in applying for Community research funding.

Strategies for Market Entry

Deciding how to operate in foreign EC markets (exporting, direct mail, sale to intermediaries, use of agents, joint ventures with other firms, licensing, franchising, or the establishment of permanent branches or subsidiaries) is a complex and problematic issue. Examples of the difficulties that might arise include the following:

- Agency laws differ among Community states, particularly *vis-à-vis* the compensation payable to an agent following the termination of an agreement. The laws of some EC countries regard agents more as 'employees' than as separate businesses. Hence, they are entitled to long periods of notice prior to non-renewal of a contract, plus recompense for lost commission.

- The use of foreign EC distributors (ie independent firms that purchase, as principals, the outputs of other businesses) involves loss of control over the final presentation and price of the product. Also, distributors frequently handle competing brands.
- Licensees might set up as rivals once licence agreements have expired. Problems may arise during a licence period in relation to control over quality standards, declaration of production levels, royalty payments, and the territories covered by the contract.
- To the extent that decisions taken by local agents, licensees or distributors bind the supplying firm, the latter could be regarded by local tax authorities as operating a permanent subsidiary, hence creating a liability for local corporation tax. Dealing with this requires accountants, solicitors, submission of documents to local tax offices and so on.

Establishing a Permanent Presence

Licensing and/or the use of foreign intermediaries enables a firm (especially a smaller business) quickly to add a European dimension to its operations. As a firm's involvement with European trade increases, however, the cost and other advantages of establishing permanent presences in foreign EC nations *via* wholly owned branches or subsidiaries become increasingly apparent.

Branches and subsidiaries
Until recently, smaller businesses have not usually found it worth while setting up foreign European branches or subsidiaries. Completion of the Single Market, however, is resulting in a significant reduction in the average size of firms engaged in foreign EC trade, with the consequence that increasing numbers of small to medium-sized enterprises are now establishing permanent presences in other EC countries. Having a permanent presence in the local market provides several advantages: the firm's products acquire a local image; employees of the branch/subsidiary will possess intimate knowledge of local markets and business conditions; competitors' activities can be closely observed; and there should be better coordination of marketing, advertising, distribution, after sales service and so on.

'Branches' are direct extensions of parent firms into other nations. 'Subsidiaries' on the other hand, are separate legally constituted entities, operating and taxed as if they were **domestic** businesses. Branches are simple to establish and to close down (no local company formation or winding-up procedures are necessary); their accounts do not have to be independently audited; and in the UK losses can be offset against the parent company's tax (in contrast to losses incurred by subsidiaries which are treated as losses made by independent businesses).

Registration of a branch is straightforward. Usually a single form has to be completed and deposited with the local tax authorities, together with the Articles and Memorandum of Association of the parent company (or comparable details if the parent is some other type of firm). The main problem, perhaps, is that complicated tax situations can arise in certain EC nations where local tax authorities are empowered to tax branch offices on profits *deemed* to accrue to the parent firm's entire worldwide operations in consequence of the branch's activities in the country where the branch is located.

Subsidiaries have limited liability, equal access to local capital markets alongside local firms, and they qualify for local investment incentives. Also, a subsidiary needs only disclose details of its own financial affairs, not those of the parent company (as happens with a branch in order that host country tax authorities may apportion tax liability for the branch's operations). Dividends from subsidiaries may be transmitted across national EC frontiers without hindrance and local employee social security and other labour matters might be dealt with more conveniently by a subsidiary than a branch.

Often the decision whether to have a subsidiary or a branch hinges on whether the operation is expected to make a loss or a profit. If losses are anticipated, a branch is normally preferable. If profits will accrue, and if the foreign tax rate is reasonably low, then a subsidiary is usually more appropriate. Other factors to be considered include:

- How the branch/subsidiary is to be financed (borrowing, share issue, transfers from the parent business's reserves), and whether the money is to be raised locally or from abroad
- The extent of planned profit retention within the branch/subsidiary and, if profits are to be retained, whether surpluses are to be invested locally
- How the branch/subsidiary will be staffed and controlled, and its performance evaluated.

Note moreover the need for meticulous tax planning prior to long-term investment in another EC nation. For example, at the time of writing corporation tax in the UK is 35 per cent, whereas in Germany the tax on a branch or subsidiary of a UK business could be anything up to 56 per cent. This seemingly militates against setting up a permanent operation in Germany. However, this ignores the extensive tax rebates, investment incentives, special depreciation allowances and regional development grants available in certain regions of Germany that could greatly outweigh the tax disadvantage (Citron, 1991).

Acquisitions
Outright purchase of existing foreign EC firms can help secure the scale economies potentially available from pan-European operations, while simultaneously providing fast and easy access to European markets. You acquire a functioning administrative system, and obtain existing marketing and distribution facilities with staff who possess detailed knowledge of local business conditions. On the other hand, the purchased firm has to be integrated into your current organisation, and implementing changes in its working methods may be difficult. Also, there is a shortage of suitable takeover targets in certain countries, as previously discussed.

Risk Sharing and Joint Ventures

Establishing a permanent presence in a foreign country is risky, and can be extremely expensive. Therefore, straightforward exporting to EC markets might be preferred. Exporting is a convenient means for *learning* about foreign EC markets: fewer resources are committed, and there is no need to share information with other firms. However, significant opportunities could be lost through not being near to local customers, and competitors' responses are difficult to observe.

An alternative method for entering a foreign EC market is the formation of a joint venture with foreign local firms, sharing the profits and the risks (which should be lower as a consequence of the foreign partners' intimate knowledge of the local business scene). Local firms can deal with local regulations, monitor competitors, help raise finance and so on. Research and distribution arrangements can be combined and developed.

The European Commission is anxious to encourage collaborative joint ventures among Community businesses (particularly for technology transfer and the setting up of joint distribution and after-sales service systems), and offers a clearing house, the Business Co-operation Centre (BCC), for this purpose. BCC aims to help small to medium-sized enterprises find 'sister companies'; that is foreign firms engaged in complementary activities and similar in size and structure to the one seeking a partner and which are capable of:

1. Acting as a local agent
2. Translating documents
3. Providing general support and advice.

The applicant business offers reciprocal facilities to the foreign partner. There are regular exchanges of information, meetings, and possibly short-period secondments of staff.

A further EC initiative intended to foster joint ventures was the introduction in 1987 of a new form of business, the European Economic Interest Group (EEIG). An EEIG is a combination of European businesses (companies, partnerships or sole traders) resident in at least two EC states. EEIGs are intended to act as vehicles for pooling common R&D or marketing activities or for managing *ad hoc* projects. They should not seek to make profits in their own right, and are not allowed to raise capital from the general public. Individual EEIG members have unlimited liability for the debts of the entire group. EEIGs are simple to register, do not need to have any capital, and are not obliged to file annual financial reports.

Selling to Europe

In the marketing field, important decisions are necessary regarding which EC markets to enter, the depth of market penetration desired, product characteristics and development, and (importantly) whether to adopt a differentiated or undifferentiated approach.

Customisation Versus Standardisation

Completion of the Single Market does not mean that Germans will cease to be German, that the Dutch will no longer be Dutch, or that the French will not be French. Cultural differences continue, and the need to 'think local' is as pressing today as ever before. It is not *necessarily* the case that promotional messages used in one national market will be unsuitable elsewhere; but it is certainly true that careful attention has to be paid to the question of whether the presentation of products should vary from state to state.

National culture affects market segmentation, consumer behaviour, household structure, and decision making within families and businesses. Cultural influences are evident, moreover, in the demographic makeups of various EC nations, in kinship patterns, social mobility and stratification, and in authority and status systems emerging from the management styles adopted within firms. Deciding how much weight to attach to cultural differences when advertising products is a major concern for companies intending to sell to other EC countries. The advantages of uniformity in presentation are that it:

1. Requires less marketing research than customisation
2. Is convenient and cheap to administer
3. Demands less creative effort.

Uniformity is possible to the extent that consumer lifestyles and perspectives are similar across the market segments in the nations in which you intend to do business. You identify comparable consumer groups in various countries, and then hope that each group will respond to the same type of message and see similar media (magazines, posters, television programmes, local newspapers) as the rest. Customisation, on the other hand, may be necessary as a consequence of cultural factors and/or differences in the backgrounds of target groups in different nations.

EC Directives on Advertising

Community legislation on advertising is already extensive, and set to increase still further. EC Directives exist in relation to: misleading advertising; labelling and packaging; the advertising of foodstuffs and pharmaceuticals; cross-border broadcasting; and several aspects of consumer protection. Additional Directives are planned for the regulation of comparative claims, tobacco advertising (both the European Commission and the European Parliament want a total ban), the use of superlatives, the words used to describe alcohol and food products, sponsorship of TV programmes (in order to prohibit sponsors from influencing the editorial contents of broadcasts), the portrayal of women in advertisements, use of speed and acceleration as selling points when promoting motor vehicles, and the advertising of children's toys. Also the Commission has openly stated that it intends becoming more heavily involved in consumer affairs generally: for example through sponsoring a Draft Directive requiring that product guarantees be honoured regardless of the customer's country of residence or the place an item was purchased; through the compulsory standardisation of the format in which credit charges are expressed (hence facilitating the easy comparison of the costs of credit in different EC states); and with the compulsory establishment in all Community nations of low-cost legal procedures capable of compensating consumers for minor damage caused by product inadequacies.

Clearly, every firm concerned with European business needs an effective system for monitoring fresh legislation in the marketing area. Assistance with this is available from companies that supply regularly updated EC information in looseleaf form, and from the on-line database SPEARHEAD of the UK Department of Trade and Industry. SPEARHEAD provides brief summaries of current and intended Single Market measures, including Directives and Proposals on advertising, health and safety at work, employee and consumer protection, and social affairs. It also contains the complete texts of all EC legislation. Information is updated weekly.

Eurobrands

Creation of a single brand identity ('Eurobrand') that presents the firm's output in exactly the same way in each of several different EC markets can be a major benefit to businesses engaged in European trade. It is not necessary to have enormous sales in order to benefit from Eurobranding, which can be as valuable for developing niche markets as for large-scale pan-European campaigns.

Intellectual property in a brand is obtained through registering a trademark (ie any word, symbol, or collections of words and/or symbols used to identify goods). The law on trademarks (and on intellectual property generally, including patents, industrial designs, computer programmes and all other copyright materials) is being harmonised at the Community level, and it is now possible to register a Community Trade Mark (CTM) which provides brand-name protection throughout the EC. A CTM has a ten-year lifespan and is renewable. Holders of CTMs may transfer their rights, offer them as security against loans, or license them to other businesses. Also, the 1988 Madrid Protocol links the CTM into the overall world intellectual property protection system.

The development of Eurobrands has implications for company pricing strategy. At present there exist wide price differentials for certain types of product sold in different EC countries, due mainly to goods having disparate positions in various markets (bicycles, for example, are regarded as a luxury and/or fashion item in some regions; as a utilitarian means of transport in others). Price levelling across national frontiers could significantly affect overall company profitability. Note moreover how the free movement of goods and people within the Community means that dealers, retailers and even private consumers can cross frontiers to take advantage of Eurobrand price differences.

Direct Marketing (DM)

Direct marketing offers a flexible, selective and potentially highly cost-effective means of reaching European customers. The UK Royal Mail provides numerous facilities for mailshots, catalogue distribution, transmission of computer disks and video tapes. A Community-wide Business Reply Service is available, as is British Telecom's Continental 0800 freefone system. The latter enables firms to quote local freefone numbers on mailshots or other promotional materials distributed in EC states, so that customers may telephone free of charge with orders or enquiries. Another option is to have the caller pay only the cost of a local call in his or her own country. Calls may be diverted to other UK (or Continental) locations at set periods, and 0800 numbers can be linked to fax machines thus enabling customers to transmit orders, technical specifications, drawings and so on free of charge at any time. Details of these services, plus help and advice with European direct marketing generally (sourcing of listing in particular EC countries for example) are available from the Royal Mail.

Logistics

Firms selling Europe need to determine how closely they wish to be involved in transport, intermediate warehousing and the final delivery of consignments. A simple solution is to use a freight forwarding company, which will manage everything from the collection of goods from a client firm's premises right up to their delivery abroad. Forwarders advise clients on the best means for delivering goods to specific destinations and assume full responsibility for all aspects of transportation, including documentation and insurance. Equally however, substantial cost savings are available to firms opting to make their own delivery and/or warehousing arrangements. Whether a business does this should depend on its resources, experience of international distribution, and the volume of its foreign sales. Note that transportation costs absorb significant proportions of an exporting company's revenues, so that no business – however small – can afford to ignore 'do-it-yourself' transportation possibilities. The return on staff training in logistics management can be extremely high.

A major corollory to the removal of EC trade barriers is the implementation of the European Commission's Common Transport Policy (CTP), which involves the total freedom to provide haulage and transport services (whether by road, sea, air or inland waterway) *anywhere* in the EC. Specific measures include the abolition of restrictions on road cabotage and the introduction of Community-wide haulage rates by transport firms. Cabotage means the local transportation of goods within national frontiers. Liberalisation of the rules on cabotage means that any EC haulage firm – regardless of its home country – can pick up and deliver loads within and between any EC member countries. The CTP will cause big reductions in the costs of freight, and maritime and air transport, making it easier to send goods long distances and to obtain inputs from other EC states.

Strategies for Small Firms

Special problems confront small businesses facing aggressive competition from European firms. The small enterprise does not have the resources necessary to engage specialist outside consultants, or to hire in-house marketing and distribution managers, export documentation clerks, accountants familiar with foreign currency trading, and so on. Nor is it likely to have first-hand experience of selling abroad. Essential measures that a small business should adopt in order to cope with the Single Market include:

- Reallocation of (scarce) resources towards the staff training necessary to equip owners and managers with the competencies required in the post-Single Market world.
- More extensive involvement with trade associations, chambers of commerce and other collective business support organisations in order to obtain low-cost access to professional advice on EC marketing, advertising, legislation and financing opportunities.
- Where possible, the accumulation of reserves to cushion the possible adverse effects of higher levels of uncertainty and environmental turbulence.
- Implementation of market information systems to identify attractive niches within foreign EC markets.

Strategies need to maximise competitive advantage (usually through conspicuous product differentiation combined with an attractive price) but *without* triggering local competitor response. Locating suitable markets is difficult, but essential for the small business that is to survive. Foreign companies are sure to launch major assaults on domestic market niches.

The Social Dimension

The European Commission has long maintained that economic progress within the Community is impossible without social cohesion. Accordingly, a number of measures affecting business's human resources strategies have been introduced, including the following:

- Attempts to harmonise employees' legal rights and health and safety standards
- Various EC Directives on the implementation of collective redundancies, employee rights following the takeover of businesses, equal pay for work of equal value, maternity leave and so on
- The proposed European Social Charter.

Britain and the Social Charter
If Britain does adopt the Social Charter it will prove expensive for many UK firms. It is important to realise that the employee benefits envisaged by the Charter – such as pro-rata pay and equal access to superannuation schemes for part-time workers, protections for the casually employed, a minimum wage, legal rights to vocational training, compulsory employee participation in management decisions – have *already* been implemented in several industrially advanced Continental states. Hence, no *additional* costs will be incurred by them when these provisions become law. Should the UK not take up the Social Charter, however, then the gap between employment conditions in British and Continental companies will widen and (critically) British firms with a permanent presence on the Continent will have to operate two-tier personnel policies and procedures; leading perhaps to bitter resentments among their lower-paid and otherwise disadvantaged UK employees.

Staffing

The free movement of labour affects company human-resources policies in several respects, notably the possibility of cross-border recruitment, new training needs, and Community pressures for greater employee participation in the management decisions of large businesses.

Cross-border Recruitment
EC (and eventually EEA) citizens may freely reside in any Community

state, are entitled to receive unemployment and retirement benefit in the nation of their last employment, and have equal access alongside local people to public housing and to education for their children.

Free mobility of labour makes possible the cross-border recruitment of workers. Hence, managements need to be able to:

- Assess the levels of skill and capability of job applications from other EC countries and utilise pan-European job advertising media and headhunting firms
- Determine the levels of pay and conditions of service necessary to attract high calibre candidates from other EC states.

'Euro-executives' will be in great demand. These are multilingual, culturally adaptable managers who are familiar with EC business practices and regulations; have generalist rather than function-specific managerial backgrounds; can work with colleagues of different nationalities; and possess first-class interpersonal communication skills.

Companies recruiting Euro-executives will need special policies to deal with the problems their engagement might create. For example, their high salaries (resulting from their short supply) could generate deep resentments among locally recruited staff. They might not fit in with conventional organisation structures (which may need alteration to avoid stifling Euro-executives' initiative and creativity), and defences against their being poached by headhunters will have to be prepared. Euro-executives, moreover, require special help with finding suitable accommodation, schools for their children, jobs for spouses, pension transfers, and all the traumas and tribulations attached to moving and living abroad.

Training

Long-term neglect of industrial training (including management training) in Britain is sure to put the country's businesses at a disadvantage when faced with intense competition from EC rivals. Eventually however, convergence of training practices is likely as companies with the worst-trained workforces go to the wall and the training, recruitment and staff development policies of successful businesses are emulated by other surviving firms. Management training needs to focus on the inculcation of pan-European perspectives, knowledge of the contents and implications of relevant EC Directives, linguistic skills, export marketing and logistics, and familiarity with EC market structures and business techniques.

Employee Participation

Implementation of the Maastricht Protocol by the 11 EC countries excluding the UK will intensify the distinction between UK and Continental approaches to industrial relations. Employee participation in management decisions and/or the appointment of employee representatives to the boards of large companies have been commonplace in Continental countries for many years (legally required in Belgium, Denmark, France, Germany, Luxembourg, the Netherlands and Portugal). Although the precise form of participation varies from state to state. Company law in Germany and certain other EC nations requires large companies to have two-tier boards of directors, comprising an 'Executive Board' of managerial employees and, above that, a 'Supervisory Board' of elected worker directors responsible for long-term strategy. In Germany any firm with more than five employees must have a Works Council empowered to approve changes in working hours and conditions, holiday arrangements, training, disciplinary procedures, and recruitment methods. The influence of Works Councils extends to the determination of staffing levels, dismissals, overtime payments and shift work systems.

Firms operating in foreign European countries must, of course, comply with local labour laws and practices, which within the next few years will be determined *entirely* by the Maastricht Protocol. Denial of 'Maastricht' benefits to the British employees of these same companies could become a major irritant to UK labour unions and the source of numerous industrial disputes. Thus, a new *philosophy* of industrial relations is needed if British companies are to survive in the post-Maastricht world. Managers of human resources have to become sensitive and responsive to Continental norms on the involvement of employee representatives in corporate decision making and to regard employees as social partners in an enterprise – not as a disposable technical resource. This new philosophy must be based on cooperation between management and labour, setting aside the confrontational practices of the past.

References

Citron, R (1991) *The Stoy Hayward Guide to Getting into Europe*, Kogan Page, London.

Collins, M (1991) *A Complete Guide to the EC's Research Funds*, Kogan Page, London.

11

Change in Central and Eastern Europe

Magdolna Csath

Introduction

After spending five years in the United States and one in the United Kingdom teaching in business schools and researching developments in Central and Eastern Europe, I recently returned to my native country, Hungary. While in the West, I followed the exciting changes in Central and Eastern Europe closely and shared in the enthusiasm for these changes that is generally to be found in the West. Now that I live in the area once again, however, what strikes me most is the general erosion of society created by the changes and the dangers this poses if change is not managed better than it has been so far. This chapter presents an analysis of the situation based on my own personal experience of life in the area, as well as on interviews with managers and politicians, company surveys and economic statistics.

Right at the beginning of this discussion it is necessary to deal with some of the main misconceptions about the situation in Central and Eastern Europe held by Westerners. In the West it is very popular to talk about the fall of Communism, the bringing down of the wall between democracy and totalitarianism and the excitement and joy Central and Eastern Europeans are supposed to feel about all these developments. I do not wish to detract from the historical importance of the change going on in the region, but if we are to understand how the region is actually changing, it is necessary to see the situation accurately and avoid making simplistic comparisons between East and West.

First it should be made clear that communism proper never really existed in the region – the economic aspect had never been properly established at all and even the political element, namely the one-party system, was not general throughout the region. For example, the one-party system did not apply to Poland, and private business and property existed in Hungary as far back as the 1950s. Communism is an ideology that was not subjected to the proof of practice. It is also superficial to put all the countries of the area into one category – the countries of Central and Eastern Europe differ from each other even more than do those of Western Europe.

Furthermore, the euphoria about change in the area that is to be found in the West is premature – anything could still happen because the changes so far made are largely 'first-order' ones. First-order changes in this context are those that benefit a narrow segment of the population consisting of the new entrepreneurs who are mostly the former leaders of the overthrown system, and foreign businesspeople who are now capitalising on the favourable business climate for foreigners, the underpaid skilled labour force and the soft environmental laws of the region. The new rulers of the region have either been too arrogant to bother educating the general public about the long-term benefits of the changes despite the immediate experience of hardship, or they have lacked the necessary communication skills. Such first-order change cannot be sustained for long in a more democratic environment and such change will be succeeded by one of two scenarios.

In the positive scenario, the leaders of countries in the region will be able to create 'second-order' change in which people outside the narrow segment described above will be involved, motivated and empowered. In the negative scenario, democracy would be demolished to preserve present positions and structures. This would be devastating for the region and for the rest of the world, but it is a real possibility. It follows that innovative thinking is required both within and outside the area in order to speed up the pace of positive secondary change through the training and development of wider groups of people and their involvement in new economic opportunities. It will not be enough to create markets – a society with integrity and a human face is essential if development in the area is to proceed instead of being reversed.

This chapter deals with the expectations aroused by the change process and with what has so far materialised. The general conclusion reached is that the outcome of change so far is largely negative as far as the inhabitants of the area are concerned and that the reasons for this are not well understood in the West. The examples I give come mainly from Hungary since that is the country I am most familiar with, but the visits I have made to other parts of the area lead me to believe that the negative consequences of change that these examples depict apply even more strongly to those other parts. The chapter then goes on to consider how these negative consequences might be overcome.

The Result to Date

As new governments came into power throughout Central and Eastern Europe, politicians made a number of promises and presented a number of arguments justifying the need for change. Typically, people throughout the region were promised democracy and freedom, as well as economic opportunities, environmental improvement and higher living standards. The expectation was created that if the economies of the region were shifted to market systems they would soon catch up with the developed world.

Consider how those promises have been fulfilled so far.

A Limited Form of Democracy, but Little Freedom

All the countries of the area have established multi-party systems, but these are still far from providing real freedom so far as their ordinary inhabitants are concerned. In a deteriorating economic and social system, democracy has made it possible for the economically stronger to dominate while the weaker drop out of a society that no longer provides proper safety nets. As far as many are concerned, the rights brought about by democracy are primarily those of dying from hunger or becoming a victim of the crime wave that has followed the establishment of democracy.

As for the freedoms of a democracy, letters in Hungary sometimes still arrive surprisingly late, opened and taped back. In Russia it still takes more than three months for a letter from the West to arrive at its destination. People are theoretically free to talk, but few employees in a company will tell enquirers how they feel about the changes and how they are treated. People fear more and more that they will be fired if they speak out – there are many unemployed outside the gates waiting to take their places. Professionals are theoretically free to publish what-ever they wish, but it is far from easy to find publication opportunities without financial support – even reputable publishers ask authors to find sponsors if they want to be published. What support there is seems to be provided for translating foreign work. While this provides opportunities for translators, it blocks the growth of local specialist expertise.

In short, where money is lacking, democracy is a slogan, an empty word. The West may attach great importance to democracy in Central and Eastern Europe, but its inhabitants are finding that democracy does not lead to freedom, food and shelter. Democracy cannot be admired in the abstract but it must be seen in its economic context.

Declining Industrial Base and Foreign Ownership of Companies

The promise of economic opportunity and rising living standards is the farthest from realisation. After a long period of economic mismanagement, the people of the region were promised wider opportunities by their newly elected leaders. But instead of wider opportunities, a process of impoverishment has begun for the majority, accompanied by a rapidly widening gap between rich and poor. The fundamental problem facing Central and Eastern Europe today is the lack of competitiveness in most economic sectors in the region. As the world economy moves toward globalisation and competition becomes fiercer, economies and companies that survive are those that build lasting competitive advantage by providing environmentally friendly, high-quality, reasonably priced products and services. However, the policies being pursued by the governments of Central and Eastern Europe are not moving their economies in the direction of global competitiveness; instead they are decreasing any possibility of achieving it.

Economic policies in the region nowadays are determined by short-term, financially based thinking, influenced by strong pressures from the World Bank and the International Monetary Fund. The importance of these bodies in policy formation was made clear recently when the minister of privatisation in Hungary said that he was not interested in opposition views on the privatisation policy – it was enough that the World Bank had approved the policy and backed its approval with a $200 million loan.

It is clear that today's short-term financially dominated thinking does not help modernise the economies of the region. Instead, the resultant policies are destroying local industry which, given time and proper management, could have survived and become competitive. The consequences of current policies can be seen in the decline of the region's industrial base and the increasing foreign ownership of what remains.

Take the declining industrial base first. In 1991 there was a 24 per cent drop in industrial output in Bulgaria, 23 per cent in Czechoslovakia, 12 per cent in Poland and 19 per cent in Hungary. And there have been further declines throughout the area since then. At the same time, the recession in the European Community tends to create economic chauvinism which makes it more difficult for the Central and Eastern European countries to export to the West. Instead of being restructured and rebuilt, local industries are being slowly and systematically demolished, throwing people on to the streets by the thousands.

And a major cause of this systematic destruction lies in current approaches to privatisation in which foreign investors are playing a large part. Foreign investors enjoy special treatment in the region and as a result state-owned companies sold in Central and Eastern Europe are going largely to foreign owners. The motivation of the new owners is to capitalise on readily available cheap skilled labour and to avoid strict environmental regulation. Foreign owners are by and large not interested in rebuilding the local economy; rather, they wish to make as much money as possible as soon as possible. A foreign owner's local business strategy is normally part of an international strategy which need not necessarily correspond with the interests of the host country. Locally owned companies find themselves at a disadvantage compared to foreign-owned companies and, as they go bankrupt at an increasing pace, more and more people become unemployed, thus further increasing the pool of cheap labour for foreign companies to choose from. And foreign advisors strongly urge governments to speed up this privatisation process, even though it is not consistent with the goal of enhancing local competitiveness. The result is a vicious circle which leads not to higher-quality products and services but to higher prices in the domestic market.

Consider some of the inconsistencies in the advice coming from the West. Professor Alan Blinder of Princeton University writes:

> Eastern Europe and the Soviet Union need role models for small-scale entrepreneurship and there is no better place to find them than in the US. We have a historic opportunity to export entrepreneurial capitalism. The US government should offer guarantees against business failure to Americans who start small enterprises or enter joint ventures with local partners. (Blinder, 1990)

Then he goes on to say why government guarantees are needed:

> Such investments face special risks . . . There is an incalculable political risk. One or more of these nations might fail to make the transition, perhaps reverting to state socialism or even degenerating into chaos. If so, American investors might find their property valueless. (Blinder, 1990)

What this advisor advocates, therefore, is that subsidised protected foreigners should be attracted to the region to teach locals how to take risks, the very essence of entrepreneurship. But those Western teachers are apparently not be required to take risks themselves – there is to be no teaching by example here.

J Wedel, a Fulbright scholar and specialist on Eastern Europe, summarises this kind of advice as follows:

> While preaching pure capitalism, and markets across the region, the private initiative of many Western firms active there consists of lobbying their governments for aid contracts. These 'free-market proponents' tend to seek monopolies and exclusive deals in countries legally and institutionally ill-equipped to monitor their activities. (Wedel, 1992)

Foreign investors are also very reluctant to hire local people to fill leadership positions and this again closes windows of opportunity for local people. It is also the practice to prefer returning emigrants to local people and this is even more resented by locals than the hiring of foreigners. J Mattock writes:

> Some joint ventures have recruited Hungarian speakers (typically the children of the 1923, 1938, 1945 or 1956 emigrants) to direct operations. This is the case with Compack Douwe Egberts (food and beverage), Ericsonn/Muszertechnika (telecom) and Gantz Hunslet (railway rolling stock). (Mattock, 1992)

Hiring such returning emigrants causes problems because such people sometimes pretend to understand the local situation although they do not: they have either been away for too long or they may even be second generation and have never been to the region.

The work practices of foreign companies often leave much to be desired in another respect: the exploitation of local cheap labour reaches unacceptable limits. I talked with a young woman employed by Unilever in Hungary – she had to work for 17 hours per day in the summer without proper compensation for the long hours. She could not complain about this because she wanted to keep her job. To take another example, a Swedish company was upset because it was not able to hire factory workers at wages lower than poverty levels. Over the radio, representatives of the Swedish company said that this was a sign of people who did not understand the value of having a job no matter what the wage.

Another painful experience is the environmental damage that foreign investors impose on the the area because of a lack of proper government regulations and their own short-term thinking. Most companies also do not train or retrain their people and this means that the knowledge of the population is not being updated.

How can local businesses compete fairly with those that are protected? If they cannot, how will local people become business owners? How will the desired local middle class emerge to fill the gap between the poor and the extremely rich?

Unemployment and Poverty

As the industrial base declines and foreign ownership increases, living standards of the majority of the population continuously deteriorate. Surveys show that living standards for more than 50 per cent of the population have declined to those of the 1950s and in today's terms those levels mean poverty. At the same time, the growing gap between rich and poor is striking and not easily justifiable. Today there are people earning more than £1 million per annum while the average income is about £1,200 and many pensioners earn as little as £500.

Furthermore, full employment, a key characteristic of the previous system, exists no more. Of course, in the old system unemployment did exist but it was concealed within an organisation. This did, however, provide a basic safety net: no one had to be afraid of losing their job and the ability to support a family. Today there are major unemployment problems in the region. In the eastern part of Hungary, where heavy industry was concentrated, more than 30 per cent unemployment rates prevail and they are increasing. The unemployment numbers are much worse in other countries of the region and the situation continues to deteriorate.

The privatisation process puts increasing numbers of people on to the streets as well. One unavoidable reason is rationalisation, the drive for increased productivity. The other reasons lie in the lack of proper management of the transition process. Foreign investors often buy factories only to close them down and start importing their own products to the markets of the region. Or they change the nature of the business entirely; for example building a supermarket in the place of a manufacturing plant. There are other similar foreign investment strategies that contribute to the shrinkage of the production base.

This process also creates an unhealthy structural unemployment: relatively more skilled workers are replaced with less skilled ones. Instead of increasing the knowledge and skill level, knowledge is losing its importance and low cost has become the criterion for success. Engineers especially are an endangered species because foreign investors immediately close down research and development departments and turn the purchased company into a 'screwdriver plant'. Although foreign owners of companies use a few excellent local 'brains', paying on average one-tenth of the salary they pay at home for the same work, most of the research is done back at the home headquarters.

The external economic and political pressures to cut long-held economic ties with neighbouring countries have also contributed to the increasing number of unemployed. Having withdrawn from former socialist countries, companies are simply not able to penetrate Western markets because they cannot meet quality standards or because of Western trade barriers.

Rising unemployment and the fear of a large segment of the workforce of being laid off in the next stage of privatisation contribute to growing tension. People have also lost or are about to lose free education, health and childcare without getting any compensation in higher wages. This is leading to a general deterioration of the already bad health of those who just cannot afford private doctors. A selection process is beginning among the young: those who have money get better education and access to schools abroad; others have to fight for foundation money or money from other sources, or simply give up and possibly increase the number of unemployed young. This number has already started climbing.

Culture is now regarded as a service to be traded on the 'market' and as a consequence theatres, cinemas and books have become very expensive, beyond the reach of the average person. As the demand dries up, cultural offerings decrease, giving way to cheap, valueless publications and mass-produced foreign films. Without doubt this process has already started and it is hard to judge how far it is going to go and what effects it might have. Opposition parties already blame the government for this new kind of 'brainwashing'. One of the most painful, embarrassing and frustrating developments is the increase in all kinds of crime. It is easy to find the causes in unemployment, desperation and deteriorating human values.

Corruption and 'Jobs for the Boys'

The behaviour of the new leaders is a bitter reminder of that of the party leaders and top government bureaucrats in the old system. For example, I was sitting in the office of a senior university official when a call came from Budapest asking him to organise a hunting weekend for Austrian and Hungarian leaders. The university official was not surprised – 'Very often the caller from Budapest is the same person who used to call in the "old system", so this is only a 50 per cent change'. There has been a change of foreign partner but not the local one. The everyday methods of using power are very much the same as they were before. The drivers of the new leaders still use official cars to take their bosses' wives shopping and their children to school.

In the 'old system' it was well known that leaders were provided with local products at lower prices or simply free of charge as 'demonstration products'. This practice has not disappeared and indeed on top of this a new pattern is arising: members of the present leadership have access to newly privatised properties at much lower than the market price. There is a closed circle in which those who prepare the valuations of state property for sale also arrange the sale either to themselves or their friends – often foreign ones. I met a university teacher who told me that he was one of the external advisers of the privatisation agency. After a short time he found the property he wanted to buy and prepared the valuation of it for himself. He is not the only person doing this.

Although bribery was widespread in the 'old system', the form it now takes leads to even larger losses to state funds. Very large amounts of state assets are changing hands at much less than their market value and it looks as if this practice will continue until all state assets have been transferred to the private sector. This corrupt method of transfer will however leave behind a bitterness on the part of those left out of a share in the spoils and therefore conflict for years to come.

Bitterness and long-lasting divisive conflict arise for another reason too; namely the manner in which the managers and top experts of state-owned companies and organisations are selected. The selection process is driven largely by political criteria – one has to be a committed member of the ruling coalition to be appointed to one of the higher positions in institutions controlled by the government. Poor performers are not removed, if they belong to the right circle, but simply moved to other specially created jobs leading to increasing layers of bureaucracy. The irony is that it had become normal in the last years of the previous system for professionals and experts to be advanced on merit without necessarily being members of the ruling party. That kind of flexibility contributed to the earlier success of the new economic and market reforms.

Furthermore, while private institutions and individuals are under tremendous pressure to economise, there is little similar pressure on government-controlled institutions. The result is poor service to the public.

A Confused Value System

So far, the governments of the region have not managed to establish and spread a new value system to replace that of the previous era. These governments keep repeating that there must be a move from central planning and a one-party system to a market economy and a multi-party system, but the failure to create a new value system is probably one of the main reasons why attempts at making this move are being accompanied by the malfunctioning of these societies. Leaders will not be able to blame this malfunctioning on the legacy of the old system for much longer. What is needed is a set of values people can believe in.

The majority cannot believe in a privatisation process that is corruptly managed for the benefit of the few. The values of honesty, fairness, openness and visibility of government activities, especially relating to the privatisation process, will have to be established if the system is not to fall apart. The privatisation process will determine property structures, living conditions and relative social status for a very long time to come and if it is based on corruption it will continue as a source of discord and instability for a very long time to come. Unfortunately, the privatisation process continues in an atmosphere of secrecy which allows rumours of bribery and corruption to abound.

The value system which is now developing has further alarming properties. The elderly are being discarded. Many who have worked for 40 years are paid pensions that are so low they have little option but to beg for food. The gap between rich and poor is widening and the social value placed on expertise and knowledge is declining – experts and professionals are paid very low salaries. The way to succeed is to operate corruptly rather than to work hard and acquire expertise. The values that lead to success in the region are those of the 'wheeler-dealer'.

Little value is placed on the human infrastructure and although the 'old system' was criticised for its insensitivity to environmental protection, the new system ignores these matters just as much. In fact Central Europe is becoming the 'Eastern dumping field' for Western Europe. And the general public finds it hard to accept being treated as second-class citizens in their own country by foreign advisors who are financed by various aid programmes. It does not promote entrepreneurial values when locals see that the markets in consultancy expertise are not 'fair' but subsidised to benefit foreigners.

The Impact of Western Assistance

The West is trying to assist in the creation of a market culture by providing consultants, university professors and other specialists to teach the locals. Wedel (1992) points out that two-thirds of US aid in 1991, provided through the Agency for International Development, took the form of 'technical assistance' for economic restructuring and the privatisation of state-owned companies. Most of this aid has gone to Poland and Hungary, and when Wedel researched its effectiveness she found that most Polish and Hungarian officials felt that their countries were being 'technically overassisted':

> While the consultants themselves are the primary recipients of the aid, they generally are unfamiliar with the institutions peculiar to the post-communist economies. Over-burdened top-level officials, often working without the benefit of trained support staff, complain that they can't do their jobs because they must spend their time meeting either fact-finders or consultants . . . (Wedel, 1992)

Wedel concludes that the form US assistance has taken has damaged America's reputation in both Poland and Hungary.

Similar conclusions apply to the aid provided by the European Community (Csath, 1992 a and b). European advisers try to 'sell' the product they already have without trying to adjust to local needs. For example, one of the aims of the initiatives of 'know-how' funds should be that of training managers to manage change better. The British contribution, however, strongly emphasises traditional Master of Business Administration (MBA) subjects such as accountancy, finance, business policy, organisational theory and management science. For example, one particpant in a British-sponsored MBA programme told me how the British professor asked her to write a case study that followed the textbook – if she wrote a case on her own company, he said, he would not be able to evaluate it. The textbook, furthermore, was out of date. This is not contributing to changes in behaviour or to the change-management skills which are most needed. Often, British partners argue that people should be sent over to Britain to study these subjects in the same programme provided for British managers, without any modifications made for those from Central Europe. It is most unlikely that programme developed in the UK social and economic environment can be implemented in countries as different as those of Central Europe.

Aid provided to the region also frequently comes with 'strings' attached. An unwritten part of the deal is often the hiring of a particular consulting firm or training institution. This practice makes it very hard for a national firm to compete with a foreign one because the local companies have no access to such special treatment. Local businesses are not automatically allowed to invest in property or shares and they cannot start a foreign business without special permission. This disadvantages the local firms. Furthermore, consultants coming from the West are paid five to ten times more than locals, even though the foreigners know very little about the region and the locals are left bearing the consequences of their advice. So, while advocating the creation of free markets, aid packages often work in the opposite direction.

Some typical attitudes and values that foreign advisors try to impose on the people of Central Europe are that:

- Everything which has been done in the region before is worthless and cannot be built upon
- Practices and methods used in the West are far superior (never mind the recession and related social problems in the West which were definitely not caused by communist governments)
- 'Quick-fix' solutions can be based on imported Western management ideas (never mind that many of them have proved to be useless in the West).

People in Central and Eastern Europe should not be treated as inferiors who have to be raised to the level of Western nations in every sphere of life. More understanding and appreciation would lead to cooperation from which both parties might learn.

Some Suggestions for the Way Forward

In the turmoil of complex changes, the most pressing need is that for leadership which creates a long-term vision and makes sure that people understand, share and commit themselves to that vision. Since clear missions and innovative actions for the future are lacking, politicians focus on a 'looking-back ideology'. They change the names of streets, remove statues, bring back old symbols, ideas and emigrants. But all this is no substitute for deliberate, future-oriented actions to get the economy moving and this will require reliance on local initiatives rather than the over-centralised, bureaucratic governments.

Government, however, still has a role. Its members should be setting an example for the values of a synergistic society and a fair system rather than engaging in continuous battles for power. Members of the government need to become much more concerned with the deteriorating social fabric. Responsible leaders in the region should also not shy away from creating development strategies just because of the perception that any planning is just the 'remains of communism'. Strategic planning is a legitimate capitalist management technique used by leaders to create the future of organisations, of regions and of countries. There is, therefore, an urgent need for a development and restructuring strategy to be developed by governments within the area. It has to be the national governments that create such a strategy, but they will require international assistance to carry it out.

A development and restructuring strategy should put emphasis on:

- Creating opportunities for the local people to become owners by making the privatisation process transparent
- Slowing down the damage of bankruptcies by offering 'breathing time' to companies that are capable of restructuring and becoming competitive
- Encouraging local businesses, especially small ones, instead of killing them with unreasonably high taxes
- Securing equal employment opportunities and practices for local people working in foreign-owned firms in order to stop age and sex discrimination
- Encouraging environmentally friendly and knowledge-based foreign companies to move into the region
- Encouraging export and foreign investment by local companies
- Negotiating better access to markets for local companies
- Negotiating the same treatment for people of the region concerning work permits in the West as foreigners enjoy in the region
- Improving the levels of education and health care in order to support long-term economic recovery and social reconciliation
- Encouraging the further development of the agricultural and food-processing sector; this is the sector most able to produce quality products for export in several countries
- Taking environmental issues very seriously by encouraging the small peasant farms created by the break-up of the state cooperatives to becomes centres for labour-intensive organically grown produce
- Building on the first-class educational level of the population to create opportunities for professionals to stay in their home country and work in knowledge-intensive areas of the economy.

By creating a long-term consistent strategy for recovery, the governments of the region could offer a vision for the people to share. Such an approach would give a tremendous psychological uplift to the people of the region. Instead of alienating them, governments could create commitment which would channel positive energies into the transition process.

To implement strategies of restructuring and recovery will of course require massive investments. The developed world, especially the European Community, has already invested but the impact has not been as encouraging as expected. The problem lies in how this money is distributed and to whom it goes. On the basis of a recent survey it appears that the major beneficiaries of foreign aid programmes are the foreign partners and consultants, businesses and universities. Through them the bulk of the money flows out of the region. As indicated above, the foreign partners who advocate free-market practices ironically do it from a safe subsidised position and as a result they make it very hard for those locals who do participate in aid programmes to compete.

If Western governments want long-lasting, sustainable and positive change in the region, then more creative and innovative approaches should be chosen to support the transition process. Keeping the aid money in the region by helping small business development, employee retraining, establishing science parks, and helping to develop environmental protection practices would be a better way of promoting the benefits of the market economy in the region.

Aid on its own has never solved any basic economic problems anywhere in the world. Opening markets for the products and services of Eastern and Central Europe would offer more practical and helpful longer-term solutions for the region.

The governments of the region should be more understanding and socially sensitive; they should demonstrate more empathy for the poor. It is now clear to everybody in the region that those who suffered most in the past system will now bear the main burden in the creation of the new capitalist class. It is not necessary, however, that the majority of the people should slip below poverty levels. It is not an attractive prospect for the people of Central and Eastern Europe to fall back to a third world economic status and such a prospect should also be unacceptable to far-sighted Western Europeans.

Increased contacts with Western Europeans make people in the region more aware of the gap between their living standards and those of the West. There is also a growing awareness that the problems people face are not simply the inevitable consequences of change but often flow from the way in which changes are mismanaged, reducing the opportunities open to the average citizen and granting advantages to foreigners who exploit the situation. This creates the strong possibility of deepening discontent. If existing trends in Eastern and Central Europe are allowed to continue, the economy, the social fabric and the environment will continue to decline and extremists will find ready audiences for their messages. The consequences for the West are unpredictable.

References

Blinder, A S (1992) *Business Week*, 29 Jan.

Csath, M (1992a) 'An Opinion: Why Central and Eastern Europe Need a Development and Restructuring Strategy', *Futures Research Quarterly*, Summer.

Csath, M (1992b) 'How Effective Western Knowledge Transfer Programs are In Helping Central Europe's Transition Toward a Market Economy', *Journal of Strategic Change*, Vol 1.

Mattock, J (1992) *The Independent*, 11 Feb.

Wedel, J (1992) 'Beware Western Governments Bearing Gifts', *The Wall Street Journal, Europe*, 14 January.

Index